HIDDEN HISTORIES

Hidden Histories

Faith and Black Lesbian Leadership

MONIQUE MOULTRIE

DUKE UNIVERSITY PRESS
Durham and London
2023

Project editor: Bird Williams
Designed by A. Mattson Gallagher
Typeset in Adobe Text Pro by Westchester Publishing Services

Library of Congress Cataloging-in-Publication Data
Names: Moultrie, Monique Nicole, [date] author.
Title: Hidden histories : faith and Black lesbian leadership / Monique Moultrie.
Description: Durham : Duke University Press, 2023. | Includes bibliographical references and index.
Identifiers: LCCN 2022040850 (print)
LCCN 2022040851 (ebook)
ISBN 9781478019114 (paperback)
ISBN 9781478016472 (hardcover)
ISBN 9781478023746 (ebook)
Subjects: LCSH: African American women clergy—Interviews. | African American lesbians—Interviews. | Womanism—Religious aspects. | Leadership—Moral and ethical aspects—United States. | Sexual orientation—Religious aspects. | BISAC: social science / Ethnic Studies / American / African American & Black Studies | SOCIAL SCIENCE / LGBTQ Studies / General | LCGFT: Oral histories.
Classification: LCC BT83.9 . M67 2023 (print) | LCC BT83.9 (ebook) | DDC 230.082—dc23/eng/20221228
LC record available at https://lccn.loc.gov/2022040850
LC ebook record available at https://lccn.loc.gov/2022040851

Cover art: (top to bottom, left to right) Dr. Pamela "Ayo" Yetunde (photo by Miriam Phields); Reverend Dr. Deborah Johnson; Reverend Dr. Cari Jackson; Bishop Tonyia Rawls; Reverend Naomi Washington-Leapheart (photo by Zamani Feelings Photography); Elder Darlene Garner; Dr. Sylvia Rhue. All photographs courtesy of their subjects.

To the memory of my grandmother,
Mildred Crews Carter

To the memory of my husband,
Rev. Eugene James Se'Bree

I am forever changed because
you both loved me.

CONTENTS

Acknowledgments   ix

Introduction   1
That Their Living Will Not Be in Vain

1   Shattering Stained-Glass Ceilings   17
African American Queer Storytelling

2   Going to Hell for My Authenticity   38
Existence as Resistance

3   Justice Is Spiritual   68
Interrogating Spiritual Activism

4   Mighty Causes Are Calling Us   103
Expanding Womanist Spiritualities

5   Doing the Work Their Souls Must Have   126
Cultivating Womanist Ethical Leadership

Conclusion   168
Leading from the Margins

Epilogue   182
Online Archives

Appendix: Interview Guide   187
Notes   189
Bibliography   203
Index   217

ACKNOWLEDGMENTS

This book has many origin points, such as my cultivated love of women's storytelling passed down to me by my mother and my maternal grandmother. My mother, Tommie Crews, was the first in our immediate family to earn a college degree, and she and my aunts recounted tales from college and their adventures in the workforce to a precocious womanish girl who hung on their every words. My grandmother, Mildred Carter, raised me to appreciate a good story and to recognize the value that our stories had in educating us about how our past, present, and future were intertwined. I learned from the women in my family that our stories tell the world that we were here and that we mattered.

Because of this awareness, when I was asked in 2009 by Mark Bowman, executive director of the Lesbian, Gay, Bisexual, Transgender, Religious Archives Network (LGBTQ-RAN), to conduct a few interviews for its website, I leapt at the opportunity to conduct oral histories and hear people's life narratives. Little did I know that a task I took as a graduate student would captivate me so many years later. Honestly, it took me a while to appreciate the gift that I had been given—access to these women's life stories—and to feel comfortable enough that I should be the one to amplify them via a book-length study. I will forever remain grateful that during a lunch with Dr. Rosetta Ross, she asked me what new research I could present to the Spelman College community, and I mentioned that I had conducted a few really interesting interviews that I would love to share. This was the first time that I tried weaving their stories together into a cohesive narrative for others, and the community was gracious toward my nascent theorizing, which propelled me to conduct further research.

Further research required further funding, and I am ever grateful for the numerous funders' financial support for this project over the years. The

American Academy of Religion awarded me an individual research grant that funded my initial eight interviews. Likewise, I received support to continue conducting interviews from the Auburn Seminary/Cross Currents Coolidge Scholars Summer Colloquium (where I was brilliantly steered in the direction of making this a book about Black lesbians), the Georgia State University Humanities Center, and my college and department's resources.

When shaping this work, I was also fortunate to receive generous support and a scholarly community in the form of the Harvard Divinity School's Women's Studies in Religion Program. WSRP provided me physical space and allowed me to teach this content as I was completing the manuscript, and Anne Braude and my cohort (Alicia Izharuddin, Monica Mercado, Jyoti Puri, and Kerry Sonia) were invaluable interlocutors who asked me early on to keep amplifying the women's stories so that their lives became the theory for the larger project. In my Leadership and Womanist Moral Traditions course the students and I wrestled with how to balance our scholarly commitments with our passions to let the women whom we interviewed shape our arguments. I am also thankful for the numerous opportunities to practice getting this balance right with academic communities: the American Academy of Religion, the Association for the Study of African American Life and History, the Society for the Scientific Study of Religion, the American Studies Association, the Oral History Association, the Queer History Conference, Brandeis University, Emory University, and Georgetown University's Berkley Center. My desire and intention to get their stories right meant I also solicited help from editors extraordinaire Ulrike Guthrie and Raedorah Stewart.

My personal thanks to Miriam Angress and the team at Duke University Press for their validation of this work. I would also like to thank my colleagues at Georgia State University (and especially Lou Ruprecht) for reading various stages of this project and to thank my graduate research assistants (Elizabeth Shuford, Shey Miller, Clifvette Webb, and Pedro Alvarez) for all their help. When I was gifted another opportunity to research in Cambridge, Barbara Revkin again provided me with a room to write in and with company while we were sheltering in place because of the COVID-19 pandemic. Being in Cambridge again also offered me the opportunity to continue to be mentored by Bernadette Brooten and Clarissa Atkinson, whose faith in me is a blessing. I am also grateful for the sage counsel of my former graduate adviser Victor Anderson, whose initial conversation on how to write a second book broke through my writer's block. For the continued reminders to keep up my writing practice, I am appreciative of the Sister Scholars' (astutely led by AnneMarie Mingo) writing space.

During the decade of collecting interviews and writing, my circle has become smaller. My in-laws Harvey and Callie Epperson both passed away before seeing the text take form. My biological mother died, and then the rock of my family passed away as I was finalizing the manuscript. Losing the light that was Mildred Carter is an immeasurable loss, and each celebration is less sweet because I am unable to share it with her. Despite these losses, I am reminded that saying their names and telling their stories show the world how much they meant to me. I am eternally grateful for my forever friends and family who made these losses manageable (Nichole Phillips, Ipsita Chatterjea, Haywood Harvey, and Jason Cogswell). Albert Smith's check-ins and ability to be a sounding board provided the organizational structure of the book. TL Gray reminds me that the world is too big not to spread my wings more. Almeda Wright and James Logan were my lifelines in a year where grief and sadness could have engulfed me. As my family circle grew smaller, our friendships grew wider and sustained us through trials and joys.

I conclude with my biggest thanks reserved for my interviewees for their trust in my intentions and gratitude for their ability to be forces of good in the world. May they continue to teach us how to be brave, authentic spiritual leaders. Finally, to my half-Bre, half-amazing partner, Rev. Eugene James Se'Bree, only you have witnessed the inner workings of this project from its earliest iteration to the final product. You have trusted that our sacrifices would all be worthwhile as we endeavored to be examples for Chandler and Jioni. You bring us back to our better selves and have always believed in our greatness. You are a constant reminder that finding a partner to share an entire life is worthwhile work. Our love is a story for the ages, and it matters that we chose daily to live in its abundance.

Introduction

That Their Living Will Not Be in Vain

Being an open lesbian in the Black community is not easy, although being closeted is even harder.

—AUDRE LORDE, "An Interview: Audre Lorde and Adrienne Rich," in *Sister Outsider*

Sexual stories about Black women are all around us, but they almost always rely on key myths, while few stories told by Black women about their own sexual lives are available.

—TRICIA ROSE, *Longing to Tell*

When I was growing up in my rural Virginia Baptist church, I was taught a conservative biblical worldview that promised fire and brimstone as punishment for same-sex attraction. The words *lesbian* and *gay* were spoken in shushed tones, and the only "out" members of our local LGBTQ community were the white gay florists in town. We seldom heard sermons or received education that discussed sexuality in any form, but when we did, heterosexuality was idealized. I was also taught that God loved everyone, and as the hymn we often sang taught us, we were to "treat everybody right."

Wrestling with this irony in practice and praise was one of the reasons I became a questioning Christian. I needed a way to deal with the castigation I was expected to direct at my lesbian and gay family and friends while simultaneously showing them Christian love. In a way, this book starts with my curious struggles with the messages I received from my Christian tradition about sexuality, and it hopes to offer the next generation of spiritual seekers a possible alternative to the domination of heterosexism.

My scholarship explores how religion, race, and sexuality intersect with gender prescriptions and normative claims within Christian contexts. In my first book, I investigated how Black women were targeted by faith-based sexuality ministries and exerted their own sexual agency. Here, by responding to the erasure of Black lesbians' sexual and sacred lives I am examining how sexual and religious actors exert agency in religious spheres. Taking seriously cultural critic Tricia Rose's assertion that sexual stories about Black women are all around us but that they rely on key myths, this text offers data based on Black lesbian women's actual stories about sexuality and faith. *Hidden Histories: Faith and Black Lesbian Leadership* examines oral histories of Black lesbian religious leaders as an exploration of womanist ethical leadership. It addresses their social justice orientation while theorizing how their models of leadership can be instructive for future generations.

As far as I can tell, this book is the first collection of oral histories of Black lesbian religious leaders in the United States. My intention is to elevate the stories of Black women who proudly claim a lesbian *and* religious identity. I recognize the dearth of scholarship on Black lesbians of faith, so my first goal is to preserve their stories for posterity. Beyond that worthy goal, I also seek to make a larger contribution to the canon of African American religion by expanding it to include the diversity of lesbian experiences in Black religious communities. The last twenty years have seen scholarship on Black LGBTQ identity that discussed religion, and there is even some recent work that focuses specifically on Black lesbians and faith. Yet these works are not typically produced by scholars trained in African American religion, and they are not often published or cited by scholars of African American religion. Whether they are ancillary because their authors are from other disciplines or whether "the gods are afraid of Black sexuality," the result is a lack of new knowledge that takes seriously the sexual identities of its leaders and participants.[1] This is particularly unfortunate when one considers the queer history that is being lost and how this erasure misshapes the subdiscipline of African American religion. Thus, the oral histories that I gathered and present here offer a genealogical bridge to interpret twenty-first-century African American religion.

I am pursuing this project to answer three main questions as I theorize on womanist ethical leadership: How are Black lesbian religious leaders incubators for social justice activism? How does spirituality animate their social activism? And how can these leaders function as models for ethical leadership for future generations? My concern with their social justice activism is correlated to my interest in their leadership styles because I contend that ethical leadership requires concern for the greater good and even the holistic well-being of the planet and its inhabitants. By examining these leaders' social justice orientation, the text ultimately explores the benefits of collaborative leadership, endeavoring to link these contemporary figures to a longer genealogy of Black female leaders for whom religion is a catalyst for their work. This historical placement also amplifies and diversifies the field of African American religion and expands current discourse on ethical leadership models.

Ultimately, I explore these questions by considering the lives of eighteen Black lesbian religious leaders whose oral histories I gathered for this project and for the Lesbian, Gay, Bisexual, Transgender, Queer Religious Archives Network (LGBTQ-RAN). The LGBTQ-RAN is a virtual archive project, and at the time of this publication it is a program that preserves LGBTQ religious histories on its website, https://lgbtqreligiousarchives.org. Initially, my work as a consultant for LGBTQ-RAN involved identifying and interviewing four Black gay and three lesbian religious leaders (including two Muslim leaders, a Pentecostal bishop, a Baptist clergyperson, a Seventh Day Adventist leader, a Unity Fellowship of Churches bishop, and a Metropolitan Community Churches elder) for the website's oral history project. After the untimely death of one of my initial participants, I realized the urgency of gathering these oral histories and decided to expand the project to concentrate only on Black lesbian religious leaders.

First, the stories of "out" Black lesbian religious leaders are valuable because in my interviews I noticed a marked difference in the leadership styles of Black gays and lesbians. These distinctions will be further explicated in chapter 5, but what I noticed was that unlike some of the men interviewed, the women's leadership and activist orientations went beyond institution building and a sole focus on the LGBTQ community. Women were certainly involved in empire building and even sat at the pinnacles of denominations, but their interests were more expansive and communally oriented. In general, Black gay men tended to establish open and affirming religious communities, and they were often tasked with the daily activities of keeping these organizations running. By contrast, Black lesbians' path to hierarchical leadership is historically more constrained such that their leadership flourishes beyond established power structures—for example, they are heralded in the community or local arenas, making their leadership often most closely aligned with community needs.

In reflecting on this dynamic, I was struck by how these female religious leaders experienced sexism, racism, and heterosexism intersectionally. Despite

FIGURE I.1. *Coalesce*, by Frederick Moultrie Jr., 2021. Used by permission.

Black women statistically being the most numerous participants in heterosexual faith communities, they are seldom the organizations' leaders. Thus, I wanted to understand how Black lesbians animated by religion or spirituality were deemed leaders in their communities. At its core, this pursuit of the narratives of Black lesbian faith leaders was an exercise to look at the some of the most ostracized persons on the margins of our religious and secular societies.

Sample Rationale

When I began collecting interviews, I was following the suggestions of the LGBTQ-RAN director on whom I should interview. Those recommendations included religious leaders at the pinnacle of their careers. Yet as I expanded the project, I realized I wanted to follow a more versatile criteria for my own work, so I included a variety of demographics and leadership positions. At the most basic level my interview pool looked for women who held some kind of leadership position—for example, they were in some position of power or authority in a religious space. Yet I found that even this simple requirement was too amorphous. I pondered whether a leader is someone who is "tied to larger aspirations for Black empowerment and social change," someone who is "fueled by a vision that [is] sustain[ed] over time," or someone who is in another category in between.[2] In the end, I asked to interview Black lesbian women who were actively integrating their spiritual and religious beliefs into their social justice activism or efforts to bring about social change. Although a few of the women were children of immigrants, all were reared in the United States and currently lived across the continent. I narrowed the selection pool by deciding to interview only cisgender women of African descent. Initially, this was a result of my snowballing sample, in which cisgender leaders referred me to other cisgender leaders, but I did not extend my research to amplify transwomen's voices. This limitation acknowledges how the absence of transgender religious leaders means that this study of cisgender female leaders is just a starting point and that it can and should provide a model for others to consider ethical leadership among transwomen religious leaders.

I interviewed only women who publicly claimed a lesbian, same-gender-loving, or queer identity because the purpose of this study is to explore Black lesbian religious leaders who were living authentically and working for social justice. Although all the participants admitted a period of life of living in the closet—being aware of their same-sex sexual attraction but not admitting this publicly—by the time I interviewed them, each woman had been self-identifying publicly as a lesbian for decades (except for the two youngest interviewees, who were in their mid-thirties and had been out on average for a decade).

Their Black lesbian identity matters to this project because Black women and especially Black lesbians are not typically chronicled in the annals of Black moral leadership. In a tradition that privileges individual male leaders, it is rare for female agents' stories to be told. In fact, when I started this project, I had a difficult time even crafting a basic genealogy of Black women leaders who happened to be lesbian, much less Black religious leaders who were lesbians. Although scholars have attempted to expand historiography to include the lesbian identity of women such as Rebecca Cox Jackson (1795–1871), Dr. Mary Evans (1891–1966), Sister Rosetta Tharpe (1915–1973), or even Pauli Murray (1910–1985), none of these women were self-identifying Black lesbians, which means that the historical record fails to help us in our contemporary pursuit of Black lesbians' past leadership.[3] Thus, the project centralizes Black lesbian identity as essential to understanding their leadership styles.

Their Black lesbian identity is instrumental to understanding the magnitude of oppressions they have overcome to break the "stained-glass ceiling" within their religious spaces. They have learned to advocate for themselves despite biases against women, Blacks, queers, and even religious persons. Their intersectional identity is key to how they approach the leadership task because they are always aware of the multiple communities to which they must be accountable. The Audre Lorde quotation at the start of the chapter references how hard it is to be out in the Black community; Lorde notes that some identities are deemed to be in conflict with one another. For example, loyalty to the Black community has presumed fidelity and perhaps even submission to Black men; thus, activism that does not privilege male concerns can cause intraracial trauma. As women who were motivated by deep religious ideologies, this is often deemed antithetical to their queer identity, for some see religion as solely a source of harm for the LGBTQ community. Those who deem women (and especially queer women) to be unworthy of religious calling challenge female leaders who are not following heteronormative leadership structures that allow for women in leadership as companions to males. Thus, women who claim their authentic voice to speak from their particular identities are also reflections of Black women's self-determination and agency.

In addition, gleaning from the lives of Black lesbian religious leaders is important because it disrupts the popular depiction of Black religion as overtly hostile to LGBTQ persons. Chapter 1 will discuss more of the publicized homophobia in Black religious communities, but the decision to research Black lesbians who were active religious leaders is a twofold response to the assertion that the Black community is less tolerant of gays and lesbians and to the research of gay male authors whose work discerns that religion does not hold as significant a role for Black lesbian women as it does for Black gay men. Performance scholar and oral historian E. Patrick Johnson's *Black.Queer. Southern.Women* reports his surprise that the women he interviewed did not enjoy going to church or find it to be a refuge, contrary to what many of his gay Black male interviewees had experienced.[4] Johnson's texts revealed women's disavowal of Black churches and their seeking women-centered alternative spiritualities instead. In *Their Own Receive Them Not*, pastoral theologian Horace Griffin contends that there is not an expectation of finding "out" Black lesbians in Black congregations because, stereotypically, lesbians have not been associated with religious attendance. My interviewees and their communities contradict such studies by demonstrating that Black lesbian religious leaders purposely work within religious spaces and find in Black religious spaces joy and space to flourish. Chapters 1 and 4 will unpack the many ways that gay male scholars miss the point of Black lesbians' religious identities, but this research is significant because it makes these varied racial and religious identities central to the theorizing of their leadership.

Research Subjects

After conducting the initial seven interviews for LGBTQ-RAN, I created a "dream list" of twenty-five potential interviewees by snowball sampling names from my participants.[5] I contacted my university IRB office and was told that my study would be exempt from IRB review because oral history activities are designed to create records of specific historical events via open-ended questions that focus on particular individuals and are thus not generalizable knowledge. I was then able to start the process of recruiting potential interviewees by either asking for a referral from a previous interviewee or by "cold contacting" the potential participant. Because the first three interviews were Protestant Christians, the sample pool was predominantly Christian. I diversified these results by conducting additional research, and this resulted in an interview with two spiritualists, a Jewish rabbi, and a Buddhist lay leader. I broadly targeted women over the age of twenty-one to explore at minimum a decade of living and working as a self-identifying lesbian religious leader. Given the focus on established Black female leadership, most of the sample pool was over the age of fifty and had a variety of leadership experience inside and outside of religious spaces. From the initial slate of twenty-five names, twenty accepted my invitation to be interviewed, and I was able to conduct eighteen interviews.

The interviewees ranged from ages thirty-seven to seventy-two. Most of the interviews were of women over the age of fifty, except for two outliers, Rev. Naomi and Rev. Kentina Washington-Leapheart, a couple who were thirty-seven and thirty-nine, respectively. Geographically, the interviewees represented the West Coast, Pacific Northwest, Midwest, Southwest, Southeast, and Northeast. I conducted the earliest three interviews in 2010 and 2011 (and updated these in 2019) and the remaining fifteen interviews between 2017 and 2019. Most of the interviews lasted an hour and a half, with five interviews lasting almost three hours. All interviews were conducted face-to-face, with the exception of two of the earliest interviews, and most interviews took place at a neutral location such as a hotel meeting room, office, church, or local library. I conducted two interviews in women's homes at the request of the participants. None of the interviewees are anonymous: the purpose of gathering their stories was for posterity. Each of the interviews was audiotaped and transcribed. The interviewees received the audio and transcript for approval, and all the interviews are housed on the LGBTQ-RAN website. I provide a biographical introduction to each interviewee the first time she appears in the book. In subsequent appearances I provide a bit of background information to refresh the reader's memory and sometimes relevant notes from our interview. Excerpts of some narratives may appear in more than one chapter. I introduce the women via the titles they preferred. Most wanted me to use their professional title rather than referencing them by their first names.[6]

As a heterosexual ally who was not a religious leader, I often found myself in an "outsider/within" scenario, as it was important for me to acknowledge that I was entrusted with these stories as a noncommunity member but also to note that there were many ways in which we were in the same community.[7] Much like E. Patrick Johnson's critical awareness regarding his male privilege, when interviewing Black queer southern women I remained vigilant about my heterosexual and class privileges as a heterosexual woman with Ivy League degrees.[8] Thus, the basic questions remained the same for all interviewees in an attempt to control any missteps that would be complicit with heterosexism or classism. Taking cues from archivist Laura Micham, director of the Sallie Bingham Center for Women's History and Culture at Duke University Libraries, regarding the ethical responsibility of the interviewer my intentions were to be a "responsible documentarian," one who was "knowledgeable about the community, but never to make the assumption . . . that you're a member of the community."[9] My efforts to be aware of when my subjectivity as a Black woman with deep faith commitments was relevant and when it was not comparable was tested with each interview. Some conversations lapsed into colloquial conversations, such as when Bishop Tonyia Rawls and I reminisced for fifteen minutes over our experiences some twenty years apart as Black female undergraduates at Duke University or the shared experiences with womanism that Rev. Kentina Washington-Leapheart and Bishop Yvette Flunder and I spent time discussing. Because these interviews often took place with only a formal introduction from someone in their inner circles, I spent time while we were not recording giving details about myself, sharing identity markers that I thought would be useful, as well as discussing why I as a heterosexual woman wanted to capture their stories. I did not use a script for these self-reflections, so I am sure the information given to each participant varied; however, I was constant in my cautiousness not to lead with my heterosexual identity too early in the conversation to avoid either privileging my story or distancing my story from their own. For the eighteen years I have been with my current partner, I seldom give pronouns and rarely used the term *boyfriend* or *husband* to describe him, yet through this project I became more sensitized to my "coming out" narrative and paid more attention to how/when/with whom I disclosed the gender identity of my partner and thus of my sexuality. This self-awareness, along with my stated womanist agenda, informed my ethical approach to conducting my oral history interviews.

Methodology

I chose to explore the lives of Black lesbian religious leaders through oral history for several reasons. First, I agreed with Rose's assertion that our knowledge about Black women's sexual lives rely on key myths instead of facts told from their own perspectives. This is doubly true for conversations around Black leadership, for it's important to hear about Black leaders' lives from their own perspectives, which in the case of this study demands a methodology that highlights Black lesbian religious leaders' stories.[10] According to the Oral History Association, "Oral history is a field of study and a method of gathering, preserving and interpreting the voices and memories of people and communities."[11] It allows a researcher to amplify the experiences of a diverse group using open-ended techniques such as semi-structured interviews concentrated on everyday experiences shaped by race, class, gender, sexuality, and religion. Because I am invested in how and why these women became religious leaders, oral history offered a means to access their thoughts, feelings, and activities.

Throughout my personal and academic career, I have placed the highest premium on listening to Black women tell their stories. Whether that was from being mesmerized by testimonies from my conservative Christian upbringing, receiving personal accolades for my public speaking, or even the experiences of hearing my grandmother weave together a story merging lessons from an earlier time with whatever instruction she was currently imparting, hearing Black women's lived truths through speech has remained significant for me. As an undergraduate African American studies student, I learned about the griot tradition and how it survived as an Africanism passed down from slavery to current generations. The import of the oral tradition is so significant that some "scholars even argue that African and African American autobiographers build upon this *griot* tradition specifically establishing connections between themselves and their communities, rather than focusing on their individual story."[12] Testifying is never just for you but to show those in your community how you have weathered the storm. I wrote a dissertation and my first book about Black women's ability to testify about their sexual lives and their faith because their stories were harbingers in their communities for past, current, and future realities. The women from my prior study refuted the "culture of dissemblance" that encouraged their silence and submission. Instead, they preferred to use their own resources of resistance against tropes that castigated their sexuality and their gender.[13] Likewise, by being interviewed and sharing their life histories, Black lesbian religious leaders shattered silence and subjugation. As these religious leaders exercised their voices, it became apparent to me that linguist Gwendolyn Etter-Lewis was accurate in saying that "it is oral narrative that is ideally suited to revealing the 'multilayered texture of Black women's lives.'"[14] Most of the Black women's oral histories that have been gathered are of heterosexual women, which made this study even more relevant and urgent.

I was also drawn to oral history because of its reputation as a method that centers the histories of persons who have been marginalized and excluded from dominant historical records.[15] In Alex Haley's famed retelling of his ancestry in *Roots*, audiences were able to learn from those whose stories had never been privileged. Following this logic, oral history offered other marginalized groups equal access to being included in the historical narrative. Ensuring the inclusion of these Black women's histories in the telling of the queer religious story was one of the reasons I wanted all the interviews to be housed on the LGBTQ-RAN website. As the African proverb states, "Until the lions have their own historians, tales from the hunt will always glorify the hunter." One cannot expect a heterosexist society or a racist and sexist community to be concerned with stories that subvert its authority. The human rights organization Voice of Witness acknowledges oral history's great capacity to produce subversive social change. It finds oral history to be a "medium that gives primary agency to the person whose story is being told, which makes it an ideal form for amplifying the stories of those who have been marginalized, disenfranchised, or harmed."[16] This is especially true for queer oral history, whose very identity markers place its stories on the fringes of history. However, capturing these stories is complex. In *Bodies of Evidence: The Practice of Queer Oral History*, Nan Boyd and Horacio Roque Ramírez wisely note that there is no guarantee that our efforts will result in the emergence of a diversity of queer experiences and desires.[17] In fact, they argue that queer storytelling has the potential for great social change but that it is methodologically tricky because we do not all inhabit the same sexual consciousness—for example, an interviewee may be proudly self-identifying now and vehemently in the closet in their earlier life. Yet a benefit of queer oral history is that it brings to the reader the endless possibilities of looking at a religion, a community, or a leader in a fully embodied way.

When I started this project, I was sure of the suitability of oral history as the main methodological focus, but this does not mean that I chose this method in a vacuum. I am aware that oral history by its nature is reliant on the interviewee for the "truth" and is dependent on that interviewee's memory of events. Thus, it is potentially a faulty enterprise if one is interested only in fitting these women's stories into what dominant culture has deemed to be history. Because their stories were never meant to be historical, there may be moments of what ethicist Katie Cannon called "structured amnesia." Oral history is nonetheless useful because even with its potential faulty memory, its "anecdotal evidence does a lot to reveal the truth as to how oppressed people live with integrity."[18] As a general rule, I took the interviewees' narratives at face value—although I had done prior research to make sure that I was at least asking questions that were based on their documented history. I also gave each interviewee the right of refusal, and I sent them their audio and transcript to make any excisions they deemed necessary.

I use my oral history lens with social justice in view, so just like the Truth and Reconciliation Commission in South Africa's commission of oral histories after apartheid ended, one of the goals of my research agenda is to pursue a healing and restorative history that includes those whose stories have been overlooked. Thus, rather than reflect a historical record simply of oppression, these oral histories will reveal a purposeful journey that also includes survival and thriving. The goal is not to present a legendary, larger-than-life lesbian religious leader. Instead, the aim is to highlight individual narratives and to analyze how these individuals' revelations and revolutions were intertwined with historical moments in religious and national communities. As such, the eighteen oral histories that I conducted were excluded from IRB review because they are not generalizable.[19]

Although similar questions prompted all eighteen interviews, because of the ebb and flow of conversation and time limitations I used flexibility in getting through my questions. I gave interviewees the opportunity to skip any questions that they did not want to discuss. The text highlights their leadership styles while also recording their journey to self-awareness of their sexual, racial, and religious identities. I allowed myself to be questioned in the interview process and found myself vulnerable in certain circumstances as I recounted my shameful past of Christian intolerance of same-sex attraction. I was equally made vulnerable by holding their stories of sexual abuse and domestic violence. Although the recordings do not often show the imprint that their sharing had on me as I kept up a dogged questioning pace, I left each interview emotionally exhausted and often unable to return to the transcripts until some time had passed.

I made some editorial decisions regarding the placement of the transcripts in this text, with full awareness that the transformation of oral speech to text necessarily involves changes in the performative and chronology of the interview.[20] I have edited for clarity but have tried to retain the cadence and rhythm of the participant's speaking style while removing some of the colloquial phrases such as "you know" and "like." Unless the interviewee requested these be permanently removed, they remain in the full transcript that is housed on the LGBTQ-RAN website so that the text matches the audio. Most importantly, I have made sure that the edits do not alter the speaker's original meaning.

Womanist Historiography

Given the interest in conveying their stories in their own words, this text also has a womanist orientation. Just to be clear, I am not stating that these leaders are womanist or would even be comfortable with me associating them with womanism. I concur with womanist ethicist Emilie Townes, who notes that although womanism is confessional, it can be used to describe a theorist or practitioner.[21] Thus, I am arguing that the framework for my interpretation of their stories is womanist. This project highlights women who used their experiences as marginalized outsiders to retain a critical posture to the structures in which they participate. Thus, to analyze their oral histories I partner with womanist historiography. This is a methodological lens taken from Alice Walker's four-part definition that describes a womanist as a "woman who loves other women sexually and/or nonsexually ... appreciates and prefers women's culture ... loves the spirit ... [and] is to feminist as purple is to lavender."[22] This womanist analysis comes from my situatedness as a third-generation womanist scholar trained by a womanist anthropologist to value the stories of living Black women. It is also bolstered by my understanding of psychologist Layli Phillips Maparyan's definition of womanism, which she identifies as the "social change perspective rooted in Black women's and other women of color's everyday experiences and everyday method of problem solving in everyday spaces." She characterizes womanism as having five features: (1) intentionally anti-oppression, (2) concerned with everyday experiences, (3) nonideological, (4) communal, and (5) spiritual.[23] Womanist theorizing relies on the everyday experiences of Black women, and because religion is so central to the lives of the Black women I interviewed, womanist thought takes seriously their spiritual concerns. Using both methodological lenses offer insight to illuminate the faith activism of Black lesbians who resist cultural invisibility and religious irrelevancy by serving as powerful religious leaders.

Womanist historiography is also a useful framework because it reflects on living agents, not fictionalized women's realities.[24] Following womanist ethicist Katie Cannon's theorizing of womanist emancipatory historiography as a "method of investigation that involves a critical, socio-ethical analysis of the past, undertaken by examining who has been silenced, marginalized, and excluded in specific historical records in order to achieve a more profound understanding,"[25] this method is automatically responsive to the voices and experiences of Black lesbian Christians who have been silenced and marginalized. Attending to the moral agency displayed by these women in spite of their marginalization gives a glimpse of the underside of history, and their histories would be incomplete without capturing not only their relegation but also their resistance to this denial of their full humanity.

Womanist Ethical Leadership

Finally, womanist historiography offers a means of interpreting the narrative histories in a way that illuminates what I see as an underlying womanist leadership structure. In her formative article "What's So Special about Women? Women's Oral History," oral historian Sherna Gluck contends that because of the creation of a new validation of women's experiences, women's oral history can be a feminist encounter even if the interviewee is not a feminist, and I assert that my interviewees are engaged in a womanist leadership style that is shaped by their intersectional identities.[26] Building on the various theories of womanism, I read their life histories as being communally oriented, justice seeking, spiritually rooted, and reflective of the fact that ethical leadership often stems from everyday acts of morality. Just as the scholarship on Black leadership points toward the griot and oral tradition as a means of understanding the charisma and clarion call of contemporary leaders, so through examining these women's oral histories I argue that their leadership also stems from womanist ways of knowing that include lessons learned from other women on similar journeys.

Business executive consultant Debora Jackson sees Black women leaders as embodying womanist values such as "survival, liberation, wholeness, spirituality, empowerment, family, community, reciprocity, egalitarianism, and extended family," and she advises that Black women seeking to lead from a womanist standpoint should embrace the stories of the women who shaped them as a means of learning from the experiences of those who were marginalized and resisted.[27] When I looked over their stories, the themes of resistance through social justice activism, spirituality, authenticity, and cooperative leadership came to the forefront. These themes were present in almost every interview, yet their narratives also demonstrated each of the tenets that Jackson presents as womanist values. In light of this, I was left to question what difference their queer identity made to their womanist leadership styles. I discovered that their lesbian identification often triggered a cooperative and holistic justice style of leading that was not always apparent when compared to heterosexual Black women's leadership. Queer Black religious leaders used intersectional frameworks for leading their groups that seemed to be elevated by their increased awareness and empathy for other perspectives. Thus, a womanist ethical leadership model that is patterned after these Black lesbian religious leaders would emphasize leadership strategies that are nonhierarchical, para-institutional, and intergenerational, allowing for leaders at any age or stage of life.

Overview of the Book

Before the book can present these eighteen interviewees as models of womanist ethical leadership, it begins by engaging some of the challenges facing these Black female religious leaders. Chapter 1, "Shattering Stained-Glass Ceilings:

African American Queer Storytelling," discusses their theological journeys through various Christian denominations or other religious traditions to land as religious leaders in particular contexts. Given that their institutional contexts vary, this chapter highlights some of their shared experiences while overcoming racial and gender oppression in religious spaces before delving into specific ecclesial circumstances where they had to deconstruct the "stained-glass ceiling." This chapter introduces all eighteen interviewees, many of whom will then reappear in more detail in subsequent chapters.

Chapter 2, "Going to Hell for My Authenticity: Existence as Resistance," examines the theme of womanist authenticity or existence as resistance by exploring how these women used the power of their authenticity to navigate ecclesial leadership structures and to amplify their calls for justice in their communities. This chapter highlights the significance of integrating their lesbian identity with their racial and religious selves, recognizing that by standing in their truths they were able to advocate for others. Drawing on philosopher Charles Taylor's theorizing on the ethics of authenticity and womanist ethicist Stacey Floyd-Thomas's theory of radical subjectivity, the chapter presents womanist authenticity as a key step in building a womanist ethical leadership model.

Chapter 3, "Justice Is Spiritual: Interrogating Spiritual Activism," focuses on the activist orientation of Black lesbian religious leaders. It illustrates how individual and collective acts of activism demonstrate larger social movements that have religious impetuses. Using Maparyan's theory of womanist spiritual activism to interrogate these leaders' faith activism, the chapter demonstrates the various ways that social justice activism is anchored within a faith leader's spirituality. By emphasizing their everyday acts of rebellion and collective community building, the chapter reflects their refusal to be relegated to obscurity and their commitment to the recognition of the full humanity of all.

Because not all of the women in the study are Protestant Christians, chapter 4, "Mighty Causes Are Calling Us: Expanding Womanist Spiritualities," examines the spiritual foci of the interviewees who were Buddhist, spiritualists, Jewish, and New Thought practitioners. Their narratives are juxtaposed with the womanist spiritualities of Diana Hayes, Emilie Townes, and Melanie Harris to help reveal that theistic connection to humanity is an important marker for womanist ethical leadership.

Although chapter 5, "Doing the Work Their Souls Must Have: Cultivating Womanist Ethical Leadership," illuminates the specific competencies required in womanist ethical leaders as reflected by my interviewees' lives, the book concludes by charting a new path for womanism and for those in leadership studies. The main aim of this chapter is to highlight specific skill sets and behaviors expressed in these Black lesbian religious leaders' lives as illustrative of some of the specific competencies required in womanist ethical leaders. The chapter provides examples from their cooperative leadership styles, noting that unlike some of the Black gay religious leaders whose leadership style has focused on institutional building and concern for assisting those impacted by HIV/AIDS, these women's religious impetuses propelled them into social justice activism that was intersectional and dependent upon coalitions.

The book's conclusion, "Leading from the Margins," challenges womanist theorizing to include a more pluralistic vision of Black female leaders that will include lesbians by pushing womanists to use living texts/living women as valid sources for analysis. The conclusion addresses current scholarship on ethical leadership in Black religious spaces and contends that ignoring Black lesbian religious activists' organizing impoverishes the scholarship and ethical models presented. The epilogue continues the expansion of scholarship noting the impact of online archives to democratize knowledge. Throughout this text I highlight the benefits of looking toward queer leadership as models for ethical management, positing that these lives are examples of the leadership required for sustained social change.

Shattering Stained-Glass Ceilings   1
African American Queer Storytelling

One thing we know as Black feminists is how important it is for us to recognize our own lives as herstory. Also as Black women, as Lesbians and feminists, there is no guarantee that our lives will ever be looked at with the kind of respect given to certain people from other races, sexes or classes. There is similarly no guarantee that we or our movement will survive long enough to become safely historical. We must document ourselves now.
—BARBARA SMITH AND BEVERLY SMITH, *I Am Not Meant to Be Alone*

To be a woman, Black, and active in religious institutions in the American scene is to labor under triple jeopardy.
—THERESSA HOOVER, "Black Women and the Churches"

It is not hyperbole to consider Black clergywomen's religious vocation as risky. Theressa Hoover's words, first published in 1974, describe the enterprise as a triple jeopardy. After conducting interviews with fifteen Black lesbian Protestant religious leaders about their ministerial careers, I concur with Hoover's assessment. What she noted in 1974 is still the case today: oppression remains even in sacred spaces. This chapter examines racism, sexism, and heterosexism in Black clergywomen's religious experiences by interrogating their intersectional realities. Specifically, the chapter provides an overview of the historical Black church's leadership structures, which have often marginalized women and queer persons. My interviewees represent both predominantly Black church denominations and mainline white denominations where Black women exert their religious leadership. Because the book explores Black lesbian women's ethical leadership paths, I also tackle the gender and heterosexist oppression prevalent in Black church spaces, an oppression often magnified by the racism that Black clergywomen experience in white religious spaces. The chapter thus sets the scene for understanding these clergywomen's storytelling as ethical acts of resistance to the multiple modes of discrimination they face as they live out their call to leadership.

The chapter centers on Christian examples of religious leadership because all but two of my eighteen interviewees had been formed in a significant way by Christianity. Although three of the eighteen interviewees were religious leaders outside of Christian models of ministry at the time of my research, I am choosing to highlight Christian leadership because for most of the participants this was their primary example of what it meant to be a religious leader. The chapter highlights the "ethical practice of truth telling" and suggests on the basis of these leaders' stories that tribulation and triumph are in fact signs of resistance.[1] Their attempts to shatter the stained-glass ceiling acknowledge that they had to create their own modes and spaces of leadership because the paths blazed before them did not always match their intersectional experiences.

Intersectionality in Sacred Spaces

Although the term *intersectional* refers to a modern theory, it is an idea with a long legacy.[2] Because of this project's focus on Black lesbian identity, understanding identity politics with the help of the Combahee River Collective's 1977 statement is particularly useful. In its predominantly Black lesbian statement, the collective argued that solidarity and joining the liberation struggle did not require subsuming one's particular struggles to the larger whole. Instead, it argued that Black women's subjectivity mattered because "if Black women were free, it would mean that everyone else would have to be free since our freedom would necessitate the destruction of all systems of oppression."[3] Ultimately, the members formed the collective to address the interlocking oppressions experienced by Black women that had not been addressed by the Black Power or feminist movement. Their organizing in secular society had shown them the dearth of attention to the plight of Black lesbians' struggles and made clear that if these systems of oppression were to be toppled, we must be attentive to the needs of the most oppressed individuals.

Acknowledging this premise is legal theorist Kimberle Crenshaw's concept of *intersectionality*, which provides an analytical framework for asserting the various ways in which race, gender, class, ethnicity, sexuality, age, ability, status, and other identities intersect to produce privileges and oppression. Crenshaw's initial use of the term in 1989 involved workplace discrimination cases, yet it is telling that she argued for an intersectional analysis, noting that Black women's "intersectional experience is greater than the sum of racism and sexism."[4] She posited that various forms of inequality operate together and exacerbate one another, creating a multilayered blanket of oppression. Yet she also recognized that there may be opportunities when the person most marginalized also retains aspects of privilege.

This recognition reiterates for this study's interest in Black lesbians' religious experiences that our identity formation matters and must be understood holistically by acknowledging that life is more than just episodes of discrimination. For those who are among the most marginalized members of society, this reminds them not to emulate the behaviors of oppressors when the opportunity arises. One of my interviewees, Bishop Yvette Flunder, describes this as oppression sickness, which is "internalized oppression that causes the oppressed to be infected by the sickness of the oppressor."[5] She warns of the seductive nature of deeming someone else inferior whenever there is an opportunity to exercise privilege and advantage over others and how ecclesial spaces are often places of monarchy, not ministry, that might otherwise be one of the few places where minority members can demonstrate and sense their value.

For example, African Americans being addressed as clergy was often one of the few signs of respect offered to a maligned population. Yet even that titling did not ensure fair and equitable treatment. Enslaved Africans could exercise their faith, but only as far as white enslavers allowed. The antebellum period allowed some quasi-independent faith expression within white-supremacist restrictions. Once emancipation occurred, Black religious spaces led primarily by Black men with strong support from Black women spread across the United States, providing sites of Black group cohesion and influence. Thus, the institutionalization of Black faith sadly repeated the oppression sickness of white religious spaces by limiting leadership to males alone.

Denominational Stances on Women in Leadership

With independent Black churches standing as a visible opposition to white racist discrimination, the formation of Black denominations offered avenues for upward mobility and prestige.[6] Yet Black male dissatisfaction with discrimination seemed to stop just shy of offering full leadership to Black women. Hoover's statement at the beginning of the chapter references the unequal burden experienced by Black women who have participated in Black churches. She notes the historical expectation that Black women remain in support roles as the backbone of the church, with the emphasis on being kept in the background. This becomes statistically significant as one delves into the practices of the various denominations.

In *Daughters of Thunder: Black Women Preachers and Their Sermons, 1850–1979*, historian Bettye Collier-Thomas illuminates in painstaking detail how the study of Black women and religion is crucial to understanding US religious authority. Writing to protest the invisibility of historical women in leadership roles, she finds it useful to document the transition from acceptance of women as clergy to their ordination and finally to their elevation to the highest positions in certain denominations. For brevity's sake, I focus only on her discussion of the struggle for ordination because it represents the moment when a woman is "officially legitimated by [her] religious tradition" as a preacher.[7] Ordination is a more modern phenomenon; it was rare during the nineteenth century (when Black faith moved from being an invisible to a visible institution) to license women to preach, much less to ordain them. When the African Methodist Episcopal Zion (AME Zion) denomination ordained Mary Small to elder in 1898, this was a watershed moment, for ordination to elder represented the "highest of holy orders"; only elders were eligible to become bishops, the ultimate authorities in the church.[8] The debate over whether a woman could be an elder was picked up in various Black denominations, their sexist readings of scripture and gender roles often preventing them from making a similar decision. By 1920, most Black denominations acknowledged women as evangelists, which was a role that promoted support for their preaching skills while limiting the scope of their leadership possibilities.

Women advanced toward ordination at different times in different denominations, and this was not rushed by AME Zion's determination. Within the Methodist theological camp, women in the African Methodist Episcopal Church were initially licensed to preach in 1884 but forbidden pastorates until they were finally granted ordination as elders in 1956. In the Christian Methodist Episcopal Church, women's ordination occurred in 1948. Yet women did not gain full clergy rights until 1966.[9] Baptist theological positions allow for individual church autonomy, so the struggle for ordination has been vast. As a result, none of the three Black Baptist denominations—National Baptist Convention, USA; National Baptist Convention of America; and the Progressive National Baptist Convention—have published stances on women's ordination. Whereas Black Baptist church membership is "at least 75% female, women constitute less than 10% of church leadership and about

1% of African American Baptist pastors."[10] Varying theological stances, belief in biblical inerrancy, and sexist societal views about women's place in society are responsible for this discrepancy between female power in the pews and ecclesial leadership. Similarly, for Pentecostals generally, and specifically members of the Church of God in Christ, the largest Black Pentecostal denomination, denying women the right to ordination is juxtaposed with the early authority given to women to exhort, teach, and missionize. The Church of God in Christ is one of the last Black denominations to still officially have prohibitions against women's ordination as "pastor, elder, or bishop" while simultaneously defining their roles as evangelists and teachers who can "have charge of a church in the absence of a pastor."[11]

The number of female pastors and bishops elected in each of the denominations is evidence of the obstacles placed before Black women seeking to exercise their leadership skills. Yet sociologist Cheryl Townsend Gilkes's *If It Wasn't for the Women: Black Women's Experience and Womanist Culture in Church and Community* suggests that looking at pastoral and higher offices as the sole examples of leadership is a mistake. Her study of women in the Sanctified Church asserts that there are multiple sites of power and authority wielded by women even while they are denied access to the pastorate. She highlights church mothers, evangelists, missionaries, prayer-band leaders, deaconesses, and teachers as alternative leadership positions in which women have excelled.[12] In fact, she contends that these positions were the "real" power brokers in churches and in the denomination, and that they wielded great economic and social power. Although I agree with Gilkes and sociologist Daphne Wiggins that sole attention to resistance to clergywomen "obfuscates other manifestations of women's power and agency," this project focuses particularly on women who held some position of power and authority in religious spaces and used this power to work for social change.[13] The majority of the interviewees in the pages that follow were or are clergy and experience(d) discrimination because of their multiple identities not aligning with stereotypical images of clergy. It is therefore helpful to have a thorough understanding of how these stereotypes were formed.

Denominational Stances on Lesbians in Ministry

However, being women was not the interviewees' only obstacle to the full acceptance of their call to Christian ministry. Each had been religiously socialized in traditions that were nonaccepting of lesbians in general, and they had no prior examples of lesbians participating in religious leadership to guide them. In general, the Black church has been rather conservative regarding sexuality, resulting in a homophobic or heterosexist view of gays and lesbians. Within the Methodist theological perspective, African Methodist Episcopal leadership "does not support the ordination of openly gay clergy," and the Christian Methodist Episcopal leadership has no official statement on the sexuality of its clergy other than that they are not allowed to perform same-sex marriages.[14] The autonomy that each Baptist church enjoys has resulted in no official stances on gay clergy from any of the predominantly Black Baptist denominations. There is a predominantly white Association of Welcoming and Affirming Baptists with which Black churches could choose to affiliate, but this is an independent choice. Finally, the Church of God in Christ has a clear statement denouncing the "sinful" homosexual practices of same-sex couples, which it considers to be "in violation of religious and social norms and . . . aberrant and deviant behavior."[15] Using biblical literalism to support its strong stance, its hierarchy prevents individual churches from expressing contrarian views.

Whereas views on gay clergy may have been only tangentially discussed by the major seven denominations, the mobilization of Black rhetoric against same-sex marriage gained traction in 2004, with numerous denominations making their first official statements in opposition to same-sex unions. This was apparently done with little coordination between the denominations but with some political pressure to speak to this "wedge" issue in the 2004 presidential election. Womanist theologian Kelly Brown Douglas sought to discover what had provoked so many Black pastors to speak out, and she posits that they did so in response to the 2003 Massachusetts Supreme Judicial Court decision that bans on same-sex marriage were unconstitutional.[16] Perhaps sensing the changing winds of social opinion as various states made same-sex marriage legal, the mounting resistance ultimately could not stop the landmark 2015 US Supreme Court *Obergefell v. Hodges* ruling, which made same-sex marriage legal throughout the United States. Within days of this ruling, six of the seven Black Protestant denominations (excluding the Progressive National Baptist Convention) made public statements denouncing same-sex marriage while simultaneously stipulating their Christian love of gay brothers and sisters.

Finding a unified voice in their heterosexism, these statements certainly reflected their conservative biblical interpretations, but they also reflected how diverse sexualities have historically been deemed a threat to Black respectability in a racist society.[17] Brown Douglas calls this a "hyper-proper sexuality": a technique that Black people adopted to mitigate concerns about their sexuality, which resulted in Black churches establishing sexist and heterosexist norms to mirror white society.[18] Acceptance of the "clobber" biblical passages that seem to disparage same-sex desire is one way that Black churches ostensibly proved their morality; they also did so through the promotion of procreative married heterosexual families as further evidence of their similarities to white unions.[19] Perhaps most perniciously, Black churches responded to their gay and lesbian congregants by rendering them invisible: ignoring their "private" lives while at the same time demanding a public performance of heterosexuality. Many Black churches demonstrate a "don't ask don't tell" policy, where Black gays and lesbians are "welcomed" to the extent that they keep certain details about themselves unspoken in the congregation. Yet ethicist Victor Anderson contends that this is hypocritical, for churches use "gay members to play music and sing songs that will set the stage for [the pastor's] hortatory ejaculations" while simultaneously expecting them to conform to church moral teachings that are disrespectful of their sexual truths.[20] Each of the interviewees remembered experiences of similar negotiated acceptance when they participated in nonaffirming religious spaces.

Lesbians in Black Churches

Just as patriarchy is devastating to women, so too is homophobia menacing to gays and lesbians. The presence of homophobia in Black religious spaces that are overwhelmingly female reminds us of Flunder's theory of oppression sickness—that those who have been marginalized seek someone over whom to wield power. In fact, the treatment of gays and lesbians in Black churches confirms Black feminist Barbara Smith's assertion that "heterosexual privilege is usually the only privilege that Black women have. None of us have racial or sexual privilege, almost none of us have class privilege, [so] maintaining 'straightness' is our last resort."[21] For some, exercising heterosexual privilege within a space where their own power has been usurped by sexist restrictions is seen as an equalizer.

Part of the premise of heterosexual privilege looming large in Black churches assumes that Black church spaces are predominantly heterosexual. Given the pervasive nature of gay bashing and heterosexist assaults, it makes sense that there are some gay and lesbian members passing as heterosexual in Black church spaces. Pastoral theologian Horace Griffin posits that Black lesbians in churches are more difficult to identify, for the "stereotypical lesbian did not have a church affiliation," instead affiliating with bars, nightclubs, street life, and prisons.[22] Griffin contends that Black gay men were stereotypically effeminate and accepted by Black churches in certain roles, whereas Black lesbians were associated with "sinful" activities outside of churches' holy grounds. I find it ironic to presume the absence of lesbians in religious spaces or to present masculine-identifying lesbians as unsuitable for church. However, I delve deeper into this assumption by arguing that the variety of Black lesbian gender expressions (femme, butch, aggressive or AG, stud, dominant, gender bender, and so on)[23] remains unnuanced by scholars such as Griffin. The presumption that only one type of lesbian exists and only as an unsatisfactory participant in the gender codes of Black churches is erroneous. Griffin admits his shock when he discovered that his elementary schoolteacher who had taught vacation Bible school and one of his church choir members were lesbians, and this shock highlights the expectation that lesbians represent in the same way that he depicts the effeminate gay choir member as the one way to express gay identity in Black churches.

Performance scholar E. Patrick Johnson rightly notes in his oral histories of queer southern women the existence of the stereotypical church-lady image as a "trope employed by 'lipstick lesbians' (i.e., feminine) to signal same-sex desire within the visual economy of the black church."[24] He also provides examples of masculine-identifying women finding space in arenas that allow them more latitude to express masculinity, such as driving the church bus, moving tables in the fellowship hall, or serving on the usher board. I concur with Johnson that many lesbians use existing acceptable gender codes to be more at home with their sexual identity and gender expression. Of course, femmes can find opportunities for acceptance in Black churches that idolize dress as a sign of sanctification and adherence to moral values. This reiterates ethicist Melanie Jones's description of the panopticon surveilling Black women's attire; she advocates for "space for Black women to flaunt their full selves in the face of unrelenting individual and collective scrutiny."[25] Ultimately, this is what full acceptance of Black lesbians in congregations looks like, not just their acquiescing in spaces where they can be free without having to speak out about their sexual identity. According to the 2015 data from the Social Justice Survey Project, 27 percent of Black LGBT survey respondents were out to no one in their religious communities, but 40 percent were out to all in their religious communities, indicating that "traditional Black churches are more accepting than commonly assumed."[26] Likewise, the majority of my interviewees were out to at least some members in their religious communities, which contradicts the notion that Black churches are bastions of heterosexuality. Thus, this project counters the notion of the invisible Black lesbian congregant by emphasizing the ways in which Black lesbians can coexist in their religious environment without having to be in the closet.

The presence of Black lesbians in Black churches also debunks the pervasive myth that the Black religious community is more homophobic than other religious or secular communities. It is certainly sexist and heterosexist, but the demarcation of being "more homophobic" stems from national research data sets, such as the General Social Survey and the Pew Research Center, which both indicate correlations between religious participation and opposition to homosexuality. In these studies, Blacks measure as more religious than the general population, with the majority identifying as Christian members of predominantly Protestant denominations. These studies also reveal a link between religious participation and intolerance toward gays and lesbians. Although there has been a gradual increase in Black Protestant acceptance of homosexuality (where now 50 percent of those surveyed in the Pew data believe that homosexuality should be accepted and even more persons support same-sex marriage), polling data seem to indicate that the Black religious community is moving too slowly in comparison to the broader population in its support of gays and lesbians.[27] However, Black Protestants are more accepting than those holding conservative Christian views, such as white evangelical Protestants, Mormons, and Jehovah's Witnesses. When the Public Religion Research Institute conducted its 2017 American Values Atlas, it found that Black Protestants were far more likely to acknowledge discrimination against LGBT persons and support legal protections against discrimination for LGBT persons than other ethnic groups.[28] The surveys demonstrate that although Black Protestants are heterosexist, they are certainly not the most heterosexist segment of the population. Thus, I find it especially futile to expend energy denouncing Black Christianity as more virulently homophobic than white Christianity because both sides pull from the same conservative interpretations of the Bible. Instead, I posit that the cultural expectation or historical memory (despite not being based entirely on fact) of the Black church as an all-encompassing justice-seeking institution conflicts with those clergy/laity who stand in opposition to the full inclusion of gays and lesbians into their communities.

Despite this opposition, Black lesbians do remain in their churches, perhaps because their conditional acceptance is enough to keep them within the familiarity of the Black religious expression. Black lesbian religious activist

Rev. Irene Monroe contends that to be "cut off from the Black church is really [to be] cut off from the Black community, the Black family . . . from your lifeline."[29] This may be one of the main reasons why Black LGBT persons do not leave their religious identities—that religion and spirituality are more important to them than to any other LGBT people of color.[30] Whereas it is true that Black Protestants are in general less likely to leave their Christian identities behind, it is worth probing whether Black lesbians may have reasons for staying within their traditions other than just a sense of community. For instance, Black churches also offer an opportunity for Black lesbians beyond Johnson or Griffin's imagination: a viable dating pool of largely single Black women. Although Johnson recalls Ann Allen Shockley's fictional account of a lesbian pastor seducing female congregants, one should also think of the many consensual and noncoercive relationships made possible in an environment that is so rich with available women, not all of whom are heterosexual. Johnson's *Black.Queer.Southern.Women* gives considerable space to the alternative religious expressions in which his interviewees participated, noting how these woman-centered spiritualities often replaced the significance of Christianity for his participants. In my small sample of eighteen women, I discovered that although women certainly experienced difficulties in their Christian communities, most of them chose to stay within Christianity instead of turning to an alternative religious expression.[31] I posit that it is their religious calling as leaders and not just participants that explains this difference.

Denominational Shopping and Swapping

This is not to say that lesbians' ties to Christianity are enough to keep them in Black Christian communities. In fact, a sizable number of my interviewees traded in the Black denominations of their youth for predominantly white Christian denominations such as the Quakers/Friends, the Metropolitan Community Churches, the United Methodist Church, and the Episcopal Church. Most of the interviewees were already aware of their same-sex desire as children but were also aware of their religious communities' opposition to their presence as same-gender-loving women. As with Black LGBTQ persons who experienced a period of exile from Christianity after coming out, my interviewees also had a season of separation. When I interviewed Bishop Flunder, she explained this religious exile as her space to open her heart to other possibilities: "I never believed myself out of relationship with God. I just knew that I was out of relationship with the Church of God in Christ."[32]

Like so many others, she still believed in God and in her Christian calling but set out to find a new space in which to exercise her gifts.

One way to be able to live out their calling was for such women to move to predominantly white denominations that had made more strides at accepting gay clergy than Black denominations. Although the shift to white denominations also happened for Black gay men, heterosexual Black clergywomen shifted to white denominations as well. Delores Carpenter's signature study of Black clergywomen, *A Time for Honor*, surveyed Black clergywomen (without specifying their sexual orientation) and discovered that 45 percent of women surveyed had switched denominations, with a significant number doing so for employment or ordination purposes.[33] Carpenter noted that 60 percent of the first wave of Black female seminarians went to work for predominantly white churches, a fact closely related to the lack of employment opportunities in Black Protestant traditions. She observed that the placement system for the two largest Black Protestant denominations (Baptists and Church of God in Christ) requires a personal invitation to become a candidate for religious leadership and that the Church of God in Christ will not appoint women to a pastorate.

Carpenter's study was conducted in 1999, and no one has updated her specific findings in a substantive way. But from the information gathered for the "State of Clergywomen in the U.S.," published in 2018, pastoral theologian Eileen Campbell-Reed confirmed that the trend of women of color finding work in predominantly white churches has continued commensurate with the rising number of Black female seminarians.[34] Thus, for Black lesbian clergy to find their way to mainline white denominations such as the United Methodist, Lutheran, Presbyterian, Episcopalian, Disciples of Christ, United Church of Christ (UCC), Reformed Church, Anabaptist, Quakers, and Metropolitan Community Churches (MCC) is predictable, given these overall trends.

Introducing Interviewees' Transitions into
Predominantly White Denominations

On average, my interviewees had been participants or leaders in at least three denominations by the time I interviewed them. Although they may have entered spaces that offered them employment and space to grow in leadership, this did not mean that these spaces were prepared to deal with the impact of their intersectional identities in the congregation. Yet they were spaces where their lesbian identity would not be an impediment to their ecclesial success.

For example, during my interview with Rev. Dr. Cari Jackson she reminisced over dealing with racism from white people who assumed that because they were gay, they couldn't also be racist. She served as an associate pastor in a United Methodist church, an interim senior pastor for a Presbyterian church, and a senior pastor of a UCC church after acknowledging her call to ministry in a Metropolitan Community church. She came to realize that despite her Black Pentecostal upbringing, "much of [her] calling has been to work with wealthy white people." That also meant that she experienced lots of "isms." Although she was in a leadership position, that alone did not mean that everyone was willing to follow her.

Several of my interviewees had at some point moved into leadership with the UCC, which as early as 1972 ordained a white gay man, and then its first white lesbian woman in 1977. For some, their start with the UCC was happenstance, as Jackson described an act of listening to the Holy Spirit guiding her to a specific church that happened to be UCC. Rev. Naomi Washington-Leapheart had been an active Black Baptist before attending Lancaster Theological Seminary. She decided to go to a UCC church because it was close to the campus. During her visit, she introduced herself as a seminarian and was invited to preach at the church (despite never having delivered a sermon before). Less than a year later, this congregation called her as part of a three-member co-pastoral team, which she saw as no coincidence but rather as the Spirit guiding her to this particular community.

Likewise, Rev. Dr. Renee McCoy has found herself pastoring a UCC church in her retirement years after decades of service to the MCC and the Unity Fellowship Church Movement, the first denomination founded for openly gay and lesbian African Americans. She was on the front lines with Unity Fellowship when she pastored Full Truth, a Detroit church that joined Unity to create a national organization. After she retired from Full Truth and the Unity denomination, she moved to Seattle, where she attended a UCC church that was welcoming. She currently serves as its interim pastor. She told me that even though she didn't know what "UCC people do," God sent her there.

Another interviewee who defected from Unity to the UCC was Bishop Tonyia Rawls. She was raised in a Black Baptist church but attended a Church of God in Christ church in her neighborhood, where she was licensed as an evangelist missionary, the highest leadership position that a woman can hold in this denomination. As she came to acceptance of her same-sex desire, she found herself at Unity Fellowship, where she was ordained, called to pastor, and elevated as bishop. However, she also felt led to move her church membership to the UCC. Like Bishop Flunder, who found in the UCC a larger community with whom to network and a place in which she could help address larger social justice issues, they both respected the congregational autonomy that the UCC provides alongside the denominational support.

Some might view these career moves as demonstrating a lack of denominational loyalty, but my interviewees expressed them as opportunities that occurred when they listened to a call from God nudging them in a different direction. Given the reality of a stained-glass ceiling in whatever direction they turned, this Spirit-led decision led them to predominantly white denominations while remaining in predominantly Black congregations. For example, when I interviewed Dr. Sylvia Rhue, she talked about her past experience as a Seventh Day Adventist and the outright racism she experienced attending a predominantly Black congregation in a white denomination. As a Seventh Day Adventist, she had been taught that Blacks were under the curse of Ham and that even Heaven would be segregated. While recovering from this bad theology, she befriended Rev. Cecil Murray, then the pastor of First African Methodist Church, Los Angeles. He had agreed to be featured in *All God's Children*, her documentary on homophobia and the Black church. Through this friendship, she found her way back into the Christian community. During her last interview with me she was a member of Bishop Flunder's City of Refuge UCC and experiencing Flunder's model of radically inclusive Christianity.

Another interviewee who had joined a predominantly white denomination but preferred her predominantly Black congregation is Rev. Dr. Pamela Lightsey. When I interviewed Rev. Dr. Lightsey, she spoke of leaving her Black Pentecostal background because of the patriarchy of a male pastor and a "strange switch on patriarchy" she experienced from her female pastor, who blocked her from being licensed to preach in that church. She was influenced by a United Methodist chaplain while in the military and joined a United Methodist church that was supportive of her call to ministry and her desire to pursue higher education. Yet with this education came the reality that she would be placed in a cross-racial appointment (meaning that she would be placed into a white congregation), but she had discerned she needed a "deep kind of relationship with members of the Black community." Even now, as one of the few Black ordained elders in the United Methodist Church with a PhD, she challenges the church to deal with its heterosexism because she believes that her privilege demands she take a stand.

Taking a stand within one's tradition often begins at an early age. Three of my interviewees learned quite early that they had to forge their own type of Christianity, one that provided meaning for them even if that differed from what their Black community deemed normative. Mandy Carter was raised in an orphanage and a foster home that exposed her to Christianity within predominantly white circles. She determined at the young age of twelve that there was "nothing there for me," an opinion she still holds today. Yet during high school she was exposed to the American Friends Service Committee (AFSC) and introduced to the Quakers, which "changed my life." She was particularly persuaded by the Quaker notion of the power of one, meaning that we all have potential to effect change, and by the predominantly white organization's commitment to racial justice. She eventually worked alongside the AFSC with the War Resisters League. There is no official hierarchy of Quaker leadership in unprogrammed Friends worship, for Quakers believe that all are ministers and responsible for the care of worship and community. Thus, because of Ms. Carter's participation in the Quaker community and social justice organizing, I gathered her oral history as a religious leader.

Another interviewee who was socialized in white denominations at an early age was seminary dean Emilie Townes. She was initially raised in a predominantly Black church in the United Methodist tradition, but her parents had made a commitment that their children would be brought up in a church that had the best Sunday school, no matter the denomination. As a result, they eventually attended a predominantly Black Presbyterian church. As a teen, she was given the freedom to choose a tradition for herself, and she decided to spend time sitting in nature at the Duke Forest rather than being in any church. She reminisced about sitting and talking with God in the forest, where she was led into a closer relationship with God. Townes experienced a call to ministry while at the University of Chicago Divinity School. She had asked to be assigned to a field education site that was in any religious tradition unfamiliar to her, and she was placed at Hyde Park Union, which was a combination of American Baptist and UCC. Although this was a predominantly white congregation, she remarked that she strangely felt that she "had come home," and it was in this community that she was ordained in the American Baptist denomination.

This experience of coming home to a predominantly white community was one also shared by my interviewee Rev. Kentina Washington-Leapheart. She grew up without really having a Christian influence (apart from the gospel choir in which she sang), and she remarked that even while singing in the choir she had no concept of church, theology, and so on. Her childhood neighborhood was heavily Jewish, and her school was quite diverse, so she was exposed to Catholics, Seventh Day Adventists, Jews, and Baháʼís, all novelties to her because her family was more "secular Christian." After college she started attending Trinity United Church of Christ with one of her sorority sisters and became quite active in the community, and this eventually led to her decision to attend seminary to further explore theology. In time, she joined an Episcopal congregation in Chicago that she still considers her church home despite having since moved to the greater Philadelphia area. In 2018 she was ordained in a very different community than she had grown to call home: The Fellowship of Affirming Ministries, a space where she could "be the pieces and parts of my most authentic self."

Affirming Ecclesial Spaces

When I started conducting interviews, I initially expected the interviewees to be leaders in gay-affirming Black denominations because I erroneously assumed that my interviewees would choose communities with higher percentages of Black gay and lesbian congregants. I assumed that their allegiances to the Black community would override denominational preferences. Yet only four of the interviewees had spent significant time with the Unity Fellowship Church Movement. In fact, it was far more likely for them to have been members of an MCC church than Unity, and perhaps this has to do with MCC's geographical density and organizational capacity.

Metropolitan Community Churches was founded by Rev. Elder Troy Perry, a gay white Pentecostal preacher whose goal was to create a church that would reach into the gay community and include anyone who "believed in the true spirit of God's love, peace, and forgiveness."[35] Over the next fifty years MCC expanded to include 172 affiliated churches. It now has a presence in thirty-three countries and participates in the World Council of Churches as well as the National Council of Churches (USA).[36] Whereas it is most notable as the first Christian denomination to serve the spiritual needs of the lesbian, gay, bisexual, and transgender community, its public messaging strives to distance itself from being just a "gay church," instead identifying itself foremost as a church of followers of Jesus. These MCC members come from a variety of mostly Christian denominations yet remain a historically and predominantly white community despite allowing significant congregational autonomy.

This congregational autonomy allows for a variety of leadership and worship styles that appeal to many Black gay and lesbian congregants. In fact, seven of my interviewees had spent significant time in the MCC community, and four of those interviewees had been MCC leaders. Each leader worked within the MCC structure to create a space for themselves, which sometimes meant attending a predominantly Black MCC congregation or forming a community for Black members in a predominantly white congregation. For example, Elder Darlene Garner rose to the highest echelons of authority in the MCC as their first Black elder, but it was still necessary for her to create the MCC Conference for People of African Descent, Our Friends, and Allies as a set-aside space for Black members. She had experience in both community spaces because she had participated in her family's Black Baptist church and attended a predominantly white Episcopal church. She recalled that her isolation in the Episcopal space was not solely because of her race but rather that their unwelcoming attitude had more to do with her sense of call to ministry at a time when the possibility of female clergy was a polarizing issue for the Episcopalians. Shortly after leaving the Episcopal Church, she found MCC and "from the very beginning, knew that I had come home" because she liked its commitment to human rights and saw it as committed to diversity of race, gender, nationality, language, and physical ability. She experienced its "religious community as being truly a manifestation of Heaven on Earth, because it included everyone." As she grew in leadership responsibilities, she maintained commitments with Black gay and lesbians in secular organizations until she was ultimately able to organize an annual conference for Black members in the MCC that generally attracts around a thousand people.

The importance of this conference in helping Black members feel at home in the MCC is not lost on Garner's wife, Rev. Candy Holmes, who served as the MCC program officer for People of African Descent and the chair of the People of African Descent Conference. Rev. Candy Holmes also had an eclectic religious upbringing that gave her experiences in predominantly white religious spaces before she united with the MCC. Although she was reared in a Black Baptist church, she became quite active in an Apostolic church, which is where she became aware of her same-sex attraction. This led to a period of religious exile. She eventually started attending a New Thought community before attending her first MCC church. Holmes recounted in her interview that when she started attending MCC, there were not a lot of Black people and especially not Black female ministers, yet she and her wife found their way into significant leadership roles within the denomination while carving out space for other Black women to follow. It is particularly noteworthy that for those who stayed within MCC, the lack of diversity in worship, personnel, and leadership was not enough of a deterrent. They made space for themselves by recognizing that they were in essence creating a "church home for Black LGBT people . . . who were marginalized by the white gay community and the Black church."[37]

Often, this home was only actualized after a period of religious exile, as was the case for Dr. Imani Woody. She grew up with a father who was a Baptist and Holiness pastor, and after an abusive childhood she had no concept of a God worth worshipping. A girlfriend introduced her to MCC, and it became a home for her despite the many cultural differences she experienced, such as women in leadership and unfamiliar worship styles. Even as an active participant in her MCC congregation as a board of directors member and a national MCC program officer for Older Adults, she told me that she does not classify herself as a Christian in a traditional sense but rather seeks to be "Christ-like as I walk through the world."

Black-Gay-and-Lesbian-Affirming Ecclesial Spaces

The MCC's autonomous structure allows congregations to choose their own worship styles, which means there is a risk that any first-time attendee may enter a space with a type of worship different from the one that she prefers. White denominations are notable for their more restrained worship styles, which sometimes seem too staid in light of Black religious expression, which typically includes shouting, dancing, and vocal and bodily performances.[38] When Horace Griffin described the emergence of Black gay and lesbian congregations, he began with those fleeing MCC, noting that for some Black gay and lesbian congregants there is just not enough commonality shared because of being gay to risk potentially encountering racism; thus, for many it is not worth "leaving the familiar, albeit homophobic, Black church worship experience."[39] Those who shared this opinion were a captive audience when Unity Fellowship Church Movement formed in 1985.

Unity Fellowship Church Movement was founded by Carl Bean, a Black gay gospel musician (with a Baptist and Pentecostal background) who moved to Los Angeles, where he started a specialized ministry for openly gay and lesbian African Americans. The movement started as a Bible study group in 1982, with a liberation theology focus advocating social justice and specifically the needs of Black gay men with AIDS. Bean's congregation formed officially as a church in 1985. It taught respect for all religious traditions, for "God is greater than any religion, denomination, or school of thought," and "God is love and love is for everyone."[40] Archbishop Bean launched a denomination that as of 2020 has fifteen congregations across the United States that draw from a variety of religious expressions, including African traditional religions, spiritualism, and Protestant Christianity. Unity has been seen by the Black LGBTQ community as appealing because it "comes from who we are, our background, our culture, what we believe, how we worship. . . . MCC could not serve that need."[41]

Unity is fledgling in size compared to MCC, but it is concentrated in urban areas of ten states with significant populations of Black LGBTQ persons (including New York City, Newark, Detroit, Atlanta, Baltimore, Washington, DC, and Philadelphia). Although there is no longer a current affiliation in Detroit, there was when my interviewee Rev. Darlene Franklin first encountered Unity. Although she was active in the Black Baptist community, she fled from homophobic content in worship and sought a new congregation. She was told about Full Truth, a Unity church led by my interviewee Rev. Dr. Renee McCoy, and Rev. Franklin joined her on her first Sunday and "stayed there every day for seventeen years." She noted the heaviness in that initial community, as this was during the worst years of people dying from AIDS, and she was introduced to ministry as literally doing something to save people's lives: providing food, housing, counseling, funerals. Unity was nationally known for its Minority AIDS Project (MAP), which was the first community-based HIV/AIDS organization in the United States established and maintained by people of color. This emphasis on social justice organizing remains significant in each of its churches.[42] Rev. Franklin was a diligent helper in the congregation, becoming ordained as a deacon, and eventually she was chosen to pastor the community. By the time I interviewed Rev. Franklin in 2018, she had left Unity like all the other women in this study and was exploring a healing ministry outside of the denomination.

Each of the women who pastored a Unity church described some experience with sexism in a community that was about freedom from oppression. Of course, this hypocrisy was not limited to this denomination and was present even in religious organizations established by women. When I interviewed Bishop Allyson Abrams, pastor of Empowerment Liberation Cathedral, she recounted a similar experience as a Black Baptist attending a United Methodist seminary and watching many of her classmates immediately be placed into

United Methodist churches. As a Baptist, her experience was quite different. She noted the number of Baptist positions that outright indicated they were seeking a man to fill their pastoral vacancy:

> So you would turn in your information to them, and a lot of those people don't even give you a call, don't send you a letter, just kind of act like you didn't even send them anything. And then some of those that you do send something to that do respond, they say, "Well. . . ." They give you the scripture, I think it's Timothy and, "This is what we're looking for." So I have so many of those, I really should have kept them all and put them in a big stack so I could show them to somebody one day. But I had so many of those. I was very discouraged for a long time, because it just seemed like, "OK, now. If God has called you to do this, why are you not able to do it?"

She started her own church and was subsequently elected pastor of a Baptist congregation in Detroit. While in this position, she felt led to train and advise pastors, so she founded Pneuma Christian Fellowship, an ecumenical coalition, and she was consecrated as bishop. Shortly afterward, she married Bishop Emeritus Diana Williams and resigned from her pastorate. As a result of the national scandal that her "secret" marriage created, the pastors operating under her in Pneuma Christian Fellowship were no longer willing to serve under her leadership, and she was ousted from her own organization.[43] She started a new nondenominational congregation in the greater Washington, DC, area called Empowerment Liberation Cathedral, and she still considers herself a bishop, believing that after having been elevated to that episcopal level in the church she should not "allow anyone to treat me differently due to my sexuality or orientation."[44]

The refusal to be treated differently, the desire to live authentically and to have ultimate autonomy over her own community, is what led Bishop Flunder to establish the City of Refuge and The Fellowship of Affirming Ministries. Bishop Flunder was reared in the Pentecostal Church of God in Christ denomination, but after accepting herself as a same-gender-loving woman she was exiled from the church for six years. She returned to church at the Love Center, an Oakland independent Pentecostal church led by Bishop Walter Hawkins where she served for almost ten years before realizing that she was "trying to live out my vision in somebody else's church."[45] She founded City of Refuge in San Francisco in 1991 as a space of radical inclusivity for women clergy, LGBTQ persons, and all persons regardless of race or social status, and as a space that would be committed to social justice.[46] Ultimately, she chose to align with UCC instead of MCC (whose lack of diversity in population and worship did not fit the congregation's Black "Metho-Bapti-costal" worship style) or Unity (whose geographical distance and insistence on not accepting clergy's prior ministerial experience were not ideal).[47]

When City of Refuge decided to plant churches, it decided to do so under its own organizational structure. The Fellowship was created in 2000 to support religious teachers and laity in a theology of radical inclusivity and radical social ministry.[48] It was later named The Fellowship of Affirming Ministries (TFAM), and Bishop Flunder was insistent in her interview that it is not a denomination but a coalition "coming to the fellowship for what the denomination cannot give us.... We're together because we want to be together." In this leadership model, autonomy is valued, as is diversity of expression. The personal freedom given to congregations and ministries within TFAM is a direct testament to the uniqueness of Bishop Flunder's organizational structure, which does not seem preoccupied with self-replication or sustainability as much as with demonstrating its core value of radical inclusivity.

The Ethical Practice of Truth Telling

All this demonstrated that there was and is no ideal faith community for Black lesbians, just spaces where infallible humans are trying to make a difference. In these women's attempts to shatter the stained-glass ceiling in various institutional contexts there were quite a few similarities in their experiences of racism, sexism, and heterosexism, which led them to create havens for others. They remained vigilant advocates for holistic justice for the most marginalized members of society but were also reflective about their own journeys from marginalization. In telling their stories, they were offering testimonies of more than just their oppression.

The late Black feminist bell hooks astutely asserted that the speech act of "talking back" is an "act of resistance, a political gesture that challenges politics of domination that would render us nameless and voiceless."[49] For hooks, speaking transforms by calling one from object to subject. One is not merely telling a story but becoming a subject worth listening to—one whose counsel can light the way for others. She highlights the significance of the oppressed speaking: "To speak as an act of resistance is quite different than ordinary talk, or the personal confession that has no relation to coming into political awareness, to developing critical consciousness."[50] When the interviewees accepted my invitation to share their stories, they were thus agreeing for their stories to be analyzed, to be theorized, and as Barbara Smith and Beverly Smith noted at the beginning of the chapter, they were willing to recognize their "own lives as herstory."

This is in line with their ancestral memory of the prominence of storytelling in Black people's perseverance through discriminatory times. Telling one's story represents the legacy of "slave narratives, folklore, and 'Black-preacher tales'" all the way to contemporary testimonials through tweets, poems, and political speeches.[51] Storytelling is a means of resistance, a way of talking back, an act of defiance to those who claim to know one's experience. Yet there is an art to this creative process. As hooks stated, it is not just a confession loosely shared. Leaders often rise to acclaim and authority because they have learned to tell their stories effectively in order to persuade persons to follow them. Thus, it was not shocking when I compared my interviews with their other public interviews or writings to find that they were strikingly similar and, in some cases, verbatim accounts of important moments for these women, demonstrating how each had perfected how to talk about their lives in such a way as to make others pay attention. Sadly, this is necessary for, as homiletician Christine Smith reminds us, "Gay and lesbian oppression is the daily experience of being silenced when heterosexual persons may speak, being made invisible when heterosexual reality is the only reality assumed and affirmed."[52]

The Black lesbian religious leaders I interviewed had shared their oral histories to speak against this silencing. They were not undone by the sexism or heterosexism they experienced by members of their own Black community. They were not slowed down by the incessant racism they experienced in their white denominations. They were buoyed and propelled forward by recognizing the necessity of their work and their voice. Just as Audre Lorde had reminded them that their silence would not protect them and that their speech was one of the first steps in their transformation, they knew that their stories would count as a "gesture of defiance that heals, that makes new life and new growth possible."[53] Thus, chapter 2 explores the topic of authenticity and the value of telling their stories in a way that is in tune with their full truth.

Going to Hell for My Authenticity   2

Existence as Resistance

And I decided that I would never again allow anything to cause me to leave any part or piece of myself, that I would engage all of ... I would enter life from a place of wholeness, not a place of brokenness, and no one would ever come between me and myself, my whole self. And that's kind of the way that I've lived since then.

—ELDER DARLENE GARNER, oral history interview, 2010

Black church is my home and always will be, always has been. It is my lifeline. I never gave up my card. I never gave up my Black church girl card, and I don't feel I need to. Just like I'm not going to give up my lesbian card. I'm not going to give up my social justice card; all of those are parts of who I am. The gift of me, and any of us is our full authentic self, so that's what I bring into all of the experiences.

—BISHOP TONYIA RAWLS, oral history interview, 2018

As a consultant for the Lesbian, Gay, Bisexual, Transgender Queer Religious Archives Network (LGBTQ-RAN), I was hired to conduct oral histories of Black LGBTQ religious leaders. I was immediately struck by what I initially thought of as my interviewees' courage to live out their callings in the authenticity of their lived realities. The more interviews I conducted, the more I began to glean that the choice to be authentic, to live their truths, and to be their whole selves was not just courageous; it was also correlated to these women's social justice commitments and desire to see others find the same path. My interest in their courage coupled with their commitment to others meant that my exploration of Black female religious leaders would focus solely on those who were "out": publicly known for their identities as lesbian/ queer/same-gender-loving. Thus, in this chapter I assess the theme of womanist authenticity or existence as resistance by exploring the oral histories of seven Black lesbian religious leaders. I examine their oral histories using Charles Taylor's philosophy on authenticity, Stacey Floyd-Thomas's theory of radical subjectivity, and Layli Maparyan's conceptualization of "standing in": staying within an oppressive system in order to change it from the inside. What I found was that these women used the power of their authenticity to navigate ecclesial leadership structures and amplify their calls for justice in their communities.

I organized my questions around the categories of race, gender, religious identity, and sexual orientation, and I asked each interviewee about which of these categories most spoke to her so that I could determine what parts of themselves they wanted highlighted, both in their oral histories and in their exploration with me of their religious leadership. Yet perhaps because of our shared experiences as Black women, race and gender were not identities that they spent a great deal of time unpacking in our interviews. They often mentioned religious identity only in passing and factually—for example, I was raised Baptist and ordained in MCC. Such brevity was not the case with sexual orientation. Discussing sexuality with "out" Black lesbian religious leaders was eye-opening. Because Black feminist scientist Evelynn Hammonds notes that the historical narrative about Black female sexuality has tended to avoid discussion of the lesbian or queer subject, often deeming her dangerous and potentially even traitorous to the Black race,[1] it did not surprise me that recovering the historical record of Black lesbian churchgoers is a difficult task. But it is not impossible.[2] If in general there is silence around Black female sexuality and if Black lesbians represent the "outsiders" within, my study asks this: What lessons can be learned from queer leaders?[3]

Black Lesbian Identity

All the interviewees were comfortable with the term *lesbian*, although some also used *queer* or *same-gender-loving*, depending on their context. This was not especially surprising, given the similar age range of my subjects, with most being in their mid-fifties. One could expect the term to have resonance with women socialized in a similar time period despite their different geographical contexts. In fact, the term *lesbian* became increasingly common in the 1970s (the formative pubescent period for many of the interviewees) thanks to a collection of women-identified-women who formed a group called Radicallesbians, which viewed lesbianism as an official "form of resistance to patriarchy" and opted to devote all their energies to their sisters as opposed to their (male) oppressors.[4] Within scholarship, equally positive was the perspective of poet and essayist Adrienne Rich's 1978 landmark essay, "Compulsory Heterosexuality and Lesbian Existence," which reminded readers that the lesbian experience should not be bracketed with other sexually stigmatized groups because it refers to a range of experiences beyond genital sexual experiences.[5]

This research supports the idea that self-identification as lesbian was also important for Black women whose narratives are even further hidden from public discourse. Self-awareness of one's sexuality as nondeviant in a society that has deemed all Black sexuality deviant is a monumental task. Historically, women and Blacks were deemed sexually loose, making Black women doubly condemned for their gender and race. For those who dare claim the identity of Black lesbian, this naming reflects Black women who are, as Black feminist Cheryl Clarke notes, "resisting the prevailing culture's attempt to keep us invisible and powerless . . . [, seeking to be] more visible . . . to our sisters hidden in their various closets." This naming signals an act of resistance for those who dare to be a "lesbian in a male-supremacist, capitalist, misogynist, racist, homophobic, imperialist culture such as that of North America."[6]

In her discussion of Black lesbian identity, Black feminist poet and theorist Audre Lorde acknowledged that being an out lesbian in the black community was difficult, which means that the act of being out and religious is subversive.[7] When I decided to focus my research on "out" Black female religious leaders, their audacity and hypervisibility in spaces that have historically and purposely not recognized them were issues worthy of documentation themselves. The importance of leading an authentic life was one of the central themes expressed by all eighteen of the oral history participants. Each woman described her desire to bring together all the various identities that made her a whole person. Each interview held a moment in which the woman being interviewed realized that living an authentic life meant accepting all parts of herself as good and divinely loved.

Let me introduce you to the first of seven such women. I introduce them via the titles they preferred.

Rev. Dr. Deborah L. Johnson is the founder and president of Inner Light Ministries, an Omnifaith outreach ministry dedicated to teaching the practical applications of Universal Spiritual Principles. She is also the founder and president of the Motivational Institute, an organizational-development consulting firm specializing in cultural diversity. In addition to being an author and instructor, she is also a founding member of the Agape International Spiritual Center in

FIGURE 2.1. Reverend Dr. Deborah Johnson. Used by permission.

Los Angeles and serves on the Leadership Council of Association of Global New Thought. She was a successful co-litigant in two landmark civil rights cases in California: one that set precedent for the state's Civil Rights Bill and one that defeated the challenge to legalizing domestic partnerships.[8]

More so than the other interviewees, Rev. Deborah Johnson included in her life narrative clear historical markers—perhaps because of our presumed age difference or perhaps to remind future generations mining her oral history for information. She seemed to want to remind me and them of the long arc of social justice that made possible her being her authentic self. She was quite moved at the outset of our interview, admitting that "I'm feeling very emotionally full that this interview is taking place and this project is even happening. I'd have killed to have this when I was [a] kid, anything that was evidence of LGBT life. I mean, there was nothing. You [ask] what was it like. There was nothing." Despite there being nothing overt paving the way for her to be free, out, and fully recognized in the world, she described her long-held hope for a "marriage between my idea of being able to just be OK, you know, and accepted, and respectable, and not second-class citizen, or second-tier. And if I had to make the environments myself, so be it."

Rev. Deborah had been "out" to her various communities at an early age but had negotiated this publicly while maintaining a private lesbian life. She recalls having the same girlfriend from the tenth grade all the way through college, but because she was so young, she was subject to her parents' disapproval of her identity (especially her mother, who believed that because Johnson was a minor, her parents would also be sent to hell for her actions). She was clear that it was not just the disapproval of her parents that shaped her identity as a lesbian at that time:

> In terms of history, to locate this, so in the state of California, the sodomy laws were on the books until 1974. [At that point] I'm halfway through college. So that any sort of affection, sexual activity between same-sex individuals was [punishable by] twenty years [in prison]. I mean we're talking a felony crime. This isn't even a misdemeanor. So you're illegal. And at the same time, '74, the American Psychiatric Association reclassified homosexuality because it had it as sick and depraved and deviant; you know, you aren't capable of being a parent or holding a job and all the rest of this.
>
> So it's this triple whammy. I have the law saying [I'm] a criminal, the church saying [I'm] satanic, and the psychiatric association saying I'm sick, so I really felt like I didn't have any other choice. It was like fight or

die. So my activism was really about [saying] you're wrong; all of you are wrong. I don't know how I knew, but I just knew, and in my mind I could see a day. It was almost like the slaves that could see freedom. I mean, I could literally see a day when it would be OK to be open; I could be proud; I really could be in a relationship; the world would accept me; I wouldn't be a second-class citizen. It was so real to me that I was willing to fight for that.

So for me it was kind of peeling away at it. My theology had to change. But first I had to literally, in my mind, be *willing to go to Hell for my authenticity*. And that was the conclusion that I came to around fourteen or fifteen, that if there was a Hell, then I was just going to have to go, because if I lived the life that they wanted me to live, I'd have been in Hell here *and* still had gone to Hell, because I knew who I was. So let me at least try to have some joy, some pleasure here because I just couldn't do it.

Part of her quest to find joy in being herself involved creating spaces where she could be accepted and embraced as a lesbian. Early in her young adult life she created a social club that put on events like cruises and plays for Black lesbians. Rev. Deborah identified this social club as the beginning of her ministry because "I created all these environments and things where we could go with dignity and pride." She recognized that there was a dearth of options for queer people of color, and she was willing to create something because the alternative of isolation and invisibility was no longer an option:

So I got to the point where I felt like my presence—and also on the gender issue and the racial issue. The males really dominated the early movement, and it was very hard for us as women to get a spot in that. And then AIDS hit. AIDS hit with a vengeance in the late '70s, early '80s. And I'm not kidding. It was like the men were sick. They were just really, really sick. And it was almost like World War II, where the women came into the factory. It was like that, where the men were so devastated the women came into power within the movement. And so much of the public perception of the LGBT community was around gay men, which had nothing to do with our lives. Even like the whatever, heightened sexuality business, like "Please . . . !" It just wasn't our life.

So it felt kind of incumbent upon me to tell the truth. Like there was a lie that was out there that needed to be debunked. There weren't many of us that were female that were "the face" [of the movement], and [there] certainly [weren't many] . . . people of color. And I felt it was just really important for the world to know that we're there; we exist. It was like this archive project or this oral history project that we're doing now. It is to say, "Hey, we're here, you know? We exist." And if it wasn't any more than just an affirmation of my own life, that I could no longer collude with the invisibility, because the invisibility was as oppressive as overt discrimination.

Integrating Fragmented Selves

Rev. Deborah's assertion that all her identities mattered and were necessary for her to feel authentic is what was most intriguing to me in conducting the oral histories. Her identity and those of the others as Black lesbian religious leaders meant that they were merging several unique identity categories. Although most of the interviewees told of periods of their lives when they felt forced to lead a compartmentalized life in which some identities could not be expressed, eventually all came to the same conclusion as Rev. Deborah—that bifurcation was not the path to authenticity. Thus, the radical pronouncement that queer identity and religious female leadership can go hand in hand shattered the silence. It declared that Black lesbians are not invisible but are invaluable members of Black religious organizations.[9] It was and is an important declaration because Black lesbian religious leaders are often in situations where others regard one of their identities as conflicting with another. For example, most of the women that I interviewed were in leadership in predominantly white settings. Although they experienced discrimination as deeply intersectional, they acknowledged that in these settings they were often viewed by their race first. Those leading in predominantly Black spaces faced obstacles based primarily on their gender. A few noted that they were either expected to deemphasize their gender or their lesbian identity in their predominantly Black organizations. Among those working for queer organizations, some commented on feeling the need to downplay their religious leadership. Those in religious institutions could experience either their queerness or their femaleness presenting challenges to how their authority was received and perceived. As one interviewee noted, these challenges resulted in a deep compartmentalization that left her "unwoven," with her strands coming apart.

My second case illustrates this compartmentalization. It concerns Elder Darlene Garner, a longtime leader in the Universal Fellowship of Metropolitan

FIGURE 2.2. Elder Darlene Garner. Used by permission.

Community Churches (MCC), the first Christian denomination to serve the spiritual needs of the lesbian, gay, bisexual, and transgender community. Garner's initial full-time ministry area was political activism; as such, she worked as executive director of the Philadelphia Mayor's Commission on Sexual Minorities and served as a member of the Philadelphia Commission on Human Relations, hearing complaints of discrimination based on persons' sexual orientation, race, gender, and national origin. She served as a pastor of several MCC churches and founded the MCC Conference for People of African Descent, Our Friends and Allies (PAD) in 1997. After decades of leadership, Elder Garner retired from the ordained ministry in the MCC in 2017 at the age of sixty-nine. Her interview highlighted both the damage she experienced from compartmentalization and the fulfillment she felt from living a whole life.[10]

My interview with Elder Garner illustrates the importance of authenticity. She had courageously taken on her family, employers, and eventually even the MCC to be fully present with all her gifts. She described her process of coming out as a "coming into self-awareness" while acknowledging what it cost her. Initially, her coming out to her family meant that her great-aunt told her relatives and church members that she had become a prostitute who had stolen money from her pimp, and this resulted in her immediate removal from their city. After accepting her identity as a lesbian, she relocated from Columbus, Ohio, to Washington, DC, and initially joined a predominantly white Episcopal church that she eventually left because she felt that the church would not welcome her call to ministry and that although it was tolerant, it was not welcoming of her as a Black woman. She recounted a feeling of "coming home" when she arrived at Metropolitan Community Church Washington, DC, and she was an active member there from 1976 until her publicly forced retirement in 2017.[11] It was in this religious space that she grew in leadership but also in her awareness that she needed a more integrated life:

> I was a member of MCC of Washington, DC . . . and with my three children had a really busy time as a member of the church. [I b]ecame a delegate to our general conference. I was on the board . . . as the treasurer of the church, and just kind of immersed myself in new theological discoveries and learned how to fully embrace myself as a beloved child of God, with no need for shame for being a lesbian. It was a wonderful time of self-discovery and discovering new things about God.
>
> But one of the realities that I faced at the time was that as a Black woman, it felt as though I had to choose between being Black and being lesbian. And so when I look back on that particular time in my life, I say that . . . I became unwoven; my strands all came apart. So . . . there came a point when my social community shifted from being my lesbian social community, shifted from being primarily through MCC, and I worked with six others to found an organization called the National Coalition of Black Lesbians and Gays in 1978. And . . . that required more and more of my time and attention and energy than I was able to put into the church. And one of the things that we did during that time was to orga-

nize an international conference for lesbian and gay people of color that preceded the first LGBT march on Washington. . . .

But it became really difficult for me personally, and there came a moment where I think all of my pieces just completely unraveled, and I actually got married to a man again, and left Washington, returned to Ohio. I had come [out] to this man. His name is Otis. And I told him that I was a lesbian and that I was tired, that I was just in pieces and I needed to rest. And he offered that if I were to marry him, that I could rest for whatever time that I needed to rest. . . . After four years (and another child), it was clear to me that I was ready to reengage my life. And so I moved from Cincinnati to Philadelphia. And the very first place that I went was to MCC. And when I walked into service that evening, there was a national committee meeting that was taking place in Philadelphia, and so when I walked in . . . I felt as though I was being welcomed back by a great crowd of witnesses.

And I decided that I would never again allow anything to cause me to leave any part or piece of myself, that I would engage all of [it]. . . . I would enter life from a place of wholeness, not a place of brokenness, and no one would ever come between me and myself, my whole self. And that's kind of the way that I've lived since then.

Elder Garner shared that even during her period of "rest," she still considered herself a lesbian, and that returning home to MCC instead of the predominantly Black Unity Fellowship Movement was a result of her desire to lead a life of integrity and to do so in a community of diversity, one that she felt was a "manifestation of Heaven on Earth." There were times in which balance or wholeness was fleeting, such as when she broke up with Rev. Candy Holmes (who is now her wife) because she was asked to take on a full-time leadership position in Los Angeles by the MCC founder and she accepted the offer before speaking with Holmes. Yet Elder Garner's oral history speaks of a life of pursuing integration for the sake of her mental and physical wellness.

My interview with Elder Garner's wife demonstrated a similar push for integration mixed with a commitment to religious leadership.

Rev. Candy Holmes was also a leader in the Metropolitan Community Churches. She initially served in the music ministry, in the healing ministries, and as planning chair for the PAD conference. Her professional activism came about through her work in the federal government in the Government Accounting Office. She

FIGURE 2.3. Reverend Candy Holmes. Used by permission.

recounts doing "one small thing"—submitting a family photograph of her and Garner for a photo display during Diversity Month in her office, and how this ultimately led to an invitation from President Obama to stand with him when he signed the presidential memorandum granting federal benefits to same-sex domestic partners in 2009. Following this act, she gave public testimony in state legislatures in support of marriage equality. She has continued her social justice activism by working with the National Black Justice Coalition, the Gay and Lesbian Alliance against Defamation (GLAAD), the Human Rights Campaign, Many Voices, and the LGBTQ Task Force. After thirty years of ministry with MCC, she, like Elder Garner, also resigned from her leadership roles within MCC, but she remains MCC clergy. Her oral history interview gave witness to the dysfunction of compartmentalized living and illustrated the possibilities that spirituality has for inculcating wholeness.[12]

Rev. Holmes described her journey to self-awareness as further complicated by her apostolic religious identity. After enjoying her first kiss with a woman, she wondered if God would be pleased with her attraction to her church member, and for a period of time she was unable to connect her physical and emotional attractions to her spiritual beliefs. She denied her attractions for as long as she could, even making compromises such as believing she could be partially lesbian—for example, not performing certain sexual acts—until she ended her denial and accepted herself. This led her to attend a Black lesbian support group in Washington, where someone invited her to a MCC church. She credits the MCC for the "beginning of me looking at not blending, but coming to terms with my sexuality, my sexual orientation and my spirituality and how they are all part of me, so that whole integration process. And it took a lot." Even as she underwent this integration process, she acknowledges that there were still boundaries to her identity formation because although she was certain about her spirituality and sexuality, she was hesitant about accepting a call to ministry. Through her apostolic training she had been taught that "women couldn't be preachers or ministers"; thus, it "never dawned on me that might be a path for me." Notwithstanding accepting a call to ministry manifested through the healing ministry and choir and even attending Interfaith Seminary in New York in 2001, she did not seek ordination through MCC until 2008. She initially saw ordination as a means of constraining her gifts because of the limited roles in which she had seen women in the apostolic church. This hesitation indicated that despite the wholeness she experienced in her sexuality, she was still working to integrate her gender and spirituality.

Within her professional life, Rev. Holmes also experienced a fragmented self. She noted in her interview that she did not feel safe at work: it was not a space that affirmed same-sex attraction. Her workforce was predominantly white, but it was from her predominantly Black and religious coworkers that she experienced particular bias:

> I did not feel like I could be out and also feel that my being gay or lesbian or [a] same-gender-loving woman would somehow hinder my up[ward] mobility in the organization. So I really felt [that,] as a Black woman, I had that already going as something of a barrier, and so then adding to that being a lesbian, and then being out, I just didn't feel comfortable for many years....
>
> I was disassociated from the world of politics and the implications of politics on my life, myself as a person. And those things that I was aware of, like Martin Luther King and the March on Washington, those kinds of civil rights, I had a place for those things or those events in my Black history part of myself, but that didn't have anything to do with being gay. I had not connected that that was also a civil right, that [this] was something that was a human right. I had not connected that. And [finally coming to that realization] had everything to do with me [under-standing] ... myself [as] ... being a full human being [who] deserved the same rights as anyone else in the US. And so it took a minute for me to connect those dots—that in the same way that Black people fought for rights, I needed to also fight for all of who I was, not just my Blackness. So I actually was pretty much compartmentalized[:] ... my Blackness was in one part; my gayness was in another part; my being a woman was in another part.

Enraged by Proposition 8, she prayed to God for strength to do "one small thing," which turned out to be sending in a photo for a display for her company's gay and lesbian employee association.[13] Again, she credits her spirituality for helping her merge her identities and notes that after taking that initial step, she became more courageous in her public witness. Although her public activism centered around federal same-sex employee benefits, she found that her role as a MCC clergyperson made her prominent as a faith leader, such that when the White House called her work number of behalf of President Obama, they asked to speak with Rev. Holmes. As more opportunities arose for her to speak about the necessity of federal same-sex employees having domestic benefits, she discovered in her witness an "indicator that her voice was important." When I asked her why she now considered herself a spiritual activist, Rev. Holmes noted the following:

> Though I didn't have all of the background as a seasoned advocate, I had my life, and so I just kept sharing my life and what it was like growing up in the church, and what it was like not knowing that I was gay. I just thought it was who I was, and I didn't know there was a name for it. And I just kept sharing those different—and it kept opening doors. I mean, it was like a snowball effect.
>
> I no longer segregate or compartmentalize my spirituality and my sexual orientation, my sexual identity, my being a same-gender-loving woman. All of that is one for me now. And so if I'm whole, a whole person, I believe that we are spiritual beings having a physical reality, so I think that our spirituality is really . . . I lead with my spirituality as who I am in this world.

Standing In

Rev. Holmes was able to access her spirituality as a way to meld her various identities and become more prominent as a religious leader. In fact, she is an example of Maparyan's theory of "standing in," for she used her newfound clout to advocate and agitate within MCC. Maparyan identifies "standing in" as staying within an oppressive system in order to change it from the inside. This womanist method, she says, defies a "fractionating tendency" by staying inside despite the difficult and personal risk to oneself.[14] According to Rev. Holmes's letter of resignation from MCC leadership, beginning in 2015 she accused MCC of wavering from its stated values of embracing diversity.[15] She asserted that she and her wife, Elder Darlene Garner, were worried about the shift in their organization and made various attempts to address the gap between the institution's values and practices. She contends that their attempts to salvage their institution were wide-ranging and even included her wife running for moderator (the top leader in the organizational leadership structure). Despite a very public restructuring and the forced retirement of Elder Garner, and despite being unwilling to continue her voluntary association with the organization, Rev. Holmes still claims an identity as an MCC clergyperson and faith leader.

Other interviewees experienced similar notions of "standing in" within their religious communities. They felt the need to stay and agitate for change while refusing to be invisible to the dominant community (whether that was the male ecclesial structure or conservative Christianity). Although Maparyan's notion of "standing in" involves personal risk, the women I interviewed knew when to stand in as part of a larger vision that was authentic to themselves, even if that meant leaving the particular community in which they had been working. One participant revealed how her reliance on her relationship with God as part of her goal of being authentic led her to stand within her community while also eventually leading her from that community.

Bishop Tonyia Rawls was elected one of the first female bishops in Unity Fellowship Church Movement, the first African American church organization founded with the mission to minister to the LGBTQ+ community. She founded the Unity Fellowship Church Charlotte in 2000 and was consecrated as bishop in 2008. She founded Sacred Souls Community Church in 2014 and is affiliated with the United Church of Christ. In addition to her religious organizing, she is the founder and codirector of the Freedom Center for Social Justice, an organization founded in 2009 to work intersectionally to support the trans community, people of color, people of low wealth, youths, and sexual minorities. Her oral history interview emphasized the costs of living an authentic life while describing the process she endured to accept all her identities as part of God's gift to her.[16]

Although she was reared in a Baptist home and was committed to her religious convictions, Bishop Tonyia Rawls found herself not living up to her full potential in service to God because of her inability to find a way to allow her same-gender-loving attraction and spirituality to coexist. She described wrestling with her sexuality and spirituality to the point where she considered marrying a "deliberate pedophile" as a way of accepting her community's acknowledgment of God's call on her life. The church leaders were preparing her to be a first lady, but she knew that she was called to ministry but could not see a realistic way to serve in that role because of her belief that her sexuality was wrong. She described a conversation that she had with God that reflected the contradictions she found in her various identities:

> I went to God pissed off, because several of my friends had gotten engaged at a similar time. We were all evangelist missionaries. I went to God and I said, "Listen, I don't get it, because it seems clear to me that you do not love your daughters as much as you love your sons. It's obvious to me. I don't see anything that suggests you really care about your daughters, because if you did you wouldn't stand by and allow this stuff to happen."

FIGURE 2.4. Bishop Tonyia Rawls. Used by permission.

Two things God wound up saying to set the trajectory for this next phase of my ministerial life. The Lord led me to know [that] number one, "I need you to know that I did not make a mistake in creating you just as you are, as same-gender-loving. This was not a mistake." The second thing was, "And I will use that to my glory one day."

I can't tell anybody that I'm still attracted to women. That never went away. God knows as much as I prayed, fasted, "Just take this away from me Lord. Take it away," it never went anywhere. The Lord was like "Well, there's a reason it didn't go anywhere because there's nothing wrong with you." The thought of God using it to God's glory, I had no point of reference for that. . . . It started my journey of growing in my understanding of who I was as same-gender-loving and others like me who loved God and loved the same gender.

Although this realization freed Bishop Rawls to imagine a life of ministry, she did not immediately seek ordination because she was still a closeted lesbian. She believed that she could not minister with integrity until she was out to her pastor and congregation, and this desire led her to a Unity Fellowship church in New York City. Once she was out in her religious community, she quickly accepted the call to be ordained. After serving with Unity Fellowship Church in Washington for seven years, she was commissioned by Archbishop Bean (the founder of Unity Fellowship) to open the first Unity church in the Bible Belt, which she located in Charlotte, North Carolina. By 2008, she had risen in the ranks at Unity to become one of the first two women consecrated as bishop in their denomination's history. In this role she experienced the costs of standing in a tradition that was not ready for change. Though familiar with sexism from her experience as a missionary in the Church of God in Christ, she described her rise to the highest office in Unity as particularly painful:

Then in 2008 I was consecrated with Bishop Jacqueline Holland as one of the first female bishops in Unity. It was an incredibly painful time for us as a denomination because we weren't ready for it. We were a denomination of old Black church kids who had men as our leaders as the background of where we were coming from. We just I think underestimated what it meant to have women in the bishopric, to have women as leaders at that level. It was incredibly painful. It really was, but on the other side of it, some of the [outcome of the] rejection and resistance was a stronger denomination. We had to do the work. We all assumed "We're so progressive; we're so amazing," but nobody ever talked to us about the woman issue fully. And definitely not women with power.

She withstood the obstacles and felt the denomination was stronger as a result of her efforts to endure the sexism. Yet she began to feel led away from Unity to join the United Church of Christ, and just as she had waited to minister until she could do so with complete integrity, she waited to announce her personal decision to her congregation until after she had dis-

FIGURE 2.5. Reverend Dr. Cari Jackson. Used by permission.

cussed it with the senior leadership of Unity Fellowship. She admitted that she had never seen a congregation do a clean break from a denomination, but she felt passionately about exploring ministry with community "in ways that weren't just about LGBTQ issues. I was concerned about poverty. I was concerned about reproductive justice. All these other issues that are queer as well, but it's bigger." Choosing to leave a denomination that she had spent twenty years building and perfecting reflected her "bold audaciousness." It also reflected her acknowledgment (reflected in the second of this chapter's epigraphs) that her greatest gift to the social justice movement is to live her life authentically and be led by all her identities to newer vistas.

Spirituality as Mediator for Compartmentalization

Agitating for justice in multiple arenas and in multiple modalities was an experience shared by Rev. Dr. Cari Jackson, my fifth interviewee. She spoke of the role of spirituality in integrating her various identities but also of the part they played in helping her determine when it was time to use her gifts in a different space.

Rev. Dr. Cari Jackson was a pastor, counselor, and organizational consultant. She pastored congregations in three Christian denominations: United

Church of Christ, where she was ordained; the United Methodist Church; and the Presbyterian Church—USA. She has a PhD in Christian ethics from Drew University, an MDiv from Union Theological Seminary, and a JD from the University of Maryland. She currently serves as executive for Religious Leadership and Advocacy at the Religious Coalition for Reproductive Choice; she is founding director of Center of Spiritual Light, a nonprofit providing spiritual counseling; and she is the president of Excellent Way Consulting, a company specializing in leadership and organizational effectiveness. Her interview was one of those most focused on the value of authenticity; she connected the importance of rejecting compartmentalization with helping advocate for others to live holistic lives.[17]

Dr. Cari Jackson's life history seems to be composed of moments when different aspects of her identity collided and were stretched beyond the limitations of what society dictated was possible. Like Bishop Rawls, Dr. Cari acknowledged the many times when clearly supernatural or spiritual help merged these dichotomies for her. She recounted that her early church experiences taught her to stay in place within classist, patriarchal, colorist environments but that in her educational and work endeavors she was discriminated against for her race and gender.[18] Dr. Cari learned to "become empowered to claim for myself who I am and what all of those things mean—to be a spiritual person, a Black person, a female person, a gay person, on, and on, and on." She recalls a direct conversation with God where she questions whether God wants her to not be gay or whether her gayness meant that God did not want her to be a minister because at that time it was not plausible to her that God could want her as she really was. When she makes peace with her spirituality and sexuality and accepts an active call to ministry, she finds that she is constantly being called to serve in spaces that are predominantly white with persons who do not think they are racist, sexist, or heterosexist. As exhausting as that seems, she feels she is a gift to those communities because of the value she places on being her authentic self. Although she often felt like an outsider, she says these experiences taught her "to just be me, be authentic to who I am." In fact, those experiences highlighted the negative effects of compartmentalization on her, for she never really fit neatly into the identity categories: she was deemed too leftist to be Black, too spiritualist to be queer, and so on:

> One of the things I think that harms people is this compartmentalization, and I grew up very compartmentalized as a person who was only gay over here and I saw the adverse impact of those kinds of compartmentalizations.

So I worked very intentionally at becoming more integrated in my own life, and that's what I seek to help other people do as well. . . .

What guides me most is [that] I talk about authenticity. I'm authentically all those things. Clearly, being a woman, being Black, being dark skinned, being someone who was shaped in a working-class context. All of those things [are] inextricably . . . who I am. It's the gestalt of the experiences from those realities and those particularities that guide[s] my life, and I can't, I really can't tweak them apart. I can say at the core of it is spirituality because I think that if I do any work affirming people in their spirituality, in their authenticity, which I think is spiritual work, I'm not primarily focusing on people who are of African descent or people who are women, or people who are LGBTQ, any of those, because I see when things are out whack socially. When there is overprivilege and underprivilege, both of those are spiritual dynamics, and I think both leave a dis-ease that needs to be addressed.

I can't imagine living any other way that would work for who I am and my understanding of who God is. I think I shared this story with you that when I was in college I met folks who did not speak in tongues the way it had been emphasized to me was important. In my early Pentecostal teachings I was told that unless a person spoke in tongues, they did not have the indwelling of the Spirit. I met people, I kept meeting people, I had to feel the Spirit of God in them, and they did not show up in the ways that I was taught one must show. So throughout my life I've [known] the multiplicity of ways that God shows up and that when each person is authentic to his or her or their own expression, that we get to see the amazingness and the varieties of God's expressions, and [that] society is stronger when we really nurture that and not just accept it and tolerate it, but really affirm that better society.

Dr. Cari believes that the work of authenticity is both individual and communal. She needs to show up as her whole self so that she can help bring others to the same realization. Thus, when discussing her newest enterprise—working with the Religious Coalition for Reproductive Choice—she similarly holds a firm belief that

> our families, our societies, our world are better when individuals live their authentic selves. It is my hope that everything that I do helps nurture a firm authenticity in others. Because there is a benefit to the individual, and that benefit then has reverberating effects in all of society. I've seen

that in my own life as I have made some challenging and at times costly choices to live authentically who I am. What I bring in all the contexts where I show up is this more fully empowered person, which then helps. You know, what's the expression about [the tide raising] all boats . . . ? And so . . . that's how the religious and the social activism come together for me.

Authenticity to Advocate for Others

This belief in the universal value of authenticity is what particularly struck me in the oral histories of these religious leaders because I was fully aware from listening to their life narratives how much living authentically had cost each of them. What I had not expected was the benefits, and particularly the joy, that they would find through helping others advocate for their own authenticity. This was especially the case for my youngest interviewees. I explicitly wanted to interview younger Black lesbian religious leaders because they displayed a different sense of hope and perhaps even a different sense of authenticity. I surmised that this might be because their generation has had more opportunities to freely express their identities than previous generations have. These next two oral histories are of a couple, both faith leaders, who placed a premium on living authentically so that they could amplify others' voices and urge them to live holistic lives.

Rev. Naomi Washington-Leapheart was the former Faith Work director for the National LGBTQ Task Force, the country's oldest national LGBTQ justice and equality group. She was a community organizer for POWER, a multifaith, multiracial network of congregations in the Philadelphia area. She served as a co-pastor of Saint Peter's United Church of Christ in Lancaster, Pennsylvania, where she was the only openly queer, licensed minister and African American at the church. She was ordained by the Fellowship of Affirming Ministries and the United Church of Christ. She currently serves as the director of Faith-Based and Interfaith Affairs for the city of Philadelphia and is an adjunct faculty member in the Theology and Religious Studies Department at Villanova University.[19]

Rev. Naomi Washington-Leapheart was the youngest interviewee, at thirty-seven years old. She was a proud transplant from Detroit who emphasized her socialization into social justice activism at an early age. She spoke of answering her call to ministry as an act of authenticity and an ethic of doing

FIGURE 2.6. Reverend Naomi Washington-Leapheart. Used by permission.

no harm. When I asked her about "coming out" while she was at seminary, she responded in a way that signaled that her decision was about more than just her living her truth:

I think that I've always known that I . . . like I remember being in middle school and having a crush on the person who was my best friend then. I didn't have any language for that. . . . In college again, I had this robust friend group of some queer-identified Christian folk who modeled for me that there's a way to be a person of faith and be queer. . . . I had models of people who were courageous. I just didn't have the courage myself to name it for myself.

Then by the time I was in seminary, I was out to myself and out to other people, but not out publicly. I think something about doing this public ministry really compelled me to say, "Listen. If I can't live fully, then how am I going to advocate for anybody else to be able to live fully? How am I going to?"

It just took a long time for me to believe that I deserved something that was healthy and whole and something that was authentic to my own sense of identity. That took a while for me. By the time I came to know myself as queer and gave myself permission to pursue a relationship, I was [in my] late twenties.

Yeah, by the time I was in seminary, again the discernment around what I was put here to do and the fact that that happened to be being in public, fighting for justice for folks who could not, who could not fight for themselves because it was too risky or needed others to accompany them on the fight, [pushed me to realize] that "I've got to be able to be me." Within the context of my being at that church, pastoring that church, being in seminary around people who were out, having mentors who could walk with me through the journey, and . . . Bishop Flunder, who could say, "You can tell the truth and survive," was what compelled me to just come on all the way out to everybody all the time.

The knowledge that she could "tell the truth and survive" was connected to her understanding that she was called to public ministry for social justice organizing. Because she would need to be out front agitating for justice for the most marginalized, she needed to do so at her full capacity, which meant claiming all the parts of her identity. When she described her grassroots faith organizing in suburban Philadelphia, she expressed a dilemma between working on behalf of her actual employer and those on whose behalf she felt compelled to work. For example, while working as an organizer in 2016, the Pulse Nightclub massacre occurred. Because of its Catholic donors, her organization had chosen not to organize around reproductive justice or LGBTQ concerns. Despite this policy, she and other members of the staff wanted the organization to make a statement about the massacre, which killed forty-nine people in an Orlando gay nightclub, and they received pushback. She discussed their hesitation and her decision that she had to speak up. Although she was angered by the organization's decision, she used her moment to make remarks to amplify that a tragedy had occurred and to stress that their community had lost one of their own Philadelphia youths that night in Florida:

> But in that moment, I said to myself, I'm not comfortable making this kind of compromise. Like, we can't say wrong is wrong because we don't want to piss off the folks who believe homosexuality is a sin, whatever they believe. And we've lost somebody. We've lost this eighteen-year-old kid from West Philly. We're in Philadelphia, and we can't name that this was our baby girl.
>
> I sort of became a little disillusioned about the extent to which I was going to be able to be authentic and actually fight for the people who need justice, all the people who need justice in this role. I was disappointed. I wasn't really looking to transition, though. I was just like: it is what it is.

Shortly after this crucial moment, she was offered the opportunity to work for a secular organization, the National LGBTQ Task Force, and she saw that job as a chance to work with congregations specifically around LGBTQ identities as opposed to having to do so with apology or pushback. She believed the job would be a site where "I could also talk about all these issues I was talking about before and be unapologetically queer and fight unapologetically for queer people." In this job and in her current position working for the city of Philadelphia, she was able to leverage all her identities to work on the behalf of others. Though acknowledging that her Blackness was a primary identity for her, this does not reflect a fragmented self. On the contrary, she insists:

> I think my queerness and my womanness sort of work together. What does it mean? I as a Black woman who loves another Black woman, like I think there's something there that really shapes my sense of self. A Black woman who loves another Black woman who's raising a Black girl. We're always talking to them about what it means to be womanish, to love deeply, and fully, and unapologetically. To let your yes be yes and no be no. That deeply shapes me.

Authenticity in Community

This communal understanding of personal identity reflects philosopher Charles Taylor's theorizing on the ethics of authenticity. In Taylor's oft-cited definition, he determines that authenticity is "self-definition in dialogue," and he rejects "self-determining freedom" as individualistic and even selfish.[20] In Taylor's understanding, our authentic selves are formed in community and "our moral salvation comes from recovering authentic moral contact with ourselves."[21] Both notions of authenticity are held simultaneously, and this is represented in Rev. Naomi Washington-Leapheart's query of how she could advocate for others when she was not ready to advocate publicly for herself. Not surprisingly, her wife shared a similar realization.

Rev. Kentina Washington-Leapheart was the former director of Programs for Reproductive Justice and Sexuality Education at the Religious Institute. She began her ministerial career as a chaplain in both health-care and clinical-care settings. She identifies as a queer womanist follower of many paths, including the way of Jesus, and volunteers her time in greater Philadelphia community organizations that work on maternal/child health and faith.

FIGURE 2.7. Reverend Kentina Washington-Leapheart. Used by permission.

Jointly ordained and married with a teenage daughter, she and her wife, Naomi, have callings that complement each other as they work side by side, though in different spheres of ministry. They both embody qualities of acceptance, self-love, authenticity, and proud queer identities as they advocate for LGBTQ policies and rights, reproductive justice, sexual health, prison reform, and religious education.[22]

Rev. Kentina Washington-Leapheart's interview demonstrated how personal identity intertwines with communal identity as she pushed me beyond my constructs of leader/activist to think about the ways that we are each called to amplify the voices and experiences of others. She placed a high value on authenticity and even delayed her ministerial ordination in search of a "more excellent and authentic way." This path forward would not require her to mute any part of herself to fit in, and at her ordination she noted that in the Fellowship of Affirming Ministries, "All of me is welcome here. All of my queer self. My Black self. My woman self. My charismatic, Spirit-filled self. My contemplative self. My multifaith-sensibilities self. My intellectual, scholarly self. My questioning, doubting self. My faithful, sure self."[23] The comfort in having all of her identities accepted at her ordination also shows up in her ministerial and professional commitments.

She describes a similar dilemma as the one her wife faced when deciding to speak from her multiple identities at work. In her role as a chaplain for Presbyterian Homes (a retirement community in greater Chicago), she was not out at work. As her pastoral team's only Black person and with only one queer staff member, she did not feel sufficiently comfortable there to be out. Although she brought her partner (now wife) to work to conduct workshops, she did not feel she could be transparent with people about who she was to her. When she decided to disclose her lesbian identity, it was because she could no longer live with this fragmented version of herself:

And so, that was when I knew this is not something that I'm going to be able to do. So part of being able to show up authentically is that my life, inasmuch as we share our personal lives . . . at work, is not a secret. And that for me is being faithful, because all of me is who I am. So . . . I know that I couldn't do a ministry assignment, whatever that assignment would be. And I don't know what would've happened had I stayed there. I think I would have gotten to the point where I couldn't keep it, sort of don't ask, don't tell. But it was becoming increasingly . . . difficult for me to be in that environment and not be fully open about who I was.

So living faithfully for me means that all the ways [that I am] who I am in the world, not just about my sexuality, but in general, are present with me. So I walk in a space, say in the reproductive justice [space] when I was doing that at work, and not be thinking about this from a perspective of being a parent and what it looks like to have to think about how you're going to pay for child care or thinking about where you live and your kid, what kind of school they go to. Like all of these are reproductive justice issues. And so, that doesn't cease to be, and actually I think it offers me a particular perspective because I'm talking about something that I've lived in many ways. So that is part of my living faithfully.

Following this chaplaincy appointment, Rev. Kentina was honored as an outstanding Black alumnus by her alma mater, Garrett-Evangelical Theological Seminary. During her interview for the award, she identified as a "womanist queer laborer for the Jesus Project" whose second career path into seminary had given her clarity about her ministerial calling. She reported a need to reject conformity and noted the following:

What is most important is to embody all of me in preaching and teaching . . . to live faithfully in my skin. When I feel most faithful is when I am operating [as] my most authentic self. . . . Sometimes those of us in ministry—whether pastoring, doing chaplaincy, teaching, or preaching—can feel the need to inauthentically conform to the context [to which] . . . we have been called.[24]

A woman of eclectic religious experience, she spoke about claiming her identities in an effort to be her own "best thing." In her oral history interview, when I asked her if she could signal which identities were more important to her, she talked about what identities she needed in order to be her own best self:

I think I realized in the last several years that so many of my identities have shifted and changed and some have even been projected on to me that aren't mine. I got married, and I'm married to someone who was very public facing, and I wasn't so much right before that. And so I've learned what that means and that identity shift. . . . And so I've been doing a lot of work around like who am I as I shift and change? So right now I think I am my best thing. So that's an identity. I am a mother of a [Black girl] teenager, which is a particular [identity]. I am a wife. I am a minister who is between calls.

I'm a Black woman—and these are in no particular order. So I'm a Black woman. I'm a womanist. I'm queer. I am compelled, a person who is compelled by the Jesus narrative and project as I call it. I'm not self-identifying as a Christian these days, even though I'm compelled by a Christ. But I feel like the Christian moniker has just been so bastardized by evangelicals. But yeah, I am on a journey. I know that sounds clichéd, but I really feel like that. And activists, like I was saying before . . . I don't know if I feel like I'm an activist, but I definitely feel like I'm trying to be an advocate.

The purpose of being her own best thing was not just to integrate her own self but also to be able to advocate for others. She was more comfortable with the language of advocacy as she united her work on herself with her work for justice in the world:

For me it was because I feel compelled to act as a voice or to help to amplify voices that get drowned out by the deluge of injustice in this world. And so whether that's injustice on a small scale, you go to a hospital and the doctor doesn't believe you when you say that you're in pain, or a large scale, you can't access abortion or live in an unsafe community where your kids are worried about how they're getting back to school every day . . . or you're living in Chicago and the teachers are on strike right now because they need to be, you know? The voices of people who nobody wants to listen to get drowned out.

And so perhaps if I could do some small part to, number one, even hear those voices, to put my ear to them, and, number two, to amplify them and use whatever privileges that I might have by virtue of my education and by virtue of my class status [and] by virtue of my experiences, I would like to do that.

This act of amplification again resonates with Charles Taylor's notion of authenticity as being dialogical. Taylor contends that our identities are formed "always in dialogue with, sometimes in struggle against, the identities our significant others want to recognize in us."[25] In a very real sense, these various parts of oneself are tied to who we want to be for others. Rev. Kentina wants to be an advocate and a social justice leader who makes space for those whose voices are muted. Amplifying experiences is most possible when the community trusts that one hears and sees them in their fullness, which at some level requires having done this work oneself.

The Importance of Womanist Authenticity

This book starts with the individual's assertion of identity independently and in community because one of my basic claims is that in speaking their truths, these Black lesbian religious leaders—Rev. Dr. Deborah Johnson, Elder Darlene Garner, Rev. Candy Holmes, Bishop Tonyia Rawls, Rev. Dr. Cari Jackson, Rev. Naomi Washington-Leapheart, and Rev. Kentina Washington-Leapheart—are exercising resistance to the many types of oppression that seek to render them invisible and unheard. Their very identities as out Black lesbian religious leaders are revolutionary. This chapter has theorized this as womanist authenticity, which refers to Black women's self-determination as agency or existence as resistance. I situate womanist authenticity within broader womanist categories and posit that this situatedness is a primary factor in reading these women's narratives as womanist.

Womanist authenticity reflects an exploration of how Black women learn to trust and integrate their various identities to advocate for themselves and the wider community. Their self-naming and self-referential disposition demonstrate what pastor-scholar Rev. Dr. Renee Hill considers to be a radical act of self-determination, which she understands as "taking the power to name oneself and to accept or reject the roles and images that society tries to impose."[26] In identifying as Black lesbians who also have a ministerial calling, my interviewees often felt conflicted within the various boundaries set to keep them in their places. Black feminist sociologist Patricia Hill Collins discusses such experiences through the lens of subjugated knowledge, which she asserts is expressed when oppressed groups have to use "alternative ways to create independent self-definitions and self-valuation . . . and knowledge."[27] Thus, the women I interviewed were crafting their own holistic self while simultaneously creating alternative avenues for others to imagine their own lives.

When I interviewed Rev. Deborah, she noted being proud that she had survived without succumbing to things that would make her unhealthy. When she made the decision at age fourteen or fifteen to go to hell for her authenticity, she could not have known how her life would unfold, but she was unwilling to live falsely. During her 2017 interview, she noted that she had done the forgiveness work to love and accept herself, recognizing that so many people are thwarted by this task. This reminded me of poet Cheryl Clarke's determination that it was time for Black lesbians to "love ourselves [, for that] is the final resistance."[28] This call to love and acceptance contains a theoretical positioning that allows their very lives to become theory. Through living fully embodied and spiritually connected lives, they resist oppressive systems that seek to negate their presence. This book is about activism and leadership but begins with what is often their first action in becoming activists and leaders—acceptance and love of oneself. Each of the women I interviewed took this first step and then used the value of authenticity as an encouragement for others to follow her example.

At its core, I also read their decision to love oneself and love the community as audaciousness. In essence, it is an acceptance of Alice Walker's definition of womanism. Walker's multifaceted definition identifies a womanist as a "woman who loves other women, sexually and/or nonsexually" and who "loves the folk" while loving herself.[29] The interviews with Black lesbian religious leaders overwhelmingly revealed women who embraced these definitional markers (even while not themselves always choosing the nomenclature). They recognized their full selves as gifts to their communities, and this self-awareness or womanist authenticity fueled their continued support of the thriving of these communities.

This concept of womanist authenticity should be familiar to those aware of womanist ethicist Stacey Floyd-Thomas's theory of radical subjectivity as the first tenet of womanism. Floyd-Thomas asserts that radical subjectivity explains the process by which Black women come to understand their own agential power to resist oppression. In her understanding, radical subjectivity demonstrates the ritual processes that aid a person in claiming their identity, and it is not a static identity.[30] Floyd-Thomas traces radical subjectivity through biomythography, a process in which Black women use their own history and myths to create a larger story that speaks to a larger community of Black women. In a way, the introduction of myth is a response to the fact that larger society views womanists' truths as lies. Yet this dismal reality does not mean we stop sharing truth. The idea of womanist authenticity concurs with her categorization, but it takes her theorizing one further step by suggesting that we rely on living texts—actual Black women as valid data to illuminate sites of resistance. Womanist authenticity is also not static, but it is intentionally communal, recognizing that actions that are liberatory for the more marginalized community members will in essence lead to the flourishing of the entire community.

As I listened to Black lesbian religious leaders' stories of resistance and gratitude for being a surviving testimony, I realized that one of the reasons their stories spoke to me was because of the attention given to survival stories or resistance narratives in Black liberation theologies. As a womanist scholar, there is a continued interest in the liberation, survival, and flourishing of Black communities. Noting that throughout history there has always existed some form of resistance for every site of oppression, womanist methodological retrieval is oriented toward validating the lives of African-descended women through more than just retelling the story. Womanism also involves constructing meaningful knowledge for today's community from the stories of the past: searching for Black women acting as catalysts for change to create future change agents.

Because there is no ontological way to be a Black lesbian religious leader, the examples I have provided from these seven women are depictions of ways in which one's existence matters: just being oneself is a resistant act. This I felt was sufficient to illustrate Katie Cannon's contention that anecdotal evidence reveals truth about how oppressed people live with integrity, especially when they are repeatedly "unheard but not unvoiced, unseen but not invisible."[31] Yet this chapter points beyond mere survival of oppression. Ultimately, as a womanist I look for examples of flourishing and thriving that can serve as beacons along the way. In chapter 3 I move further into examples of thriving by exploring womanist spiritual activism, the everyday acts of justice seeking that promote the greatest good.

Interrogating Spiritual Activism

With Proposition 8, it was like, well, you know, I had to do something. And I didn't know if it would jeopardize my work or not, but I knew I had to do something. And so at the desk, at my desk, I said a prayer. I said God, I don't know what to do, but if I could just do one small thing. And so when I just said that prayer, I remember it like it was yesterday, and I glanced up at my computer, and on the screen was this email about a gay and lesbian employee association. They were doing a project for Diversity Month. And this particular year they decided they wanted to put our families on display because of all the stuff that was starting to brew around gay people, and gay people having families, and wanting to get married, so they thought this would be one way to show that we do have families and it's important to acknowledge that we have families.... [After calling Darlene,] I nervously picked one of our [best] pictures and sent it in. I was all kind of nervous about it, but I figured, well, what's a picture.

—REV. CANDY HOLMES, oral history interview, 2017

I think that [area] grew organically into the other very easily, organically, if you understand what I'm saying. It happened organically. One of them grew into the other; we started with the HIV work, which led us to the housing work, which of course later, yeah, got us out there around social justice work, you know, which moves us to women's issues, which moves us to, you know, prison reform, which moves us to border work, which we're doing . . . now. Once you start doing justice work, you begin to see the intersections of the evil that oppresses all of us and particularly oppresses people of color and anyone else marginalized.

—BISHOP YVETTE FLUNDER, oral history interview, 2019

In chapter 2 I examined how several of the activist interviewees were able to claim their authentic voice to advocate on behalf of others. This chapter also starts with a concern about activist orientation. Through synthesizing elements from Black lesbian religious leaders' lives, I highlight their faith activism as a necessary component of their radical religious leadership. Their actions and beliefs are the standpoint from which they approach their social justice work, and it is through their faith that they describe how they understand and interact with society. This chapter explores everyday activism and shows how individual acts of activism illustrate larger social movements that have religious impetuses. Using Patricia Hill Collins's understanding of activism as an everyday Black woman's daily resistance to oppression and Layli Maparyan's theory of womanist spiritual activism as spiritualized social change, this chapter interrogates these leaders' faith activism, demonstrating how faith and social justice work together to assist these women in advocating for their communities.

Black Women and Social Justice Activism

It is outside the scope of this chapter and even this book to offer an exhaustive discussion of the long history of Black women and social justice activism. Just as women are currently at the forefront of the Black Lives Matter movement, so too has every path toward Black liberation depended on the expertise and labor of Black women. Women's notable leadership has been present in every social movement in the United States, and in particular the impact of Black women's participation in broad Black, feminist, and lesbian social, intellectual, and artistic resistance is a legacy embraced by those I interviewed.

Their Black lesbian activist leadership is most aptly noted within the framework provided by the Combahee River Collective, which situated Black female resistance as a radicalization borne from their awareness of "identity politics," a term that is believed to have been coined in their forty-five-year-old statement. Identity politics is key to understanding the history of Black women's social justice organizing because it was "not just about who you were; it was also about what you could do to confront the oppression you were facing."[1] Recognizing that all of their identities were grounds to become politically active and aware is perhaps most poignantly described in the collective's statement, but it was also surely evident in the activism, writings, and artistic expressions of historical Black women.

Beginning with enslaved African women's resistance to their capture and controlled agency, there are documented reports of women destroying farm equipment, pretending to be ill, running away, and even committing infanticide as forms of resistance to their enslavement. In the nineteenth century, there is plenty of recorded evidence of individual and group efforts to thwart slavocracy and ensure a better life for themselves and their communities. Examples include individual heroines such as Jarena Lee, Sojourner Truth, Rebecca Cox Jackson, and Harriet Tubman, whose activism ranged from spiritual engagement and encouragement, to seeing themselves as divinely created and human, and to leading revolts that demanded corporeal freedom.[2] The nineteenth and early twentieth centuries also witnessed collective activism, as demonstrated in the mutual-aid societies and Black women's club movements. An example is the National Association of Colored Women, whose local clubs served the immediate needs of their communities by providing everything from education and health care to burial services. Again, there were numerous individual women in leadership within these movements (as well as those working outside of moral reform movements), among them Ida B. Wells-Barnett, Mary McLeod Bethune, Anna Julia Cooper, and Mary Church Terrell. Female participants within racial-uplift movements actively addressed a wide range of issues, such as suffrage, lynching, sexual violence, and working conditions for the newly emancipated Black community.[3] Continuing to strive for full democratic participation in US society, Black women also played significant roles in resisting southern apartheid during the civil rights movement. Their actions during the marches, bus boycotts, sit-ins, voter registration drives, and desegregation efforts reflected individual as well as collective agency. As the focus of historiographies of activism in the civil rights movement expanded beyond male elites, the lived faith of women such as Ella Baker, Fannie Lou Hamer, Septima Clark, and Diane Nash has illuminated the community-building work long spearheaded by women resisters.[4] Black women's contemporary participation in activism includes the digital/hashtag activism that propelled the Black Lives Matter movement, which emerged in 2013 after the acquittal of Trayvon Martin's killer. The expansion of resistance tactics beyond protests and marches to include the realm of social media and the leadership models produced by out queer leaders show that these contemporary movements are in the lineage of prior agitations for justice and are examples of a new type of Black-women–led resistance for the current generation.

Despite highlighting individual and collective actors for social change, the increase in feminist historiography has not always paid sufficient attention to the spiritual and religious motivations of Black women activists.[5] It is ironic that the fields of religious studies and African American studies, which have excavated and elevated the narratives of Black men such as Frederick Douglass, W. E. B. Du Bois, Martin Luther King Jr., and even Bayard Rustin, exploring their religious cartographies, has been slow to consider seriously the role of faith in female and queer activism.[6] Yet in each of the individual examples cited in the previous paragraph, there have been studies published that examine the spiritual impetus of female leaders. These cases provide blueprints for this current research on Black lesbian religious activism.

Whether examining the social reform of early nineteenth-century Black women or contemporary leaders, spirituality is a key factor to understanding how they seek to ameliorate social ills using resistance tactics. Womanist ethicist Emilie Townes described nineteenth-century activists as living their spirituality in such a way that took seriously the moral responsibility to create and maintain a just world.[7] By valuing the spiritual and religious ideologies of a Black woman activist, one is made aware of her motivations as well as what sustains her in the long strides toward justice. In fact, for each of the women whom I studied, her spiritual foundation is often her basis for acting in spite of multiple oppressions that ironically may include her religious community.

Bettye Collier-Thomas's *Jesus, Jobs, and Justice: African American Women and Religion* notes that scholarly work on Black women activists has focused on narrow groups—for example, club movements and the National Baptist Convention—and then tried to make these limited examples illustrative of the experiences of all Black church women or all Black women activists.[8] Her text is a stunningly diverse and exhaustive reporting of individual and collective Black women's organizing and faith, yet my book is concerned with the activist orientation of eighteen Black lesbian religious leaders from a variety of backgrounds and with a variety of missions, women whose experiences should not be presumed to be representative of the entire Black female community. Instead, this project adds to the diversity chronicled by Collier-Thomas as the first collection of oral histories of Black lesbian religious activists. Attending to the moral agency displayed by these women in spite of their marginalization gives us a glimpse of the underside of history, a view amplified by the lens of emancipatory historiography. Their histories would be incomplete without capturing both their relegation to obscurity and their resistance to this denial of their full humanity. Thus, the chapter unfolds by concentrating on individual and everyday acts of rebellion as well as acts of collective community building.

Everyday Activism

To begin this discussion of everyday resistance, I will discuss four such women who direct their everyday activities to making a difference. The epigraph at the beginning of the chapter describes the simple act of sharing a family photo as an example of activism because it was the catalyst for significant social justice work for Rev. Candy Holmes. In chapter 2 I describe her path to finding her full self while describing the activism that followed her decision to publicly disclose her sexual orientation at work. As she reflected on the moment that launched her social justice activism, like many other interviewees during the oral history she disclosed the much longer process of knowing she needed to be an agent of justice in the world. For instance, in describing her early childhood to me, she said that even when she was very young, her church's ongoing response to injustice and hypocrisy taught her that "it's only right to do right," which as an adult she translated as justice. Even before she had the language to articulate the feeling of injustice or the awareness of the need for a just world, she told me she "had this justice streak, so . . . I d[idn't] understand why it is that we . . . do right on Sunday but we [don't] do right on Monday through Saturday. And so my response to that was resistance." Her resistance started with everyday tasks like telling the truth even when it was unpopular or recognizing hypocritical responses and refusing to participate in them. Thus, it is ironic that she said she had never had leanings toward activism or advocacy before she found herself a public champion for same-sex marriage in adulthood. In fact, on reflection Rev. Holmes noted that her "justice button" had been nurtured throughout the years. It was in her full-time federal job that her activism was aroused, prompted by being discriminated against by being denied federal benefits as an LGBTQ person:

> Proposition 8 changed that all for me because I could not understand, even with my limited awareness and knowledge about politics, how a group of people, their rights could be voted away, that they could get married, because they could get married, and then because a group of people said no, we don't like that, for their reasons, their right to love and to participate in marriage was taken away. That so incensed me; it pushed a button in me that I didn't know was even there. But it had been nurtured all along. I just didn't pay any attention to it, that justice button. It showed itself in different times in my life. But this time Proposition 8 pushed that button so that [that injustice] unraveled me; it rattled me. It

gut-punched me. It woke me up, [and] I realized I had to do something. And I didn't know what I was going to do because I had no skills; I had no tools. I was not out [at work]. But it pushed me to the edge of what I now understand as being in denial.

Often the something that can be done is a small preliminary action that allows a burgeoning activist the space to gain traction on an issue to expand her platform. This is what happened for Rev. Holmes. From that small act of resistance, she went on to become one of the public faces of DC Marriage Equality, then to testify before Congress, and finally to stand beside President Obama as he signed a presidential memorandum allowing federal benefits for LGBT employees. Perhaps what is most striking is how quickly she progressed to acting in a broader way. Before becoming an activist, she understood civil rights as being what Martin Luther King Jr. did or the march on Washington. After her consciousness raising, she found herself able to advocate for human rights for all. She recognized that her "voice was important . . . [in helping herself and others find] freedom from oppression, freedom from things that would bind us, freedom from things that will take away our hope." She often spoke about not being a seasoned advocate or activist but not letting that limit her sphere of activism, given that the goal was freedom for all. Indeed, she recounts that "I had my life, so I just keep sharing my life and what it was like growing up in the church, and what it was like not knowing that I was gay. . . . So it wasn't one thing that helped me to go from being someone who was not active to someone who was very active, but it was like I progressed [as I told my story]." Telling her story one picture at a time, one person at a time, was enough to launch her into social justice work, which provided resources to combat the trauma experienced by activists. She uses her own pain and life experiences to connect with others in the long-term pursuit of justice. She has learned that achieving social justice demands long-term strategizing and that this attitude is particularly important when there is backlash or when those seeking justice do not win.

Likewise, when examining everyday activism or daily acts of resistance, these actions demonstrated that whatever helps people view themselves as human is an activist orientation. In 1990 Patricia Hill Collins introduced Black feminist standpoint theory. This theory emphasizes the role of ordinary Black women as subjects worthy of study. Collins did not build her theoretical model around the Black women's club movement, suffragists, or civil rights leaders. Instead of grand public gestures or the actions of well-known public figures, she investigated how domestic workers, teachers, preachers, and mothers go about acts of resistance. She was concerned that the existing notions of activism were too limiting, for they typically considered actions like voting, taking office, or participating in collective movements. Her time studying "everyday Black women" showed her that a more expansive depiction of activism was needed. She posited that "private decisions to reject external definitions of Afro-American womanhood . . . and Black women's everyday behavior . . . [are] a form of activism [because] people who view themselves as fully human, as subjects, become activists, no matter how limited the sphere of their activism."[9]

The next interviewee, Dr. Sylvia Rhue, champions precisely this: the importance of everyday actions that help others view themselves as fully human.

Dr. Sylvia Rhue is a writer, activist, filmmaker, and producer. She was raised a fourth-generation Seventh Day Adventist, and after attending Oakwood College, a Seventh Day Adventist College in Alabama, she went on to earn a master's in social work from UCLA *and a PhD in human sexuality. She is perhaps best known for co-producing the film* All God's Children, *which presents an analysis of the political, social, and religious values of African American Christian gays and lesbians. After many years as a gay organizer in organizations such as the Black Gay and Lesbian Leadership Forum and the National Black Justice Coalition, she was the executive assistant to Bishop Yvette Flunder, the founder and senior pastor of City of Refuge United Church of Christ. She is currently the Education and Outreach director for SisterReach, a reproductive justice nonprofit.*[10]

Like Rev. Holmes, from an early age Sylvia Rhue had an almost innate sense of justice. She recounted meeting Dr. Martin Luther King Jr. while she was in high school and how he was an early mentor to her. She and her friends raised funds for his civil rights efforts, realizing even at their young age that they could assist in the movement. She acknowledged that she was already on the way to a life of justice seeking but noted that there were certain encounters (like meeting King) that left indelible marks on her consciousness. She was also prompted by her realization that the Kennedy family had a developmentally delayed child whom they hid away, which led her to think that "people who are given so much gray matter need to help people who have problems with being able to think and function in the world." She committed to a masters of social work program and became the first Black social worker in South Central Los Angeles, where she worked with the Regional Center for the Developmentally Disabled. Later, again in response to seeing

FIGURE 3.1. Dr. Sylvia Rhue. Used by permission.

a need, she trained as a sex therapist through UCLA and opened the largest sex-therapy clinic for African Americans in southern California. She went on to earn a doctorate in human sexuality but realized through her everyday job duties that the African American community was being underrepresented and underserved in sex-therapy films, so she created a documentary called *Women in Love: Bonding Strategies of Black Lesbians* to offer better resources to her community. As a result of this film (which she made as part of her doctoral dissertation), she was asked to participate in the making of the film *All God's Children*.

Although a film involves a production crew and thus goes far beyond one person's response to a social injustice, making *All God's Children* is nonetheless an example of Dr. Rhue's everyday activism. Once again, this particular work of justice was her response to filling a need. Using empirical research, her studies, and her everyday experience, she had the knowledge to help the community. Regarding the creation and vision of the film:

> In 1995 Dr. Dee Mosbacher and I started doing *All God's Children*, which was the video that Phill had a vision for. And we knew that we would be able to . . . well, actually we said if we don't get any ministers involved, we don't have it, so the first ministers we went to said [they] would gladly be in this. So that opened the door. And we knew if we were able to get some parents, politicians, preachers . . . on our side to be affirmative in our orientation, that that would go a long way. Also with the music that we used that I picked out. And it came true because when I started taking it around the country, people would cry and people would say, "Now I can go home for Thanksgiving. Now I can go home for Christmas" to change people's lives, change their thinking, and to educate them, raise their consciousness.

As a result of that one movie, filmmaking became both a hobby and a passion as she leaned further into her activist identity.

Dr. Rhue has had a multifaceted career whose central thread has been quite simply to go and do what's needed. At the time of her interview, she was the executive assistant to Bishop Flunder, whom I introduce in the next section of this chapter. Dr. Rhue joked about never being able to retire because she feels driven to keep working until everything is right in the world. In her role as assistant to Bishop Flunder she found a new purpose, a purpose that nonetheless still derives from just showing up with her talents to do her job. With great joy she said that "running Bishop Flunder's life is now my activism because she is such an international star and I interface with everyone she interfaces with, and if I can help her do her work, then I'm doing my activism." Although at first this might make it seem as if in her new job she is a step removed from direct action, when one considers the global ministry of Bishop Flunder, it is evident that Dr. Rhue is really on the front lines fighting for justice.

The import of doing one small thing or playing one's part as an activist reflects a signature value that Dr. Sylvia Rhue expressed. When I asked her of what she was most proud when she surveyed her life, she paraphrased Erma Bombeck and said she was proud to have "put every ounce of talent into doing things, activities, writing, producing films, whatever, to help people feel more connected to being a human being." Whether her justice work has come in the form of making films, doing therapy, or managing Bishop Flunder's calendar, all her endeavors have been in line with her desire to promote awareness of the divinely created nature of each person she encounters.

In this, she reflects Black women's activist religiosity more broadly. Explains ethicist Rosetta Ross, "Black women religious activists are examples of persons who, in the midst of their ordinary lives, use critical analytical and reasoning skills to assess the usefulness of traditional religious conceptions and to construct new ways of making religion functional."[11] I asked each of the interviewees a question about social justice and their own everyday participation in such actions. I was perhaps most surprised by the following testimony of interviewee Rev. Kentina Washington-Leapheart. As we shall see, in addition to her participation in on-the-ground social justice movements, she also spoke about justice as a personal, daily lived experience.

Rev. Kentina Washington-Leapheart is married to Rev. Naomi Washington-Leapheart, a more public-facing activist. Yet in her own more localized activism, she mirrors similar passion and concern for justice. When I conducted the interview with her, she spoke of herself as a "minister who is in between calls," for she had recently stepped down from her position as director of Programs for Reproductive Justice and Sexuality Education at the Religious Institute. She had recently been ordained within Bishop Flunder's Fellowship and had prior experience working as a chaplain but was taking a break to figure out how she should next work for good in the world. Thus, her discussions with me about justice included her past experiences as well as imagining new possibilities for her future.

She spoke about the importance of family as a justice issue, describing how as a child she watched the news with her grandmothers and talked with them about political engagement. She noted that although they did not necessarily call that social justice, thanks to her grandmothers and others she recognized from an early age the importance of awareness of politics, women's rights, and racial issues. This awareness followed her into her chaplaincy work, which she started while in seminary. In describing her chaplaincy role, she remarked how the position demanded she cultivate deep listening and not "run out of the room" when things got tough. This skill set of deep listening and being keenly present translated into her activism and advocacy work. This often gets lost in movement spaces, she said, where doing tends to take precedence over being. She told of how, in marketing herself for the position at the Religious Institute, she realized that

> it's one thing to be talking about, for example, reproductive justice, sexual health and all of that, and the difficult or complex decision making . . . that women and families are doing related to pregnancy. . . . Completing a pregnancy or not and everything kind of in between[—it's] one thing to talk about that and protest about that and rail about that. And it's another thing to actually have sat with and spent time with and walked through those experiences with human beings who are making them, who are people of faith in many ways. So I think that [my chaplaincy experience] uniquely prepared me. My pastoral sense was key to how I showed up in that work.

Rev. Kentina also discovered that justice work is deeply connected to her own familial and personal life. In the conversation on authenticity described in chapter 2, she talked about what it meant for her to live faithfully in her ministry calling. On the individual level, authenticity was about being all of herself in any given space. Yet when discussing how that factored into her justice work, she remarked that this meant that she showed up for her reproductive-justice advocacy work from the perspective of being a parent. She also spoke about justice showing up in her home life, for she insisted on establishing boundaries and maintaining a work-life balance. She was aware that justice work is never ending, and particularly because she and her wife were both working for justice movements, she learned to insist on downtime and reflective space:

> Because it will be a situation where the constant necessity to work and the constant for us in particular, when we were both working in movement spaces, the constant having to be angry and outraged about the latest thing, like getting paid to do that. Right? And I'm like, I can't; I can't. And it doesn't mean that there isn't something to be mad about every day. There is! But at some point you got to be like, I'm about to watch something on Netflix and eat this chicken wing and I'm not, I can't do this [activism thing] right now. And so I do, I turn off . . . and that's a privileged space. Like I know that I have some privilege and [am privileged to be] able to be like, I'm not doing this today. But I think that the social justice industrial complex

requires you to constantly be outraged. And I know that for me or whatever my next move is in terms of my vocation, that's not something that I'm able to do for my own sense of mental health and well-being, as well as so that I can show up in a particular kind of way for my spouse or for my child and for my friends.

The transparency she shared regarding what she described as the potentially all-consuming social justice world shows her awareness of how she wants to live and display her faith, how she wants to be as a whole person. She recognizes that for her well-being she cannot be "on" all the time. Trans activist Frances Lee warned against the dangers of "performing activism more than doing activism" and noted that this hyperperformance of rage against injustice is unsustainable for activists.[12] Consequently, it becomes necessary to set boundaries in one's life and tend to one's own well-being.

Boundaries are also sites of everyday activism for Rev. Kentina because of her commitments to her family. She discussed how it was important for her to be her own "best thing" for herself and her wife and child. She was leery of pouring out all her energies in other spaces and having little left for her family:

> My spouse and I talked about [this] all the time: what good is it if we're out doing justice in the world—whatever that looks like—and we're not doing that in our own relationship? I don't think it has to be that you are a brilliant activist and a terrible spouse or a brilliant activist and a terrible parent, or a prolific pastor and a terrible. . . . I think that there has to be some intentionality. I think that institutions, whether it's a church or a nonprofit or a university, will own you or treat you like they own you [unless you decide to say that that's not going to happen]. And I don't say that to make it seem like it's easy, but I refuse to be owned.

Maintaining boundaries—by advocating first for herself—is how she is able to show up in the movement spaces and advocate for others.

The interview with Rev. Kentina was particularly noteworthy because in prior conversations, older Black lesbian religious leaders all spoke about when an individual burned out or became unraveled because her commitment to her causes proved too great. As the second-youngest interviewee, at age thirty-nine, Rev. Kentina showed an ability to bracket and protect herself while being an advocate that was admirable. Furthermore, it reiterated how her being led by her faith (which to her meant being compelled by the Jesus Project) had an actual impact on her social justice advocacy.

FIGURE 3.2. Dean Emilie Townes. Used by permission.

Next is another example of everyday religious activism, this time a narrative shared by Dean Emilie Townes.

Rev. Dr. Emilie Townes is a womanist ethicist and the dean of the Vanderbilt Divinity School and the E. Rhodes and Leona B. Carpenter Professor of Womanist Ethics and Society. She has taught at Yale University Divinity School, Union Theological Seminary in New York, and Saint Paul School of Theology. She was the first African American woman to serve as the president of the American Academy of Religion, which is the largest professional society for scholars of religion. She has forged networks between Afro-Brazilian feminists and US womanists. Her research focuses on economic justice, gender, race, and poetry. She is an ordained American Baptist clergywoman.[13]

In her interview, Dean Townes reflected on her childhood history of social justice concerns, as well as connecting social justice to doing right in the world. She grew up in Durham, North Carolina, in a home that gave her freedom to cultivate a personal relationship with God, which she did by sitting in nature in the Duke Forest and talking to God. Her parents were concerned that she should receive a strong moral formation, and they raised her in a United Methodist home, but they did not mandate that she attend church. Despite finding a closer relationship with God outside rather than inside the church, she credits her childhood pastor with helping her connect social justice with her faith. Her pastor preached the necessity of having a "strong spiritual base if you're going to have a strong social justice base," and she carried that message into her approach to seeing injustice in her youthful world. In our interview she recalled being in high school during the desegregation of schools in Durham and experiencing a sense of outrage at class inequalities:

> And I didn't really know [or] understand class dynamics. But what I saw consistently was [that] the students who came from poorer backgrounds or less socially prominent backgrounds, no matter where they were, Black or White, were the students who got the short end of the stick on a consistent basis. And I was taught that that wasn't right, so I became a student activist, trying to right the injustices of the system. My mother used to always say, "You're out there trying to save the world." I said, "No, I'm just trying to make it right because it's wrong, what's going on." You know, my parents couldn't dispute it when I would describe what I'd see. But I know that where I got that from was from church. You stand up and speak out when you see wrong happening, and you don't let people suffer without saying something and trying to change it.

Because her parents were college professors, she was not directly affected by the kinds of income disparities and inequalities that she saw. Even so, at that early age she determined that it was important to stand up for her classmates. When she described spearheading activities like conducting surveys to better school conditions for students with lower economic means, she talked about using her privilege to advocate for equity.

Dean Townes's social justice championing remained tied to how she was living her faith and also was a part of her scholarly interests. While completing coursework for her doctorate at Garrett-Northwestern, she began researching Ida B. Wells-Barnett and through archival research found that Wells-Barnett had a deeply religious worldview that motivated her nineteenth- and early twentieth-century activism. This connection of faith and activism that she was tracking in an early Black women activist is also a hallmark of her own scholarship. When I asked Dean Townes how she viewed her scholarship, she stated that her scholarship was activism:

> My job is to bring a whole bunch of people along with me in this journey, not just faculty, not just students, and not just staff. . . . And if they've got some kin, they can come along too, but I really do understand that the work of me as the dean . . . is to open up doors. As many doors and

windows as I can for folks to be able to have their say. I want to create a structure and opportunities for people to be able to have their say about their lives and their witness, and I'd like to have my say too.

Or my PhD students, I know they're going to make an impact on the academy. That, to me, is activism. And they can do things I can't, so [together] we have a bigger impact.

For her, bridging the academy and religious spaces is an activist move that connects heart and mind. As one who is currently situated with the academy, she helps to train the next generation of religious scholars and practitioners. She reiterates that dismantling historical injustices takes group organizing, self-consciousness, theorizing, and negotiating various systems. She warns that what her parents and her lengthy career in the academy have taught her is that in academia everybody's expendable if the university feels threatened. Rather than cower before that vulnerability, she vows to cast her lot with the people rather than with the institution.[14] Her everyday activism continues to mirror the lessons she learned as a teenager—especially the value of and responsibility to speak up for others.

Collective Efforts toward Social Change

The four women introduced thus far have primarily exemplified individual activism, individual acts of expressing their faith and seeking social justice in society. This next section spotlights collective efforts to bring about social change. Here the emphasis is on tracking resistance strategies that are a part of larger-scale movements such as the Black Lives Matter movement and LGBTQ activism. Both movements were created with women-of-color organizers, but the specifically religious motivations of these social justice activists have not been widely investigated. It is easy to understand why Black lesbian religious leaders would show interest in both movements. What I found novel were the ways in which the interviewees drew on their faith as the foundation for their activism.

Much of the scholarship and media attention surrounding the organizing of the Black Lives Matter hashtag, coined in July 2013, has centered on the activism of queer women of color. Unfortunately, Black religion scholars have interrogated this movement and its incorporation into Black religion without adequately examining the queer lived realities of its founders.[15] This chapter cannot do this large topic justice. Instead, I focus more narrowly on the queer religiosities of the Black Lives Matter movement and its non-Christian leanings before highlighting the activism of two Black lesbian Christian leaders more locally involved in digital activism.

Following the social media activism of Patrisse Cullors, Alicia Garza, and Opal Tometi in the aftermath of the acquittal of Trayvon Martin's killer, much physical organizing and demonstrating occurred across the country. As murders of Black people by police were chronicled and protested, word spread that this burgeoning movement was being led by queer Black women who were not associated with the traditional Black church. The presumption that they were nonreligious actors motivated by social justice principles who had little time for the protest leader model of the Black male preacher—as exemplified by Rev. Al Sharpton at the microphone. Yet further investigation into the spiritual practices of Black Lives Matter protesters revealed that women and men were in fact relying on such African spiritual practices such as ancestor worship, Ifá rituals, and Buddhist meditation.[16] This realization of the absence of Christian rituals highlights that, unlike conservative religious actors who are the primary producers of their activist rhetoric and social justice activism, progressive religious actors often take Black Lives Matter practices back into their religious networks.[17]

This was apparent when I explored organizing around Black Lives Matter with my interviewees. Many of the women were participants in a variety of social justice movements over several decades, so tracking to see if they were participating in this contemporary liberation campaign was noteworthy. I introduce you next to one such participant—Rev. Dr. Pamela Lightsey—whose interview and scholarship connect Christian faith and social justice activism.

Rev. Dr. Pamela Lightsey is the first out Black lesbian ordained elder in the United Methodist Church. She is the vice president of Academic and Student Affairs and associate professor of constructive theology at the Meadville Lombard Theological School. She formerly served as the associate dean of Community Life and Lifelong Learning at the Boston University School of Theology. She is a veteran of the US Army, a former pastor, a former civil servant, a social justice activist, and scholar whose research interests include just-war theory, womanist theology, and queer theology.[18]

Rev. Dr. Lightsey grew up in a household that had ongoing conversations about freedom and Black liberation. Her deep connections to the Black community instilled in her a pride in Blackness and commitment to the thriving of the Black community. Although she was not reared in a particularly churchgoing

FIGURE 3.3. Reverend Dr. Pamela Lightsey. Used by permission.

home, her parents ensured that she and her siblings heard about God from them and learned to have a personal relationship with God. She entered the military at age eighteen; while enlisted, she had a mystical experience with God and felt called into the ministry. She was attending a Pentecostal church whose female pastor licensed her husband but not her, and she recognized that the civil disobedience and resistance methodology of the civil rights movement was the strategy for undoing the sexism experienced in the church. In addition to making up her mind to fight against sexism (and changing denominations), she decided that from that point on she would listen only to God and not to what humans said about God. This resolution led her to the Interdenominational Theological Seminary as she was preparing to pastor full-time for the United Methodist Church. During seminary she was in a lesbian relationship and was struck by the homophobia present in a school ostensibly so dedicated to liberation for the Black community. She rejected the normalization of this discrimination as well, and by the time she received her call to pastor her first church in Chicago's Southside, she had a full liberationist foundation. In that congregation she became more vocal in her commitment to LGBTQ justice and particularly HIV/AIDS outreach. She recalled that the church was eager for younger members, which she gained by outreach to the gang members in her environment. She was aware the church probably did not have in mind those kinds of new members, but "they got what they wanted; I got what I needed. And what I needed was that continued, deep kind of relationship with members of the Black community that are often spoken ill of and are forgotten about.... It was in keeping with how I was raised—that is, stick with your people."

Rev. Dr. Lightsey's willingness to serve her people is ultimately what propelled her into Black Lives Matter organizing later in her career. After completing her doctorate at Garrett Northwestern and working there as dean of Students and vice-president of Student Affairs, she accepted a position at Boston University School of Theology as associate dean of Community Life. While there, she was moved by seeing the murdered body of Michael Brown on the news and wanted to become actively involved in the protests. She felt that she was well equipped to help as a military veteran, as someone who had lived through the civil rights movement, and as a woman who had experienced poverty. She went to Ferguson, Missouri, as a representative of the Boston University School of Theology and the Reconciling Ministries Network (a United Methodist social justice group) communication staff "without a clue ... but [with] a sincere commitment to justice." She recorded hours of footage of day-to-day interactions between the protesters and the militarized Ferguson police. Her interviews with activists and citizens of Ferguson illuminated how police brutality, public policies like ticketing schemes that unfairly penalized poor Blacks, and denial of proper health care and quality education were all conditions that the Black Lives Matter movement was seeking to alleviate. Ultimately, she was convinced that just as she was stirred into action by seeing what was happening on social media, her Livestream broadcasts could influence others:

> I was also interested, as a womanist scholar, about the ways in which women were leading in the movement compared to what had happened during the civil rights movement. So I really wanted to find the female leaders, where were the sisters who were leading, because I didn't want the story told in the future that this was a movement that was largely led by men, when in fact that wasn't the truth. So I paid particular [attention] to ways in which the women were leading, serving in leadership capacity in Ferguson as a woman. I was also wanting to know theologically what the people thought justice looked like, would look like for them. So I had all those sensibilities when I went down to Ferguson.

As a womanist scholar, she was committed to bringing forth a perspective that centered the experiences of women as well as highlighted the role that religion was playing (two topics that she felt were being obscured in the media surrounding the protests). She was able to draw attention to the "rich theology present in the Black community" that was being articulated on the ground but was not being recorded or communicated by the national secular media.[19]

Her womanist lens and approach to activism not only highlighted religion and women's leadership but also demonstrated generational gaps and fissures within coalition building. She discussed a teachable moment that she experienced while filming in Ferguson as she witnessed an exchange between residents about Black spending power that became a bit heated. Men were raising their voices and becoming really passionate in their conversation when two Black women joined the conversation, matching the same octave and passion. At that moment, a younger Black man intervened and asked the women to quiet down:

> And I yelled out, before I could catch myself, the activist in me, the womanist in me, I said, "Wait! You didn't stop the men when they were talking. Why are you trying to stop the women?" And in another corner a sister yells out, "Oh, don't come down here with that feminist bullshit." And I'm struck by this, you know.
>
> And my body begins to shake until another sister says, "Oh no, she right, she right, she right, she right." Well, by then I'd had all of these kind of quick internal conversations in my head about context, you know, about my own privilege, you know, my own privilege, and how, you know, I opened a door and stepped, you know, how I stepped into, put myself into the community that was my community, but not my community, you know.
>
> So as an activist, that moment reminds—I go back to that moment in my mind because it helps me to teach people about privilege, about class privilege, helps me to teach people about sexism. It helps me to talk to people about the difference between womanist and feminist. Right there on the street, you know, all of that came into being.
>
> Secondly, that moment reminded me of why I really should be there, and what the presence of a scholar, and the immediacy, what being immediately connected as a scholar, as a theologian in protest movements can and must do. And the danger of doing that, too, you know, the danger of

doing that. So by inserting myself, I'm, you know, just a response; inserting myself brought a conversation for the community about sexism. And that was good. It was a dangerous moment for me, but it allowed them to continue that conversation about women, Black women.

She incorporated her experiences in Ferguson into her book *Our Lives Matter: A Womanist Queer Theology*, committing to make the book accessible to those participating in activism movements on the ground. She expressed great joy in knowing that her book could be useful to the LGBTQ community and activists in general. She recounted an activist highlighting the book, placing it in his pocket, going to a protest, then following up with her to ask questions about the text. She sees her scholarship much like Dean Townes does—as an extension of her collective and individual activism.

Another interviewee displayed a similar personal commitment to Black Lives Matter organizing, seeing it as co-constitutive of her queer and religious activism. In my interview with Rev. Naomi Washington-Leapheart, wife of Rev. Kentina, it became clear that she also had a calling to Ferguson that gripped her and spurred her into action.

Rev. Naomi was my youngest interviewee, at thirty-seven years old. She was described by her wife as a workaholic whose identity was deeply intertwined with her participation in social justice movements. Similarly to Dean Townes and Rev. Dr. Lightsey, she experienced her teaching as activism but was also familiar with on-the-ground protest. This commitment to social justice organizing was likewise forged early on in her life. One of her childhood memories is of watching the trial after the murder of Miles Green (a Detroit resident who was stopped by the police and beaten to death) and being instructed by her mother that Black people needed to stand up because white people could not keep killing them. In college, she felt this same push to stand up for her community when she was learning to connect the "dots between what the Bible says, what Jesus did, and the vocation of social justice." Immediately after college, she spent some years working in urban education, where she fought for resources for underserved students. She was aghast that although her students were experiencing trauma, she was expected to teach them algebra as if their traumas were not affecting them. In response, she created a social justice math class in which the class looked at redlining and statistical analyses of stop-and-frisk incidents in the city of Philadelphia as both social justice concerns and mathematical problems to solve. When Trayvon Martin was murdered, she was working with youths who were trying to earn their GED, so she had them learn from the Constitution about the right to bear arms. She saw her classroom as a space to contextualize what they were seeing in the news. Shortly thereafter, she entered seminary at Lancaster Theological Seminary, and then Michael Brown was killed. She had just accepted a unique three-pastor team appointment at a United Church of Christ congregation and was completing her first year of seminary when she was nudged into action:

> Michael Brown is killed. I am activated. I am frustrated that nobody at the church is saying anything about it. I go to his funeral because I just felt led to go. I spend my own money, and . . . I came back and I said, "We need a social justice ministry here in this church. We no longer need to be silent about the issues happening right here in Lancaster. We don't have to go to Ferguson. Right here in Lancaster, there's a police brutality issue. Black and brown people in Lancaster feel targeted in a certain area. We started a social justice ministry at the church, and we organized protests. People would meet me in the fellowship hall and make signs, and we would go down there, and I would speak at the line, and there would be the members of the church standing right there. That was what helped me to know that perhaps this is what I can do. This is what I can contribute to the work of the gospel here in this community.
>
> We did some really great work together around mass incarceration and reentry of people coming home from Lancaster County Prison. We did some work around, of course, [the] Black Lives Matter movement. The congregation was involved in protests and then having events at the church. We were involved in LGBTQ advocacy. We hosted the Transgender Day of Remembrance ceremony a couple of times. Went down to the courthouse steps to do a trans affirmation. Got the city involved. In that way in seminary, as pastor of this church, I came to know myself as a person who could do . . . who was called to kind of public ministry for justice movements, and that I could pastorally do that as well, because people in the movement still need pastoral care and they might not go to church to get that, but they will go to the protests. If I can be a person that they can talk to, I can walk alongside them at the protest, then I would do that. That's what I've been doing.
>
> It's not coincidental that the Black Lives Matter kind of movement started or coincides with the beginning of my seminary journey such that I now see no separation between the work I'm doing as it relates to justice

and the work I do. . . . I mean my training as a minister happened at the same time as my training as a kind of justice-seeking person.

As mentioned in chapter 2, Rev. Naomi's social justice work was not just limited to her Black Lives Matter organizing. In the same way she was activated around community organizing after the Mike Brown murder, she was also catapulted into advocacy for LGBTQ persons after the Pulse Nightclub massacre. She left local organizing for the greater Philadelphia area to take a position as the Faith Work director for the National LGBTQ Task Force. Her advocacy is reminiscent of the Combahee River Collective's 1977 statement of beliefs because the writers of the statement realized that "the only people who care enough about us to work consistently for our liberation are us."[20] All of the women I interviewed expressed similar sentiments, for they all did some organizing for the LGBTQ and/or specifically Black LGBTQ community. Yet each of the women realized the necessity for their work to be connected to their full liberation. For Rev. Naomi, this was possible in her position as Faith Work director:

> This was an opportunity to work with congregations around the issue of LGBTQ justice without apology and do it intersectionally such that we're not just talking about marriage for example, but we're talking about queer kids who have no place to live because they've been kicked out of their home and church communities, or we're talking about trans women who are engaging in sex work for survival and don't need to be criminalized for such, or we're talking about queer people in prisons who are harassed and assaulted on a daily basis. It's not just about LGBTQ affirmation in a kind of basic sense. It's also about queer people are also living in poverty, are also criminalized because of their gender identity, are also experiencing disenfranchisement at work and being fired because they put a picture of their spouse on the desk. I mean, so it just seemed to me to be a place where I could also talk about all those issues I was talking about before and be unapologetically queer and fight unapologetically for queer people.

In that position she worked with denominations, lobbyists, state campaigns, and persons with wide-ranging theological positions. She was also able to develop Free Indeed, a project that targeted historically Black Christians regarding the notion of religious freedom, highlighting the connections between religious freedom's early use as a means to preserve segregation to its current use to deny services and products to LGBTQ people. She focused the project on what freedom in Christ or biblical freedom means for Black persons, and this project is an example of the integration of her various identities and how they propel her to connect religion to activist responses.

Likewise, Rev. Dr. Lightsey's activism reflected a need to have her Christian faith fully activated for the work of justice for LGBTQ persons. She has been a vocal and long-standing advocate addressing LGBTQ inclusion within the United Methodist Church. This work began when she was a pastor and had HIV/AIDS ministries, but her participation increased beyond service providing. She and others have united around changing the United Methodist Church's *Book of Discipline*, which currently states that the practice of homosexuality is incompatible with Christian teaching and prevents clergy from being practicing homosexuals.[21] Rev. Dr. Lightsey is an ordained elder in the tradition, is committed to its longevity, and thus feels obligated to help it be at its best:

> I took up the cause of LGBTQ activism in the United Methodist Church because I felt that I have the cover to do so. Let me explain what I mean by cover. First of all, the United Methodist Church has already repented of its discrimination against Black people, so as a Black person and queer and lesbian, the United Methodist Church, I mean, the right wing of the United Methodist Church, I felt would be taking its chances to attack a Black woman. They already take their chances, horribly so, to attack LGBTQ persons.
>
> You know, the church has been good to me. I'm one of the few ordained elders, Black ordained elders, in the United Methodist Church with a Ph.D. Not a D.Min., but a Ph.D. So I wanted to use my achievement, my accomplishments that have been supported by the church to help make the very church that supported my education better. And I thought it important for me to do that. This is my way of thanking the church for being committed to helping to improve the lives of its laypeople, its clergypersons. So what better way than to help the church live out the principles that it articulates.
>
> Secondly, I do this because I want Black clergy in the United Methodist Church and Black people in the United Methodist Church to understand that homophobia is illogical, is an illogical place to lay their hat, to hang their hat as people who have been oppressed. I mean, come on, Black people . . . being homophobic? Yeah, it happens, but why should we? We

of all people ought not be oppressing people. So I use my theological education to make that point.

And I use what clout I have in the church. But you only get so many minutes of fame, you know, and so I'm trying to use my few minutes of fame to make life better, not just for our church members, but for people who have been hurt by the church and who walked away from the church. I want them to know that God loves them. And unfortunately, when people talk about LGBTQ persons, in the Black community I've heard it too often where they say that's a white man's problem. I'm trying to help people to understand that Black people are part of the LGBTQ community. And I'm also committed to saying and we really do matter.

As a Black lesbian religious leader advocating for LGBTQ equality, Rev. Dr. Lightsey sees the efficacy of having her spirituality intertwined with her activism. Ultimately, she sees full integration into society and religious community as a moral imperative.

Lightsey asserts that oppression must be resisted in any format that it appears. She posits that a queer womanist theological framework reveals a "commitment to whole people existing in the wholeness of their given bodies; free bodies, sensual and spiritual in nature."[22] In praxis, what this means is that there is an expectation that persons expressing this kind of activism will work toward the good of the many.

Womanist Spiritual Activism

The examples of Rev. Naomi's and Rev. Dr. Lightsey's integrated scholar-activist-pastoral lives underscore the contention of psychologists Thema Bryant-Davis and Tyonna Adams that activism is integral to womanism because the desire to fight for the wholeness of all people demands intentional actions to bring about transformation. They argue that womanist activism is inherently based on resisting oppression but is also grounded in spirituality, for the spirituality of a womanist "motivates her to act for justice and to create sustainable peace."[23] They rely upon Alice Walker's definition of womanism here, particularly her description of a womanist as one who "loves the Spirit." But I conjecture that womanist activism also reflects Walker's characterization of a womanist as someone who "loves the struggle."[24] Womanist activists like the women whom I interviewed and presented here do not shirk from a fight; they wage battle and regroup to fight another day.

Scholarship on womanist spirituality is beyond the purview of this chapter.[25] Most US-based womanists have followed the theological academy's interpretation of reading womanist spirituality through the lens of Christianity. However, instead of this lens—which was explicitly not Walker's lens—I turn to Maparyan's understanding of womanist spiritual activism, which is crafted in a religiously eclectic manner reliant on her own blending of African religions, religious science, Kabbalah, and Kemetic tradition rather than Christianity. She argues that organized religion is institutionalized but that spirituality is individualized, and that if we want to study the practices of individuals, we should look more closely at their personal faith practices.[26] Her argument is persuasive because at its core her understanding of womanist spiritual activism centers the experiences of everyday women who use their religion to produce social change. This project seeks to do similar work.

In *The Womanist Idea*, Maparyan defines spiritual activism as key to womanist praxis. She contends that spiritual activism is social or ecological transformation rooted in a spiritual belief system that literally puts spirituality to work for positive social change. She predicates her concept on three theories: the innate divinity of humans and creation, the existence and lawfulness of invisible realms, and humans as energy transformers who can perform miracles by learning and applying metaphysical laws.[27] She writes about spiritual activism as a social change method that helps one to interrogate the two basic principles for creating social change: change yourself (inner work) and change the world (outer work).

When relating this method to what my interviewees told me, I was pleased to find it applicable to their experiences with social justice activism. It was also a self-categorization for some of the interviewees. For instance, Rev. Holmes introduced herself in her bio as a spiritual activist. When I asked her to describe what that meant for her, she stated:

> I lead with my spirituality as who I am in this world. And how I express myself is an expression of my spirituality. And so as a spiritual activist, I express myself now as an activist, in other words, someone who is active and actively pursuing justice, and that that is an outgrowth of my spirituality.
>
> It is not that I have some political agenda that's inspiring me. I'm inspired by my spirituality to be an activist, to be a change agent, to see that the world we are living in is about other spiritual people as well, no matter where they fall on the spectrum in terms of the[ir] politics, but

that I can bring my spirit and my spirituality and my humanity, all that's combined and integrated, and I bring that to the table, and that is the alchemy that I think helps activism, for me, to be impactful, because I don't leave that at the door, I bring that in the room with me, or I take that to the mic, or I put that in the articles that I write, or whatever the expression of activism it is.

My spirituality is not so much me being a minister and wearing a collar, but it is that spirituality, the gift of my spirituality and the gift of my sexual orientation are just that, they're gifts, and they're part of who I am. And being an activist is to say that I lift all that up for the cause of justice in the same way that Jesus did. And so I see Jesus as a spiritual activist. And I see myself in that same way.

Because she is a spiritual activist, her faith animates her to make significant strides for social change, but she notes that she first did the inner work of learning to accept herself as a Black lesbian religious leader. It was only after that, and through using those identities, those gifts (as she put it), that she could move out into the world to agitate for justice.

Likewise, Rev. Dr. Cari Jackson was also comfortable with categorizing her justice- seeking efforts as spiritual activism. Dr. Cari described a life of never quite fitting in and this creating an empathetic impetus. Her parents were both civically conscious and believed in helping the community strive to be better, so she found herself volunteering at an early age. Before she was out of high school, she had participated in voter registration, environmental justice campaigns, prisoner reentry programs, and other service-oriented work. By the time she graduated from college, she went to work for the United Way because she had connected the need for civic awareness with community service as a way of life. The world of helping others gave her a sense of belonging, for she came to realize that her "spirituality is the most important part of my being." Although her race was important, she recognized that her various identities were ultimately societal constructs but that her spirituality was not a construct; it was real.

In her oral history she shared that she was always involved with a range of justice or spiritual activism because "I can't from my perspective as a spiritual person not be engaged in justice work. . . . If spirituality is to make any difference, it is to see the Divine in others . . . whether it was the young girl working in the Children's Hospital or working with juvenile offenders. . . . I see the Divine in other people, and I seek to create space where people can see that within themselves." Whether in her secular work or her ministerial calls, Dr. Cari is animated by her spirituality to work for social good, be that fighting homelessness, prison reform, death penalty abolition, or now her current work in reproductive choice. Envisioning Dr. Cari as a spiritual activist is useful because she demonstrated an awareness of the connection of spiritual activism as individual and collective:

> Well, for me the spiritual must always be social. That was not teaching from my earliest religious tradition within Pentecostalism. Very individual, but spirituality for me is both individual and communal. The scripture that really guides me in terms of social activism is from the Lord's Prayer: "Give us this day our daily bread." It's the communal aspect of that. It's not "God, give me my bread and screw what happens to the other people." But it's our bread, and so whatever I have in my life I see it as Spirit gifting me to be a conduit to help share those resources with the community. . . . And I feel that way in terms of people who I have never met; I feel a responsibility to them because we share our humanity. And so it's spiritual and it is social for me.

This effort to see the divine in others and a connection to others means that one is motivated into working fervently so that all thrive, which is a basic foundation of womanist spiritual activism.

Another interviewee that demonstrates this concept of womanist spiritual activism is Bishop Flunder.

Bishop Rev. Dr. Yvette Flunder is founder and senior pastor of the City of Refuge United Church of Christ and presiding bishop of the Fellowship, a multidenominational fellowship of more than a hundred primarily African American Christian churches that practice radical inclusivity. Flunder was heavily active in the Church of God in Christ denomination until she realized that being same-gender-loving and also an active member of her denomination would cause conflict. After a self-imposed exile, she went on to serve as associate pastor for Love Center Ministries before feeling a call to plant a church, the City of Refuge, in Oakland, California. One of her church's main purposes is to unite gospel and social ministry, and it is particularly known for its work with AIDS and transgender communities. Flunder earned a master of arts degree from the Pacific School of Religion and a doctor of ministry degree from the San Francisco Theological Seminary, where she focused on providing a framework for her work in the AIDS and transgender communities and for her activism on marriage equality.[28]

FIGURE 3.4. Bishop Yvette Flunder. Used by permission.

Bishop Flunder was born and raised in San Francisco in a middle-class family that was heavily active in the Church of God in Christ denomination. She led a life devoted to social justice from an early age, which could be seen as ironic given that she was reared in a somewhat isolating Pentecostal home. Reared as a fundamentalist to not worry about the world, she told me that part of her early religious training emphasized staying saved, which was the opposite of social justice motivation because if "you're always afraid you're going to lose your salvation, you can't really concentrate on the needs of other people, because every altar is for you." Bishop Flunder had perhaps earned the most notoriety for her social justice activism with prominent honors like giving the keynote address for the White House's World AIDS Day in 2014, which she credits to a deepened spirituality and connection to her faith. In her initial interview with me, she indicated that she felt that she had always had a "social justice bent," and in our follow-up interview in July 2019, she reiterated this formation, noting that despite her upbringing preparing her for the coming of Jesus, she made time for social consciousness because she felt "it was my responsibility, not just to get to Heaven, but to bring Heaven to Earth."

Similarly to Maparyan's claim that the inner work is the first step to outward social change, Bishop Flunder's acceptance of social consciousness and interconnectedness is instrumental to how she helps actualize social change in her community. In her response to my question regarding how she created City of Refuge, I was intrigued how Bishop Flunder was able to amplify this personal sense of responsibility to make it a corporate sense of responsibility for her church. She told me that she had a few goals when founding her church:

> Well, I certainly wanted to create an environment where we could celebrate our relationships as same-gender-loving people, and I wanted to create an environment where we could be very focused on justice issues as our primary concern. Love Center's badge in the world is a church that excels in the arts. And it's not that I didn't enjoy it, you know what I mean? But what is really my passion is for social justice and human services, and getting people wrapped around finding ways to fight for their own freedom and for the freedom of anyone who has been marginalized. And it was hard for me to exercise that passion in an arts atmosphere where the principal concern was, again, for music and arts. And I don't say that pejoratively; it's just that I didn't feel that to be my primary call. And the other thing is, as I said before, I wanted to create a situation where same-gender-loving people could come and be fully who they are, who we are.

She did not diminish the difficulty involved with getting others to share her vision but noted that moving from a small New Testament–like home cell to a flourishing community involved meeting the needs of the burgeoning community and expanding its vision as the community recognized the intersections of evil oppressing them.

Bishop Flunder founded City of Refuge as an independent religious community in 1991, and she remembered that the time of the church's founding was at the height of the AIDS epidemic, particularly in San Francisco's Tenderloin District and the demographic that the church served. Initially, the church grew as people came for access to the services it provided, such as housing, food, case management, and spiritual support for the LGBTQ community and for those infected with HIV/AIDS. She reminisced about how much stigma there was around HIV and how many of the providers of care were women, "unseen heroines" who engaged as healers in a particularly ostracized community. By committing to the "least of these" in their communities, City of Refuge was linked to a vision of social justice that was animated by faith.

In our interviews, I appreciated the capaciousness of Flunder's vision and the vastness of her spiritual calling. Whether it was the on-the-ground activist work spearheaded by the City of Refuge or the connectivity of the many churches associated with the fellowship and its social justice leanings, Bishop Flunder was continually reaching outward to the community, propelled by her understanding of her ministerial call. In her response to my follow-up question regarding why she felt so passionately about linking social justice and her faith, she spoke about the need to take Jesus back from those who tried to use Christianity to marginalize others. City of Refuge has also expanded its seat of spiritual power to include ancestral practices: she instructs congregants that "it is holy to go forward, and it is also holy to go backwards" to receive gifts from the ancestors to help achieve a theology of liberation. She speaks of this task as by its very nature expansive because "what we are called to is to have people that give us comfort and strength so then we can go back out into the larger world and do the work that is necessary to help people who may be quite different from us."

Holistic Activism

What Bishop Flunder is describing can be theorized using Monica Coleman's womanist framework of "making a way out of no way," which is a means of creative social transformation. Within Coleman's theorizing she uplifts the goal of justice, survival, and quality of life as a challenge to the existing order. Her discussion of salvation is closely aligned with notions of justice; she posits that both serve the purpose of changing our world. Creative transformation can come in the form of saviors, but this "constructive womanist concept of salvation comes from the new vision that God provides to Black women, who have significant agency in moving the future towards a just and participatory society." One of Coleman's key examples is the leader of God, Self, Neighbor Ministries (GSN Ministries), Rev. Dr. Kathi Martin, a Black lesbian religious leader living with mental and physical health challenges. Rev. Dr. Kathi Martin founded GSN in 1999, and it disbanded in 2005. She founded the ministry with social justice as a significant aspect of its vision. Her goal was to energize outreach activities that would focus on the most marginalized community members. Coleman casts Rev. Dr. Kathi Martin as a savior because she leads in creative transformation. What I find persuasive about Coleman's articulation of Martin's ministry is that salvation is communally oriented: she suggests that there is no salvation "unless the entire community is saved."[29]

Coleman's choice of Rev. Dr. Kathi Martin as a savior is a precursor for this research highlighting Black lesbian women actively engaged in social justice activism. Coleman's model reflects a holistic activism that necessitates a world that is just for the most marginalized members of society. One such leader exploring this type of holistic activism is Bishop Tonyia Rawls.

Bishop Rawls demonstrated a long-standing commitment to social justice enterprises that was animated by living in the aftermath of riots in Newark, New Jersey, after Dr. Martin Luther King Jr. was assassinated. She was warned by her mother about turning anger inward as an activist, which left an indelible mark. Unlike many of other interviewees, Bishop Rawls did not report on secular social justice activism as an outlet for her early commitments. Instead, her early organizing occurred in religious spaces, and now her later organizing occurs primarily in secular spaces. While in her first pastorate with a Unity Fellowship church, she beamed with pride over her socially active congregation. The city's first out elected official was a member, the area Gay Prides were birthed out of the congregation, and she noted that the congregation was involved in everything from domestic violence to educating youths. She recounted that having a congregation that was committed to social justice was dependent on a theological position that cast Christianity as a revolutionary religion that required communal awareness and a desire to love and serve:

> [I teach] that Jesus really was a revolutionary and to be OK with that. With us being revolutionaries. In the ways that love drives that action. Love drives that work; that's a lot of what we do as we're focusing on that kind of building and the like. It is assumed that Black people in particular are powerful and that we have much to offer the world. That I can be a have-not, but I'm also a have in many ways. The goal is finding where those connections are and then walking in the fullness of it. . . .
>
> When it was time for us to have the church, we also followed those principles of the fact that if I am to be a true Christian, caring for my neighbor is a core part of what we're called to do. In caring for my neighbor, that may mean and likely means I have to step outside of my comfort zone. Yes, I even had to step outside of the church. Everybody in our congregation understands that's who we are. Somebody had said to me very early on in my ministerial life, it was an older pastor. He said, "You know, I see that

you're very active in the social justice efforts and in fighting the school system and all these kind of things." He said, "I get all of that, but I want to suggest you'll need to make a choice and the choice is this, you can have a large church or you can have an active church."

What he was saying was "but it is nearly impossible to have both." I didn't understand it at the time because I was such a young pastor. But I later grew to understand what he was saying. What he was talking about was some people just want to come to church. They don't want you challenging them about doing stuff. They don't want you dragging them to marches and stepping on their toes about life and these kind of things. That's not what they want. They just want to feel good. They want to hear some good music. They want to hear some exciting preaching and go home and just write a check. But if that's not who you are, then know there is also a price you pay for that.

For Bishop Rawls, commitment to social justice is part of what it means to be the church, and her love for the church demands that it live up to its full potential. As she notes, achieving this goal means leaving our comfort zones to be, in King's language, an enactment of the "beloved community." In doing this self-reflective work from the leadership throughout the religious community, she realized that when she asked her trans members what their experiences were in that community, she was not prepared for their responses:

The responses were revelatory and devastating at the same time. [Their responses were] the most difficult things I've had to hear as a pastor. It was person after person, and I realized what many of us in the church had done in these affirming spaces was we would look at the trans community and say, "Oh, girl, you better go on. You're looking fierce; you're looking fine."

So much of who they are for the mind outside of their true experience was for people's entertainment and people's enjoyment, whether it was to look at them, to have sex with them, to be entertained by them, but nobody was talking to them about their life, about who they are as people of faith. It started that trajectory of my work. Now my work with the trans community is one of my larger bodies of work. Part of it is because my belief is once we make sure trans people are OK, everybody else will be fine. It's like going to that farthest edge and saying, "How inclusive are we really? How loving are we really? How grace filled are we really?" To understand we've got a long way to go. Unfortunately a long way to go, as lesbian, gay, bi, people—we're some of the worst because their expectation would be that we would be there for them.

Bishop Rawls's desire to "make sure trans people are OK" reflects an understanding of holistic activism that is not just based on identity politics. It spreads beyond the experiences of the leader and asks who still needs to be liberated and saved.[30] Yet the persons in need of liberation are involved in their own salvation. This is not a model of activism that privileges isolated saviors; instead, this argues for the necessity of being in community and allowing collaborative leadership models to dictate where resources and personnel are allocated.

Some of this resource sharing is done within the religious space, and some is done outside of the church in her nonprofit, the Freedom Center for Social Justice (FCSJ), which she founded in 2009. Its mission is to be a "culture-shifting organization committed to growth, safety, and empowerment of marginalized populations." It is a collaborative organization that partners with other social justice organizations to advance the rights of specific populations. She discussed her work with the Freedom Center as liberating because it gave her access to different skill sets while working toward a similar calling:

> There's a freedom [being an executive director], and I get to be unapologetically activist in that kind of way. As a pastor, which I love pastoring, but it comes with certain kind of responsibilities and also some limitations in terms of what is reasonable to do. With the nonprofit, I have an opportunity to build that team, build that body of work, and it's all similar in that it's all freedom-based work. Culture shift work, because I consider the faith work I do culture shift work. The complement of the two is wonderful; it really is. It's a lot of work, but it works for me in terms of my commitment to helping to ensure that the poor, LGBTQ, people of color, trans people, that's my primary groups that we focus on and people of faith. That those intersections are where we've been able to accomplish some amazing things. It's an unlikely place, it's an unlikely intersection, but it is one that actually I find quite beautiful, challenging, yes, but beautiful.

Many of the Black lesbian religious leaders I interviewed had experience with secular organizing for social justice, and a sizable number were able to create 501(c)3 foundations or organizations to sustain their social justice work. Bishop Rawls does so in a bivocational way and is a leader in both the religious space and in her secular organization (most of the other interviewees had separate leaders for the secular foundations/organizations). What she deems culture work is an effort to produce social change with the "least of these" in mind. This activism with the most marginalized at the center necessitates organizing beyond the sacred/secular divide. Bishop Rawls pursues justice within her church and the Freedom Center for Social Justice with intersectional analyses.

Patricia Hill Collins posits that because we now have flourishing analyses from feminists and womanists, "Black women can move beyond their particular experiences without losing sight of the specificity of their experiences."[31] This is what Bishop Flunder has in mind at the start of the chapter when she says that her church grew organically from one area of justice work to another. Their vision expanded beyond the impact of HIV/AIDS on the Black LGBTQ community to address women's issues, prison reform, and now border work. Her vision for City of Refuge was intentionally intersectional: Bishop Flunder explained that they were called to address the "intersections of evil that oppress all of us." This is what Coleman is referencing in her notion of creative transformation as salvation. Arguably, this is also what Maparyan's discussion of womanist spiritual activism seeks to present. If "old forms of activism are not enough,"[32] then contemporary times require activism that creates coalitions between communities, making womanist spiritual activism a bold move.

Bishops Rawls and Flunder indicated that they simply just got involved in areas that would affect the most sidelined members of society. From Bishop Flunder's simple acceptance of the need to let her faith motivate her to act in the world, she has been trying to create Heaven here among us. For her, this is manifested in seeing "people who are finding their way to their own personal freedom in God," and it is demonstrated in her hope that her work helps the marginalized, disenfranchised, abused, torn, and ostracized people find their way to full faith and confidence in God. Her call is a quintessential example of the inner and outward work expressed by womanist spiritual activists:

I always apologize for the interesting life that I have, to say the least, but as I often also say it's kind of the life of a prophet, of a trailblazer, and it's all over the place simultaneously. And I make an effort to try to tie things down. I don't always do so well, but I'm at it, you know, I'm doing [*laughs*] the best I can, given my circumstances. I hope that the generation that is coming after us will know us to be the trailblazers, and know the personal cost, but also the personal joy that it has been for us, and if nothing else, that we can provide a path for them through this wilderness so that their way will not be nearly as difficult, in many ways, as ours has been. Then I know that our living and our working hasn't been in vain.

Many of the leaders that I have profiled in this chapter are aware of their role in Black LGBTQ history but see their contributions as just part of many that helped change the tide.

The utility of spiritualized social change is foundational to the prototype of a womanist ethical leader. This chapter has focused on understanding the various ways that social justice activism is anchored within a faith leader's spirituality. I have deliberately looked at everyday resistance as well as collective action as sites for social change. Ultimately, the chapter concludes that a womanist spiritual activism is oriented toward intersectional justice for all. Although I have largely accepted Maparyan's notion that "spiritual activism is key to womanist praxis," chapter 4 moves into the practical skill sets expected for a womanist ethical leader.[33]

Mighty Causes Are Calling Us   4
Expanding Womanist Spiritualities

Mighty causes are calling us—the freeing of women, the training of children, the putting down of hate and poverty—all these and more. But they call with voices that mean work and sacrifice and death. Mercifully grant us, O God, the spirit of Esther, that we say: I will go unto the King and if I perish, I perish—Amen!

—W. E. B. DU BOIS, *Prayers for Dark People*

My spirituality is really the most important part of my being. My race is important, but so much of that I understand is social construct. My spirituality, how I've shaped it, is not social construct. It started that way and over the years, how I understand myself as a Black person has shifted also as I've reclaimed and not just focused on the social construct in the relationship. Each of those things I've had to become empowered, to claim for myself, who I am and what all of those things mean to be a spiritual person, a Black person, a female person, a gay person, on, and on, and on.

—REV. DR. CARI JACKSON, oral history interview, 2018

When I initially created my vision board of Black lesbian religious leaders to interview, I relied on referrals by snowball-sampling names from my participants. This resulted in a predominantly Protestant Christian sample pool, with the exceptions of my interviews with a Jewish rabbi, a Buddhist lay leader, and a spiritualist. Early in my study I thought of these three interviews as "outliers" and decided that they would fit in the book as a coda reflecting new vistas awaiting scholars and practitioners. Yet as I explored womanist spirituality and its relation to social justice activism (see chapter 3), I discovered a more expansive understanding of spiritual activism and spirituality that was evident in the oral histories of not only these three seemingly disparate narratives but in two of the "Christian" interviewees. Thus, this chapter further examines how social justice activism is animated in diverse religious expressions. In particular, this chapter explores expansive understandings of how these Black lesbian religious leaders used Christianity, New Thought/ Religious Science spiritualists, Judaism, and Buddhism to create a more-just world. I assess their oral histories as examples of the moral wisdom found in womanist spiritualities, positing that theistic connection to humanity is a marker of womanist ethical leadership.

At the onset of this chapter, it is necessary to note that this exploration of alternative spiritualities reflects the book's pursuit of religious leaders' everyday faith practices and expressions. The adage "religion is about the day we die and whether we will go to heaven or hell, and spirituality is about what we do with our time now" is apropos for this study because each of the interviewees was concerned with the ability to live out her faith to produce social change in her current reality.[1] This chapter was written during the summer of 2020 as the world tried to survive the COVID-19 pandemic and was forced to deal with the impact of anti-Black racism. As millions took to the global streets to organize against police brutality and other injustices affecting Black Americans, past religious leaders such as Rev. Al Sharpton came to the forefront, heralding tactics from prior generations like the planned August 2020 march on Washington. The movement for Black Lives leaders seemed to respond respectfully to these attempts while forging ahead with their own leaders and actions, and being supported by spiritual-care doulas and other alternative spiritualities. These efforts to build a new social reality undergirded by new spiritual practices resonate with the examples set by several of my interviewees, which followed a unique call that sometimes led them beyond their traditional Christian practices.

One such participant who was able to traverse beyond the solitary practice of Christianity was Rev. Dr. Cari Jackson, who despite pastoring in three different Christian denominations also managed to counsel persons from various traditions in her Center of Spiritual Light. In previous chapters I have discussed Dr. Cari's feeling that she stood out from her religious tradition because of her eclectic perspectives. She recounts an auditory connection to Spirit, which she never discusses as solely the Holy Spirit discussed in Christianity. Although she was reared in the Black Pentecostal tradition, she told me of her early remembrance of being "ushered into this oneness with the cosmos" as she learned that "God comes in lots of different ways to us."[2] This has been a hallmark of her religious leadership, for she contends that she has always been spiritual more than religious.

Despite leaving the Pentecostal church for connection with Metropolitan Community Churches (MCC), she recalls saying yes to God about ministry but never presuming that this ministry would be solely within the tradition of Christianity. She stated that she knew her calling was not to MCC because "there are many religious and spiritual traditions that speak to me." She found it perfectly acceptable to practice with a Buddhist community and attend her Christian church on Sundays, indicating that sitting with the Buddhist community during the week and then attending church on Sunday morning was nurturing for her. In addition, during the Lenten season she spends an intentional period of spiritual practice guided by Sadhana, a Hindu/Buddhist meditation. She is not limited by her race, class, gender, or sexuality, as she noted in this chapter's epigraph; she is instead grounded and led by her sense of spirituality.

Perhaps because of Dr. Cari's expansive understanding, others were drawn to her Center of Spiritual Light for counseling. When I asked how she managed this community with her other often full-time Christian commitments, she indicated that what she had created was an "alternative space [for] very inter-spiritual folks" who were learning to integrate Spirit into "every aspect of their lives." This Spirit integration did not indicate a Christian understanding or even a theistic understanding. Dr. Cari indicated that she would counsel persons who were Jewish, Muslim, Buddhist, and even atheist who were seeking spiritual care. Although some might find offering an atheist spiritual care unusual, Dr. Cari believes that being an atheist just means that their "spirituality is not theistically oriented."

Dr. Cari is aware that the capacious way she approaches Christianity is different from others. While in seminary she even questioned God regarding this spiritual journey and recalls the Spirit telling her that she had been given the "gift of tongues," which was unlike the glossolalia she was familiar with from her Pentecostal background. Her interpretation of this gift is that she was endowed with the ability to "speak in languages that resonate spiritually for different people who are plodding along in different ways on their own spiritual journeys." This broad interpretation of her Christian call to ministry is also an impetus behind the call to social activism: she sees society as a collection of spiritual folks needing to integrate Spirit in their lives to create an opportunity for thriving.

Another Christian with an expansive understanding of the Christian call is Bishop Flunder. During her exile from her Pentecostal faith tradition, she acknowledged being estranged from the church but still in right relationship with Jesus. She indicated that during that time she oriented her life toward a deeper/inner spirituality. In City of Refuge, the church she founded, her goal is to lead the congregation to become less religious and more spiritual. Yet this call to spirituality includes indigenous experiences with the divine. She recounted in our interview how she is teaching her congregation to notice the parallels between Pentecostalism and Candomblé, Yoruba, and Vodun. Each of these traditions validates experience with the spirit realm, and she considers it holy work to teach people to go back to connect with the gifts of their ancestors.

In addition to the work of integrating African diasporic religious practices into her community, Bishop Flunder also has started working with the metaphysical communities Unity and Centers for Spiritual Living. She has been particularly influenced by Religious Science philosophies, for she recognizes that "Pentecostalism is metaphysical and metaphysical is Pentecostal."[3] Bishop Flunder discussed the stigma that is associated with "new age" and Pentecostal communities, and she sees this being overcome by more reliance on spirituality. She indicates that the possibilities provided by connecting her Christian practice with Religious Science are numerous:

> Ernest Holmes and Charles Harrison Mason walked around on the planet at just about the same time. Ernest Holmes was a white man, very wealthy and elitist, and they were prejudiced. They were anti-Black. New Thought didn't help them not to be great, by the way. William Joseph Seymour, the father of the Azusa Street movement, this Black preacher who was in many ways the beginning of the whole thing and of evolution and revolution in 1906, 1904, they couldn't get together because there was, the divide was too wide. Nope, no amount of Spirit could do something about racism or sexism. All that Holy Ghost and all that New Thought couldn't talk them into getting together. I think that we are what I call the Third Pentecost because we have an opportunity to sew these things together into a tapestry.

For Bishop Flunder, this generation of Christian believers has the ability to learn from past mistakes and to embrace their metaphysician attributes. When persons do not get hung up on labels, they can realize that "I'm a metaphysician [is the same as] saying I'm a spiritualist."

Historian Darnise Martin explores the connection that African Americans have with Religious Science because it is not a Christian religion in orthodox terms (despite sharing Christian symbols and scriptures).[4] Martin's discussion of African American Religious Scientists reflects the mixture of African American spirituality with Religious Science as a historical trend, citing leaders such as Father Divine, Rev. Ike, Daddy Grace, and contemporary Prosperity Gospel leaders such as Rev. Fred Price and Rev. Creflo Dollar, who use New Thought principles. Those following such leaders find this syncretic approach to Black religion normative. Although Martin does not document Holmes's racism, she does detail Holmes's doctrine of Oneness as a Spirit available to any who recognized it. The logic shared in Religious Science is that humans are an incarnation of Spirit or Universal Mind and that all things can be accomplished using this mind.[5] For practitioners like Bishop Flunder, this reflects the understanding that humans are "spirit people." This is also significant because Bishop Flunder notes that this contemporary generation is more comfortable being known as "spiritual and not religious," and she believes to reach them takes an acknowledgment that the "move of the Spirit is greater than race, that it is greater than the conversation about sexuality, that it is greater than nation borders." This movement of the Spirit may be represented by Christianity, or it may be reflected by Christianity plus other faith expressions.

This is an accurate depiction of the faith journey of Rev. Dr. Deborah Johnson. She grew up Pentecostal and even experienced a call to ministry while in this tradition but recounted never believing its doctrine. She just knew there was always something whispering, telling her something else, and she eventually realized that she was much more metaphysical, having a universal spirituality in her heart. She leads Inner Light Ministries, an omnifaith congregation dedicated to practicing spiritual principles. She preferred *omnifaith* as her descriptor because she believed that "interfaith conjures up major religions all coming together, and I'm not really about religion, per se."[6] Omnifaith offered her flexibility in thought and practice because she felt it spoke to the "ever presence of faith wherever that is and however that comes." Despite this rationale and going through the trainings to be an ordained practitioner in Religious Science, she still personally feels "like Jesus was [her] main man."

Rev. Deborah was introduced to Religious Science and Science of the Mind, and she was even able to find a predominantly Black Religious Science church to attend. She helped Rev. Michael Beckwith to found the Agape International Spiritual Center, and although both Beckwith and she were ordained as Religious Science ministers, they also embrace New Thought philosophies. Technically, Religious Science is a denomination of New Thought practices that affirms the "nature of reality to be based upon thoughts or ideas" and states that the universe operates through principles, or basic laws like cause and effect/laws of attraction, that work for everyone. California is an epicenter for New Thought practitioners, and Religious Science in general has a preponderance of female religious leaders,[7] making the community hospitable for Rev. Deborah to grow her ministry.

Much like her mentor Beckwith, her congregation is a multicultural spiritual community. Yet Rev. Deborah feels a bit unusual in that she is a Black female pastor of a predominantly white and heterosexual church. Because it is in Santa Cruz, a predominantly white demographic, the church is diverse in its cross section of people and faiths represented. Within this mix of faith and ethnicities, Johnson presents her Religious Science perspective with a particular Christian emphasis. Having been reared in a Christian household, she rejected some doctrinal views about Jesus such that she "had to make a distinction in [her] mind between the religion about Jesus and the religion of Jesus." Her incorporation of metaphysical principles in her understanding of Jesus expanded her spirituality:

> The idea of us being cocreators with God and how we use our energy to me spoke to what Jesus was talking about, how it's done unto you as you believe. So ironically enough, in my mind, this more metaphysical version of Christianity to me was truer to Jesus. So in my mind, I didn't see myself as walking away or leaving my Jesus. I felt the opposite. So that's how it looked to me, like I was actually being a better Christian, not leaving my Christianity.

Her ability to infuse what she sees as Jesus's spirit of respecting everyone fits with her belief that God has no favorites, and in fact the "character of Jesus is the human embodiment of Christ consciousness," a figure or archetype who learned to connect his "deepest intent" with the "Inexhaustible Supply" of Spirit to make miracles happen.[8]

Rev. Deborah's belief in Oneness is appealing to persons from varying faith communities and those who are spiritually unaffiliated. She is clear that Oneness is really the thread connecting all of creation, and even while she educates her congregation on how to apply the Universal Spiritual Principles associated with Religious Science, they are taught to delineate the differences among spirituality, religion, and the church. In a divine transmission from Spirit she was instructed to inform the public several truisms: (1) spirituality is your innate divinity that is One with me (Spirit); (2) church and religion should be the servant of Spirit; (3) to perceive one's own divinity, one needs healthy self-esteem; (4) religion is a culture's accumulated beliefs about spirituality; (5) religions should be the spirit of the law, not an institution; (6) spirituality must be above religion and religion above the church; (7) the church is to support religion, which is to support spirituality; (8) spirituality never changes, but religions and churches always do; (9) as people grow in spiritual understanding, all systems must change; and (10) some reject their spirituality, protesting religion and church.[9] These revelations are meant to unify communities and expand religious understandings.

Expanding and adapting Christian logic to match a multifaith population demonstrates one of the benefits of Black lesbian participation in metaphysical communities. As nonexclusivist religious groups that teach that the material world is irrelevant, they tend to be indifferent toward sexual orientation, thus making them appear more accepting and welcoming to LGBTQ members.[10] Although one can ponder if perhaps there is something about the queer embodiment of LGBTQ members that resonates with these spiritual communities, groups like Religious Science and New Thought communities provide spiritual resources that empower LGBTQ persons. This sympathetic relationship is noted in sociologist Mignon Moore's research on Black lesbians in Los Angeles, where she documented strong support among middle-class Black lesbians for Religious Science/New Thought. In Moore's research, Black lesbians were drawn to Rev. Deborah's mentor's spiritual center because they felt a sense of familiarity with the religious community and experienced a feeling of full acceptance. Moore noted the importance of having a spiritual leader with a similar racial and cultural background and that New Thought offered them more agency within themselves as opposed to depending solely on a higher power.[11]

Alternative Spiritualities

Relying on a new or alternative spirituality is a part of Black women's faith experience in the United States. Black feminist activist Akasha Gloria Hull argued that there was a new twenty-first-century spirituality emerging that spoke to Black women's political and social awareness, merged Christianity with New Age metaphysics, and enhanced their creativity.[12] This logic would explain the experiences just described by my three "Christian" interviewees. Yet I concur with womanist ethicist Melanie Harris that Hull is recording just one "public" moment in a continuous history of Black women's fluid

FIGURE 4.1. Rabbi Sandra Lawson. Used by permission.

spirituality. Scholars of African American religions are aware of the hidden faith practices of many people of African descent who since slavery melded their faith into the dominant traditions forced upon them. Scholars have also documented Black women's participation in diverse religious traditions that are distinct from Christianity. Harris discusses these evolving spiritualities as "spiritual plateaus," the process that incorporates past wisdom to create a perhaps lifelong journey of becoming spiritually aware.[13] Harris is most concerned with describing the fluid spirituality of Alice Walker and how that should impact womanists' understanding of non-Christian spirituality, yet her viewpoint is useful in this study's exploration of the prevalence of theistic alternative spiritualities for the interviewees.

This chapter explores theistic alternative spiritual expressions because all of my interviewees indicated a belief in a higher power, which many named God/Spirit, or some connection to a force greater than themselves. One such interviewee who expressed a connection to a non-Christian concept of God is Rabbi Sandra Lawson.

Rabbi Sandra Lawson is the director of Racial Diversity, Equity, and Inclusion for Reconstructing Judaism and formerly associate chaplain for Jewish Life and Jewish Educator at Hillel at Elon University in North Carolina. She was ordained from the Reconstructionist Rabbinical College in 2018. Rabbi Lawson is also a former military police officer, investigative researcher for the

Anti-Defamation League's Southeast Region, and personal trainer. Although she is perhaps most notable as Snapchat's Top Rabbi and through her other social media and public facing offerings, her vision of ministry is to help build a more inclusive Jewish community.[14]

Rabbi Sandra Lawson explained to me that she had loose Christian ties as a child and that as an adult she stopped attending church because services did nothing for her. During this time she felt that she had no spirituality, and she was not actively searching for her seemingly missing faith. Having been raised in a military family that moved often, it seemed that what Lawson craved more than a theistic connection was community. She found that sense of community during her military enlistment, but she had to remain guarded because being gay in the military was cause for dismissal and even jail. Thus, when she left the military, it was important for her to be in environments where she could be fully herself and find others with shared experiences. Ironically, this call to community is what led her to Judaism.

After the military she worked as a personal trainer and had a Jewish girl-friend and Jewish clients who exposed her to the faith. One of her clients, Rabbi Josh Lesser, invited her to his synagogue, and she recalls that there was "something about the space where I felt like I could be my whole self." She was not sure that she got the Jewish part of it, but she felt at home in the space. She was particularly moved during her first visit that the service ended with a prayer that began "We as gay and lesbian Jews," even though the synagogue was only half LGBTQ. The embrace of everyone in their midst was welcoming enough for her to keep going back. She realized that to have full membership in the community, she needed to convert to Judaism. Shortly after converting, she said she expected to be a "Jew in the pew," but she was quickly tapped for board leadership because of her active level of participation in the community. In short time she had gone from someone with no spiritual grounding to someone deeply enmeshed in the Jewish faith. At some point she recognized that community members were turning to her for lay leadership, and she was being sent outside of the community as a representative of their synagogue. She decided if she really wanted to be able to create and effect changes in the larger Jewish world and in interfaith religious spaces, then she would need the experiences and title of rabbi.

Because her initial synagogue had made her feel like she belonged, she was ill prepared for how many questions about her Jewishness she would face from the outside Jewish and non-Jewish world. According to Brandeis University's American Jewish Population Project, an estimated 11 percent of the Jewish population is made up of people of color, and a sizable number of this population are persons born into the tradition, not converts.[15] Controlling her own public narrative was one of her coping strategies for the invasive and intrusive questions about her identity, including constantly having to explain how she was Jewish. She created a website devoted to her "Jewish story," acknowledging that this gave her a safe way to talk about her complex Jewish path. Her narrative does include an Ethiopian Jewish ancestor, but she avoids the terms *converted* or *Jewish by choice* because she believes this just represents "another way to separate out people who are different in the Jewish community"; instead, she feels like she is "back where [her] family should have been all along."[16] When she made the decision to attend rabbinical school, it was with the intent to unite her various identities to be a bridge builder for all her communities. Rabbi Lawson often introduces herself as the first openly gay Black lesbian rabbi (even though it is a disputable claim, for Black lesbian rabbi Georgette Kennebrae graduated a year before her), and part of this self-disclosure is an effort to bring all the pieces of her identity to the forefront.

When Rebecca Alpert writes about the first generation of white lesbian rabbis, she notes that they were women who refused to choose between their Jewish and lesbian identities and were pioneers who experienced a "double burden" because of their gender and sexuality.[17] When Lawson's alma mater, the Reconstructionist Rabbinical College, started ordaining gays and lesbians, it signaled support yet did not equate this support to promising job prospects for its gay and lesbian rabbis. As she approached graduation, Lawson noted her concern about whether she would be "un-hirable" because her combination of identities may have proved too much for future employers. Her former employer, Elon University, found her finesse with social media and ability to meet Jews wherever they were as attractive skill sets, which means by taking control of her narrative she was also able to make herself more marketable.

This action seemed to be following the legacy of pioneering rabbi Denise Eger, the first lesbian to serve as rabbi for the first gay and lesbian synagogue, Beth Chayim Chadashim. Eger also felt called to take the "rabbinate beyond the walls of the synagogue" and go into the community where people worked and played.[18] For Lawson, heeding this lesson meant finding people via SnapChat, Facebook, YouTube, podcasts, blogs, or even in vegan cafes. This expansiveness is an important marker of her leadership style: she realizes that Judaism is changing, and this next generation will experience Judaism outside

FIGURE 4.2. Dr. Pamela "Ayo" Yetunde. Used by permission.

of traditional settings. She uses nontraditional means to spread Jewish content because she does not want to duplicate the model of the synagogue, where people pay large dues to come only to High Holidays.[19] Instead, she hopes to create sacred spaces wherever people are—making her a guitar-playing, bodybuilding, tweeting rabbi who teaches Torah in repurposed ways to college students and unaffiliated Jewish adults. As a reconstructionist Jew, she believes that is her duty to find ways to reconstruct her tradition to make it more relevant today.

My interview with Dr. Pamela Ayo Yetunde also reflects someone who is trying to make her religion relevant to a more diverse audience and through nontraditional settings.

At the time of her interview, Dr. Pamela "Ayo" Yetunde was an assistant professor of pastoral and spiritual care and counseling and assistant vice president for Faculty Community Relations at United Theological Seminary of the Twin

Cities, in Minneapolis. She earned a JD from Indiana University School of Law and a ThD from Columbia Theological Seminary. She is a community dharma leader, certified by Spirit Rock Meditation Center in Woodacre, California. She is trained in the Insight Meditation community, and as an interfaith Buddhist practitioner, she also teaches at the Upaya Institute and Zen Center in Santa Fe, New Mexico.[20]

"Dr. Ayo" is a pastoral-care counselor using Buddhist perspectives to treat clients and educate students. For example, she created www.dharmacare .com, a website designed for Insight Meditation practitioners to learn how take their Buddhist practice into spiritual care and counseling. Typically, this training is done in educational settings, chaplaincy programs, or even at Buddhist retreats. By embracing an innovative and cost-equitable model, she is able to present Buddhist lay leaders with resources in a new format. Part of the appeal for Dr. Ayo is that she is "passionate about seeing people being treated well, being treated with respect and dignity, having their human rights respected. And I'm passionate about people treating themselves well." Overall, her theistic connection to humanity compels her to compassion and to offer aid in as many modalities as will be useful.

This desire to help persons achieve respect and dignity is borne from her own struggles to obtain that within her own life. She described being instructed early in life to believe in a creator God and salvific son who protected and cared for people, yet her life experiences showed her that this understanding of God was too simplistic. She had been raised in a United Methodist church but had not really taken it in upon herself to read the Bible or do any spiritual searching until she was leaving college. After a rift between her mother and herself, she was feeling lonely and in need of spiritual support, so she decided to open the Bible, searching for connection. When she began reading, she said that by the third story of war and killing she knew she needed to close the book because she "was not on the right path." After spending a summer in Zimbabwe in a refugee camp, she had even more questions about the Christian God she had been taught to believe in, and as she pondered her spiritual questions and what her role would be in the world, she resolved that she wanted to "be able to speak to this world being a better world, a safer place for people, just in terms of dignity."

This was reinforced by an experience with a cousin who was dying of AIDS, when she realized that her Christian family would not visit him because of his disease. She knew that it was the Christian thing to do, so her decision to visit him must have meant that she had a different understanding of Christianity than her family did. She found herself a member of Glide United Methodist Church in San Francisco because she was drawn by the focus on liberation presented by the pastor, Rev. Cecil Williams, and the fact that the congregation was interracial and pro-gay. Her time there helped her become open to spiritual community, which ironically led her to Buddhism.

Initially, this pull to Buddhism came from a promise that she had made to herself when she was with her cousin dying of AIDS. Her cousin died in hospice, and she wanted to be the "kind of person who could do that for strangers," so she called hospice organizations in the Bay Area asking to be trained in hospice care. The Zen Hospice Project had a year-long training program. Even though she did not know anything about Buddhism, once she entered the program, she discovered that it was what she should be doing with her life. She found that the Zen Buddhist teachings made sense to her in a way that the Bible had not, and she found herself at peace in Buddhist meditation. This calling to be with the dying led her to chaplaincy training, which led her to a doctorate in pastoral care and counseling, where she specialized in Buddhist approaches. Eventually, she chose to complete a two-year program in community dharma leadership from the Spirit Rock Meditation Center, which qualified her as a Buddhist lay leader who could start meditation groups and lead retreats.

Dr. Ayo's goal of helping persons achieve respect and dignity is one of the reasons she became a community dharma leader, realizing that the "absence of people of color who are dharma teachers has meant that the Insight Meditation communities were virtually silent on the subjects of justice, pluralistic scriptural interpretation, interracial dialogue, and critical race social analysis." Acknowledging and healing from her own traumas within her Christian family and recognizing that liberatory religion could in fact heal (as she experienced at Glide United Methodist Church), she set out to bring Buddhist wisdom and freedom to others. As a lay leader and a scholar, she has devoted her time to demonstrating that African American lesbians have perspectives on how Black people can survive.[21] Her path has included Buddhism, but she has been a strong advocate that although African American lesbians may leave Christianity in search of safe spiritual home in Buddhism, this can be the case only when Buddhist communities deal with their members' racism. American Buddhist scholar Wendy Cadge has noted that lesbians and gay men were comfortable in Buddhist organizations founded by white people because Buddhist texts are read as being neutral about homosexuality, and there is little antigay discrimination and prejudice in US Buddhist centers.[22]

Cadge speculates that this is because the vast majority of attendees of these Buddhist organizations tend to be upper-middle-class, well-educated persons who are presumed to have less prejudices toward homosexuality. Dr. Ayo's research with Black lesbian Buddhists and her own personal experiences in Buddhist communities indicate that although they may not hold as many sexual prejudices, they can still hold racial biases. Thus, her scholarship and pastoral-care practices seek to inform practitioners on ways to notice if Black women are being rendered invisible in their spiritual-care communities.

In this regard, Dr. Ayo, like other interviewees, promoted finding rituals and practices that tend to the whole person rather than making them choose which identity gets validated. Each of the interviewees in this chapter has encouraged herself and others to see their spirituality as a daily practice and as a means of experiencing the divine in their lives. Black feminist anthropologist Marla Frederick noted in her seminal study of Black women and faith that spirituality "embodies both the personal and public areas of life"; she contextualized how spirituality conveys the ability to move beyond the limits of religiosity. For the women she studied, spirituality evolved over time to match the experiences of the individual. Thus, spirituality "comes from inside the person and it's a reflection of how they live."[23] Spirituality must consider all the various aspects of a person and their environments as they seek to create a connection between humanity and the divine. Womanist homiletician Khalia Jelks Williams relies on Frederick's discussion of spirituality as the basis of her own argument for an embodied Black women's spirituality that seeks "wholeness in the community."[24] For Williams, this spirituality again comes from within and is reflective of the whole woman. Both of these studies are centered around Christian understandings of spirituality, but their work is useful in speaking to the ways that my interviewees depended on themselves, the richness of their life experience, and connection to communities as guides for social justice action.

Womanist Spiritualities and Faith Activism

Chapter 3's discussion of the spiritual activism of Black Lives Matters' Black lesbian organizers pointed out that these women felt rejected or even pushed out of their Christian communities and found solace in indigenous spiritualities that emphasized the interconnection of humanity and divinity. They were encouraged to interpret their resistance on the behalf of the Black community as part of the healing work of their spirituality. As womanist ethicist Elise Edwards surmises, this "African American form of spirituality addresses the practical aspects of what it takes to stay alive and flourish."[25] Gleaning from the spiritualities displayed by my interviewees, there is definitely an expectation that evidence of spirituality is one's commitment to working for the thriving of the community.

This sense of individual and communal spirituality is reflected in womanist ethicist Emilie Townes's book-length study of womanist spirituality. She argues that it is "embodied, personal, and communal." She describes it as a dynamic process that integrates faith and life through daily practices. Townes contends that womanist spirituality "advocates a self-other relationship" where "wholeness can be found for African Americans" while offering future hope beyond oppression.[26] Although Townes's womanist spirituality is specifically Christian, her analysis is relevant to the narratives expressed in this chapter because of the attention to overcoming individual and collective oppression and to restoring dignity and respect to marginalized persons.

In fact, womanist ethicist Melanie Harris suggests that Townes's discussion of womanist spirituality can be used beyond Christianity because of the evolution of Townes's own thinking: in later works, Townes discusses spirituality as encompassing a multiplicity of religious understandings across the African diaspora. I also turn to Harris because she heralds third-wave discussions of womanist spirituality that extend beyond Christianity. She is an expert in Buddhist-Christian dialogue as well as womanist humanism, both of which are important support for understanding my interviewees within womanist discourse.

Harris's discussion of womanist Buddhist dialogue centers on healthy self-love and compassionate justice for all. She contends that Buddhism is an appealing factor for many Black women because it offers an invitation to "overcome oppression" and transform self and community. Harris posits that Buddhism provides Black women with a means of honoring and even divinizing the self—gifts that Christianity has not always provided.[27] Whether one learns to honor the self through humanist praxis, via acceptance of one's authentic identities, or by merging prior Christian beliefs with other spiritualities, Harris is confident that the path to communal transformation starts with self-love. This concept of a dynamic womanist spirituality that progresses and stretches beyond its formation is why I turn to the lens of womanist spirituality as a means of interpreting my interviewees' narratives.[28]

Chapter 3 takes up the concept of Layli Maparyan's womanist spiritual activism and uses it to theorize the actions of several of my Christian interviewees. In that discussion I note how Maparyan's understanding of the term is decidedly not Christian, and I demonstrate why it can still be applicable in those examples. In this chapter I return to Maparyan's theory and expand it, using some of her original parameters, as I articulate how it can be applied to the five women introduced here. Maparyan premises her theorizing of womanist spiritual activism on her articulation of spirituality, which she contends is eclectic in that it comprises diverse elements, is synthetic as it brings together these elements creatively, and is holistic in that it creates a new spirituality from these various sacred wisdoms. Her spirituality does not begin with Christian roots; instead, Maparyan starts with ancient and indigenous spiritual practices. In her expanded viewpoint, spiritual activism represents those practices that are conducted to bring about optimal change for individuals, communities, and the planet.[29]

I return to Maparyan's interpretation of womanist spiritual activism because of all of my interlocutors she is the only one to predominantly use contemporary women's lives as the examples for spiritual activism. Unlike other womanist scholars, who rely on fictional works or women's activities of the nineteenth and early twentieth centuries, Maparyan's rendition of spiritual activism resonates because she also dares to write on the modern subject, whose views and actions can change rapidly. Relying on living subjects and not fictional women leaves both our projects vulnerable to the whimsies of real life, where sometimes individuals do not live to see their social change bear fruit. Yet this reliance also makes the moral wisdom garnered from their narratives more applicable for future generations.

Finally, Maparyan's theory is useful in interpreting my interviewees' narratives because many of them are eclectic, synthetic, and holistic in their spiritualities. Dr. Cari and Bishop Flunder merge Buddhist, indigenous, and metaphysical principles into their practices of Christianity in ways that are creative and produce a new wisdom for their communities. Dr. Cari births the Center for Spiritual Light, and Bishop Flunder founds The Fellowship of Affirming Ministries. Rev. Deborah incorporates Christianity into her Religious Science spiritual principles. Dr. Ayo is also a multifaith Buddhist pastoral counselor, and Rabbi Lawson has merged Judaism with social media technology to present those ancient teachings in diverse new formats. Next, I investigate the spiritual activism presented through their particular spiritualities.

Buddhist Spiritual Activism

Some western Buddhists practice socially engaged Buddhism as depicted by Thich Nhat Hanh. This mandates that Buddhist practitioners actively work toward making the world a better place. Yet this outward working begins within: "activism, however configured, focuses on peace and acceptance from within" because this is seen as the path of enlightenment.[30] For Dr. Ayo, this process began as she made peace with herself as a lesbian. She then realized her interest in activism; in fact, she went to law school to become a more effective political activist. As a pastoral counselor she has written about Black Lives Matter and Buddhist principles, she actively speaks about classism and racism in Buddhist retreats, and since the impact of COVID-19 and the summer of 2020's racial unrest, she has created content for a meditation app called Liberate that offers meditative assistance for persons dealing with microaggressions, racism, and so on. One of her more popular offerings, "Unveiling Your Deepest Goodness," gives viewers a guided meditation that includes a visualization of women who have cared for you as a circle of self-love, and in the same app she gives a dharma talk on transgender solidarity based on the teachings of Thich Nhat Hanh. These efforts are her realization that "nothing that I do in terms of social change, social action, I will do by myself. So it's got to be done in community and a supportive community that is willing to share the risks, the burdens, the responsibilities, the joys. I've learned that if there's no community behind it, it's not going to get done."

Womanist ethicist Jennifer Leath writes about Buddhist-Christian relations as well, and she concedes that the quest for freedom for oneself and one's community remains paramount and that by broadening the landscape of womanist scholarship and praxis, we can observe how people are bringing forth freedom in their own lives. Leath rightly imagines a "radically new exploration of non-Christian Afro-Diasporic faith traditions . . . through which Orishas, ancestors, and 'others' might speak."[31] Thus, when examining Dr. Ayo's work to get herself free, it is also apparent how this freedom also spurred her to advocate for others. Dr. Ayo has since gone on to add competencies in interreligious counseling and served as director of the United Theological Seminary's Interreligious Chaplaincy program, which trains chaplains to accept a diversity of religious belief so they can provide their clients with respectful and appropriate assistance.

Jewish Spiritual Activism

This call to communal advocating is also present in Judaism in the concept of *tikkun olam*, a term that refers to the "repairing and healing of the world through acts of justice and reconciliation."[32] Rabbi Denise Eger believed that the call to justice and community are a central part of Judaism—from its texts that taught about a God of justice to the concepts of *tzedakah* and *mitzvah* terms that connoted God-sanctioned just actions. Eger felt that social justice action is how she was to express her spirituality and do the work of healing the world, and in my interviewee with Rabbi Lawson it was clear that she shared a similar understanding. Whereas Eger mostly advocated for the concerns of the LGBTQ community, Rabbi Lawson's intersectional identities required that she be committed to a much more pluralistic sense of community.

For instance, before Rabbi Lawson went to rabbinical college, she worked for the Anti-Defamation League as an investigative researcher answering questions from law enforcement about extremist groups and conducting qualitative research on hate groups in the southern United States. She worked as a victim outreach specialist for the Georgia Council for Restorative Justice and helped create a new interfaith organization to advocate for civil and human rights. She organized gay and lesbian activists to keep the Georgia state legislature from adding a ban against gay marriage to the Georgia constitution (which, unfortunately, they were unable to prevent). She said she felt like every Black queer person she knew in Atlanta was in the social justice arena, and she did not feel that we had the "privilege to not be ... [because] there was always some issue affecting the larger Black community." Yet this situation is why coalition building was so necessary: to provide a larger pool of persons advocating for a cause. She remarked sadly to me that after devoting a great deal of her time to grassroots activism in Atlanta, she "left activism to go study." Ultimately, she felt that she needed to go to rabbinical school to complete her training so that she could do a better job as an advocate.

While in rabbinical school she kept her focus on social justice. She realized that "Judaism gave me language and a value system that I didn't have before." She learned through her coursework, internships, and experiences as a Jewish woman that the "faith part sort of married with the social just part

[and] gave me tools I didn't have access to before." Namely, through her work with *T'ruah*, the Rabbinical Voice for Social Justice, she learned how to be a "social justice rabbi" as she learned how to use Jewish terms to tell people to care about topics that they may not have seen as relevant to their lives.

One such example was her writing on Black Lives Matter for *T'ruah*. Her earliest childhood home was in a community that was on the border of Ferguson, Missouri. After the murder of Michael Brown, she reflected on his killing in the frame of a prayer that is called the *Hashkiveinu* prayer, a prayer that is said at night for God's protection. She was able to use her rabbinical voice to explain the terror that the protesters were experiencing at night: the pepper spray, tear gas, weapons, and assaults. In the prayer she contextualized:

> It was written when the night was scary, and it asks for God to protect us. Spread over us your canopy of peace. And when people realize, when they read this prayer . . . they were like oh my gosh, like they got it. And I didn't have to do a lot of explaining. I didn't have to articulate you as Jews need to care about this. They could see where the prayer was written, and they could add it into their liturgy. . . . And then my friend Josh told me that—and also Deborah Waxman, who is the president of our denomination—that that prayer was the first time for many that they understood why it was an important issue, why they should care. Because I put my own narrative in it.

She wrote that prayer while she was still in rabbinical school, but it gave her a sense of the kind of rabbi she hoped to become.

Metaphysical Spiritual Activism

As Rabbi Lawson endeavored to bridge her faith and social justice work to create a more just society, this is also evident for the interviewees who relied on metaphysical principles as a part of their spirituality. In sociologist of religion Margarita Guillory's research on early twentieth-century African American spiritual churches and social transformation, she purports that healing served as a "form of social activism" because there was a symbiotic relationship between spiritual transformation and sociopolitical activism. Guillory understood spiritual leaders as using spirituality to address the tangible social, political, physical, and emotional concerns of Black people such that an individual's personal turn to a metaphysician was never just about the individual. There was always a corresponding relationship where metaphysical principles were used as ritualized resistance for wholeness in the community.[33] This logic is also shared by many New Thought/Religious Science practitioners. Although founder Ernest Holmes taught that Religious Science is an individualized program, this does not mean that the individual's transformation does not have a larger impact. In fact, if their logic system holds, by changing oneself one is in essence changing the environment.

Contemporary followers of spiritual principles use them to directly address social realities. For example, Rev. Michael Beckwith, mentor to Rev. Deborah, founded the Association for Global New Thought, an organization that brings together individual ministers for engagement in a "mission of spiritually motivated social activism."[34] It has projects on such issues as racism, gun violence, climate change, global poverty, homelessness, women's rights, refugee rights, and access to quality health care, and the ministers call upon spiritual activists to explore these topics using spiritual principles. Rev. Deborah serves on the Association's Leadership Council and for decades has incorporated her social justice activism with her metaphysical practices. Spiritual Director Liza Rankow contends that Rev. Deborah represents a new generation of spiritualists whose "grounding in the social consciousness of the Black Church and their participation in liberation movements of the sixties and seventies informed their interpretation and practice of New Thought."[35] Rankow rightly observes that Rev. Deborah extends individual healing and transformation into social healing and transformation of communities.

Rev. Deborah has a lifetime of commitment to activism, including being a litigant in two landmark civil rights cases in California. She frequently brings up social justice issues to her congregation because she sees activism as fundamentally a part of who she is, not just what she does for a living. In this congregation she recognizes that

> I have people who are in fact connected to other faith communities like Jews or Catholics or Muslims or whatnot, or Buddhists, but I have a lot of those non people, or spiritually unaffiliated, and I have a fair number of people who are atheists who come and really like it. And people who do Wicca and Burning Man, and who are more Pagan, earth-based, that kind of thing. It speaks to my activism because I believe in the oneness. I believe in the wholeness. I believe in the integration of us all and that if we're separate and we're siloed, we can't heal and we can't get the synergies that happen in community when there's real communion. I'm all for putting the commune back in communication and community.

So for me the activism part of it is that we are firmly committed to environmental sustainability; we're firmly committed to social justice. I tell them sometimes that, you know, we've got everything up in here. We've got homeless people and millionaires, we've got carnivores and vegans, and 12-steppers and club hoppers, you know.... Somehow or another we're going to work this out. And to me, that's what the activism is about. I'm not about just promoting this group, that group. I'm not about just the civil rights for this group. But I am about the beloved community. That's what I'm about. I'm about bringing forth that world where everybody can excel and be who they are.

Although she is dedicated to helping raise the consciousness of her congregants to spiritual principles, she realizes that her call is also to create the beloved community.

When Rev. Deborah starts receiving messages from the divine in the form of sacred letters, she finds that even these missives are social justice oriented.[36] Within the first volume, she has messages for those incarcerated in the Pleasant Valley State Prison, where her congregation runs the IMPACT program. She is sent messages to offer them empowerment through the form of spiritual enlightenment and forgiveness but also to provide them life skills such as healthy decision making and anger management. She publicly fought for marriage equality in the state of California, and she received divine messages urging the queer community to move beyond these gains to seek transgender equality. She spoke publicly about the US involvement in Iraq as well as offering divinely gifted messages of safety after 9/11. Wherever she offers spiritual principles, she also offers tangible examples of activist steps to achieve those principles.

In her understanding of her role at Inner Light Ministries, Rev. Deborah accepts divine instruction that the congregation she founded was meant to be a collection of ministries. Yet she means this in a way that follows metaphysical principles. She teaches that ministry is about consciousness and that as such she is not the head of a hierarchy; rather, she is a part of an "infrastructure umbrella that allows people to answer that call and develop into that greater yet to be that pulsates and reverberates at the center and core of their being."[37] She is listed on the Inner Light Ministries website as founder, but its homepage indicates that she is *frequently* the featured speaker during their Sunday service. In keeping with Religious Science principles, as a practitioner she is just one of many who can offer messages and healings to the congregation.

Womanist Spiritual Wisdom as Marker
for Ethical Leadership

Regarding the interviewees' discussion of spiritual activism, Rev. Deborah's divine message suggests that she thinks of her work a bit differently. She asserts that "this work of publicly standing for Oneness instead of divisive polarization [is] *sacred* activism, not merely spiritual activism."[38] She takes this to mean that she is called to be a bridge builder in the same way that Rabbi Lawson describes her role and Dr. Ayo mediates as an interreligious counselor. Dr. Cari described her spiritual activism as a responsibility to people whom she had never met because we all share humanity together. Bishop Flunder's assertion that we are all "spirit people" compels her to see the connection between everyone, so she feels called to serve. Each of these interviewees demonstrated the capacity to function as spiritual activists, using their spiritual foundations to animate social justice. They also each reflect Du Bois's notion in the chapter's epigraph of following the spirit of Esther (and I would argue Vashti), who spoke truth to power and used her spirituality as a catalyst for her work and sacrifice for her people.

These spiritual foundations are found in what Townes describes as the moral wisdom of African American women. *In a Blaze of Glory* provides many attributes of womanist spirituality. Townes states that this spirituality arises from Black women's lives and that this moral wisdom is found in the "autobiographies, speeches, novels, poems, sermons, testimonies, songs, and oral histories" of Black women.[39] When mining the oral histories and life narratives of these five interviewees, moral wisdom does appear. This wisdom perhaps more closely aligns with Alice Walker's initial intent when she referred to a womanist as one who "loves the Spirit" because it honors Walker's own fluid sense of spirituality and nonreliance on Christianity as the basis for morality. It also relies on Walker's attributions of womanist as one who wants to "know more and in greater depth than is considered 'good' for one."[40] By plunging into the depths of these Black women's wisdom, it is possible to understand their motivations for being moral leaders.

Gleaning from the morality crafted as these women listen to their divine source provides a compass for why they all share a similar social justice calling. Their theistic connection to humanity motivates them to create a just world for others, not just to enlighten themselves. They innately feel and respond to the "mighty causes" calling them. For example, Rabbi Lawson's experiences in Judaism include struggles to be accepted as a community member. Her moral wisdom spurs her to envision a "more inclusive Jewish community where all who want to come are welcomed, diversity is embraced, and [people] come together to learn, to pray, and to eat."[41] For Dr. Ayo, her moral wisdom comes from her willingness to "seek out wisdom from African American lesbians on how to create safe spaces for themselves" and others.[42] Their wisdom on how to survive and thrive inspires her to keep doing what she is passionate about, doing the work with the people who are willing to assist. Bishop Flunder gains power from linking to her ancestors and their divine knowledge, recognizing that her DNA contains Cherokee, Celtic, Irish, and Black ancestors whose stories of survival can be folded into a theology of liberation for herself and others. Rev. Deborah receives divine messages from Spirit, but she is careful to note that this does not make her special because Spirit is equally available to all.[43] Her purpose for connecting to Spirit is to reflect back missives for humanity's thriving. Similarly, Dr. Cari's moral wisdom comes from direct connection to Spirit as well. She has an "auditory" relationship with Spirit that reveals directions for her own life and often for others. When she described hearing from Spirit that she needed to start a Wednesday-night worship service at someone else's church, she obeyed despite the seeming oddity of the request. In response to her obedience, she was able to host her worship service at the church, and hundreds of people of all spiritual faiths came for a participatory and collective spiritual boost. Because they are leaders of various religious and spiritual communities, these women's moral wisdom, inspired by their differing spiritualities, is a reason why they appeal to followers. Chapter 5 will highlight other such practical skill sets and behaviors that are expected for a womanist ethical leader.

Cultivating Womanist Ethical Leadership

I guess I think that people actually need somebody who can speak up for them, and sometimes they may not have anybody else who has the voice and platform. And so . . . you have to be willing to step out and sometimes speak out on the difficult issues, and to be willing to risk some things to bring about change. . . . I think it's important to always do the right thing, do it for the right reason, and know . . . that you've done it in good conscience. So I think that that helps me, and to know that I might be able to help somebody always is going to motivate me.

—BISHOP ALLYSON ABRAMS, oral history interview, 2019

Leadership [is] not a series of qualities that prepares one to lead or to give leadership to people in the world, but . . . the best kind of leadership emerg[es] from social movements as reflecting collective ideas and collective aspirations.

—ANGELA DAVIS, "Leaders as Teachers"

As a child in my conservative Baptist church, I often heard sermons from Numbers 22: 21–38 that referenced Balaam's speaking donkey. These sermons always seemed to appear right before Women's Day, a day where our worship service would typically be led completely by women, including the sermon for the day. Perhaps inadvertently, the message I heard was that women in religious leadership were just as out of place as a speaking donkey but that God would use them *anyway*. I was in college before I read the accounts of Rev. Jarena Lee, the first woman authorized to preach in the African Methodist Episcopal Church, who used the very same scripture to explain that "maybe a speaking woman is like an ass—but I can tell you one thing, the ass seen the angel when Balaam didn't."[1] The lesson that I took from Lee's rejoinder was that Black women have a second sight or even a special call to religious leadership that, despite being ignored by patriarchy, is not ignored by God. There was no *anyway* to their role as leaders; it came as naturally to them as leadership did for men. When I started this research project exploring lesbian religious leadership, I likewise found this to be true.

Initially, I interviewed gay men and women and was given a slate of potential interviewees, who were predominantly male and gay because LGBTQ-RAN was interested in capturing the "early leaders" in religious movements. I recalibrated my expectations and processes, realizing that leadership was something done not only by those who were "in charge" of denominations/churches/ institutions. I remembered my own religious experience watching women literally run the church while not having access to any titles or credentialing that would reflect their actual power. Katie Cannon's mantra "Do the work your soul must have" came to my memory, and I realized that I needed to look outside of denominational hierarchies for queer women leaders; I needed to look for where the "work" was actually happening. Thus, this chapter explores women who went about the work of transformational holistic justice in their immediate communities and beyond.

When I decided to write a book about these interviewees, it was not merely to expose a larger audience to these women's herstories. Although this is a valid goal, I assert that these women's lives point toward greater possibilities. They illustrate moral leadership or what I deem a better model: womanist ethical leadership. This book's preceding chapters have covered the traits of an ethical leader—for example, authenticity, social justice consciousness, and spirituality—as I set out to differentiate how Black lesbian religious leaders' leadership styles are instructive for future generations. This chapter focuses on how these traits are cultivated to create examples of womanist ethical leadership for others to follow. In particular, the chapter examines womanist ethical leadership by highlighting skill-set development, which occurs via training and formation, honing charisma, and consensus building. After discussing these skills, the chapter presents the final trait necessary for womanist ethical leadership: collaborative leadership models, a leadership style that yields transformation and holistic justice.

Ethical Leadership

Ethical leadership is a burgeoning field of study that runs the gamut from theory to corporatization. There are numerous leadership theories— authentic, transformational, servant, values-based, spiritual, moral—that reflect the evolving definitions of leadership since the twentieth century. Early twentieth-century leadership studies were concerned about power and domination, whereas those of the mid-twentieth century focused on influence. Twenty-first-century leadership studies emphasize distinctions among types/processes of leadership. But as demand for ethical leaders arise, many in the field admit they really only "know it when they see it," mirroring Supreme Court Justice Potter Stewart's famous definition of pornography. If trained ethicists know ethical leaders but have such varied definitions on what they "know," what hope does that leave for the everyday religious practitioner who simply wants to trust their religious authority?

Because there is such a variety of definitions in the discipline, this chapter engages Walter Fluker and Robert Franklin as its primary interlocutors. These two scholars were chosen because they are experts on Black leadership models and because they both present the standard depiction of Black leadership as male and religious.[2] Fluker served as executive director of the Morehouse Leadership Center and recently retired as professor of ethical leadership at Boston University. Franklin holds a chair in moral leadership at Candler School of Theology and was formerly president of Morehouse College and the Interdenominational Theological Center. They write on ethical leadership and moral leadership, respectively.

Fluker defines ethical leadership as the "critical appropriation and embodiment of moral traditions that have shaped the character and shared meanings of a people," contending that ethical leaders are formed through the development of character, civility, and community.[3] He argues that most leadership is moral (morality being a consequence of our contexts) but that not all leadership is ethical. In his estimation, ethical leaders are created from our particular lifeworlds, our habits and traditions, in the moments when the leader decides to act for the collective good.[4] Fluker is a renowned scholar of mystic Howard Thurman and Martin Luther King Jr., and these two men figure prominently in his model exemplars of Black leadership. Despite his scholarly allegiances, Fluker looks to these past "race men" as courageous visionaries steeped in the Black church tradition who can inspire and guide others to lives of service and sacrifice. To be fair, it is not their maleness or even their religious authority that makes them worthy examples; Fluker conjectures that they "present themselves to the world as symbols" who have been transformed into "apostles of sensitiveness," hopeful agents of compassion.[5] Yet Fluker's texts do not always interrogate their male privilege as a mechanism for how they are able to become these beacons for others. Both leaders make universal claims about Blacks that do not consider the specifics of gender and race, and both surely benefited from systems of untold women leaders' support, a caveat that remains unexplored in Fluker's promotion of Thurman and King.

Franklin also relies on King and Thurman as examples of moral leadership. Franklin's definition of a moral leader emphasizes those who "live and lead with integrity, courage, and imagination as they serve the common good, while inviting others to join them."[6] He chooses King's life to examine at length because he posits that King's flawed leadership is instructive for understanding how one develops moral character and agency. In fairness, he also highlights Ella Baker and Dolores Huerta, but both female leaders are given considerably less attention than King and even Thurman in *Moral Leadership*. In his discussion of Baker, Franklin notes that her legacy is special because although she was crucial to the development of three prominent organizations (NAACP, SCLC, SNCC), she was an outsider to their inner circles.[7] Franklin's text highlights the role of moral leadership in sustaining institutions; thus, it is not surprising that he gives Baker less attention than male leaders who organized within institutions.

Much like Baker, the women in my study often found themselves as outsiders in their organizations, so the emphasis on understanding queer women's religious leadership is more than just swapping out a male perspective for a female one. Patricia Hill Collins contends that oppressed group members produce subjugated knowledge that provides alternative ways to resist oppression. Such knowledge from the underside is a complicated, layered knowledge, one that demonstrates how Black women had made "creative use out of their marginality—their outsider within status" in order to advance the common good. Thus, Black lesbian religious leadership comes from a specific standpoint, one that brings to leadership the awareness of intersectional experiences.[8]

Distinctions in Black Gay and Lesbian Religious Leadership

There are certainly similarities among Black gay and lesbian religious leaders' approaches, not least that those who started working in the 1980s and 1990s undertook the necessary ministry of working with many persons who were dying of AIDS. The HIV/AIDS pandemic brought many leaders to direct service work, yet in my interviews, Black lesbian religious leaders articulated a lengthier and more intimate duration of their work with those affected by HIV/AIDS. They recounted washing the bodies of the sick, preparing their food, helping them take their medications, and eventually preparing their bodies and officiating at their funerals once they died. When I spoke with Black gay leaders regarding their work with those affected by HIV/AIDS, they often reminisced about providing direct services such as medical management, housing, food, and employment, services that were just as needed but did not require the same level of in-person care. Whether from personal preference or the misogynistic assumption that women would do the caregiving, Black queer leadership was contextual in its approach to AIDS.

Another difference I observed from my interviews with Black gay religious leaders was their early acceptance of a call to religious leadership. Although many men objected to call language, they experienced something that prompted them to advocate for others to have a particular religious experience. None described a hesitancy to accept this positioning because of their sexual orientation. Yet every woman I interviewed wrestled with public acknowledgment of her call to religious authority whether because they are female or because they are female and lesbian. Privately, most of the women accepted that they were being drawn to deeper levels of participation in their faith, but many delayed publicly fighting for their right to proclaim themselves as someone whom God had specifically called for a purpose. The result of this dichotomy is that men have many more years of religious experience among supporters than women do. This experience has built credibility and authority to which women lack similar access.

A final distinction between the male leaders I interviewed and the women leaders is men's emphasis on participating within institutions, whereas Black lesbian religious leaders were on the peripheries of many institutions. Men were actively involved in their religious hierarchies as leaders; they often worked within systems created and sustained by other gay men. Their investment in these systems was also an investment in how the hierarchies helped them serve their constituents. Most of the lesbian leaders I interviewed worked within larger structures that they did not control and, in the case of several women, that were not even controlled by Black men. Thus, they had learned to navigate systems that were not structured with their needs in mind and in fact presented obstacles to their thriving in their leadership roles. This led most of the women to engage in para-institutional leadership. Bishops Flunder and Abrams were notable exceptions to this experience, but those whose leadership opportunities were constrained by sexism and/or racism have much to teach us about their leadership decisions.

These gender differences correspond to observations in contemporary leadership studies. In her stellar book *Women and Leadership*, Deborah Rhode surveyed decades of research on gender differences in leadership and found that female leaders are "more participatory, democratic, and interpersonally sensitive than male leaders."[9] She noted a preference for collaborative leadership, not because women were incapable of "leaning in" but rather because collaboration was seen as an asset in most leadership scenarios. When factoring in racial considerations, research indicates that Black women proceed from collective standpoints and lead for community empowerment, just as Angela Davis's opening epigraph notes.[10] Thus, examining the leadership experiences of the Black lesbian religious interviewees means understanding their leadership through the lens of the wider scholarship on gender and race.

Womanist Ethical Leadership

Whether leadership styles are viewed as para-institutional, cooperative, or independent, being a Black lesbian is often an important factor in how she leads and what she considers ethical. My own contextual definition of ethical leadership is a merging of these prior interlocutors' views, for I posit that ethical leadership requires concern for the greater good and the holistic well-being of the planet and its inhabitants. For that reason, community is essential to unlocking their leadership gifts. Fluker asserts that the work of ethical leadership begins and ends with community; I wonder what it means to imagine community from the margins.[11] The Black lesbian religious leaders I interviewed create community from their vantage point of the margins of society. Their race, gender, and sexuality can result in their isolation: not being central to the thriving of communities despite the centuries of Black female experience as the backbone of societies. As essential members who are often forgotten or maligned when they speak for the community, Black lesbian religious leaders reassess community with its most marginalized members at its center, uplifting their experiences such that thriving in the community is driven by what thriving looks like for the most vulnerable.

At its core, this is the hallmark of womanist ethical leadership—deliberately resisting oppression that prevents holistic well-being. My articulation of womanist ethical leadership is more than just adding the term *womanist* to my previous definition of ethical leadership.[12] I am a "Walker womanist," and my womanism is informed by Walker's 1983 womanist definition in *In Search of Our Mothers' Gardens.* She describes a womanist as someone who is "committed to survival and wholeness of entire people, male and female" and who "loves the folk."[13] This commitment to the everyday folk—the least and the left out—is an energizing addition to leadership scholarship.

Both Fluker and Franklin emphasize the common good and promote community, yet the starting point of their work is the perspectives of men who are leading the community.[14] By contrast, my interviewees reflected a different way of leading that aligns more closely with the community. In fact, these interviews demonstrated Ella Baker's perspective that the "very idea of leading people to freedom is a contradiction in terms. Freedom requires that people be able to analyze their own social position and understand their collective ability to do something about it without relying on leaders."[15] Imagining community as cocreating its own leadership is what commitment to the wholeness of a people entails because wholeness is all encompassing. It does not establish or enforce hierarchies because everyone is equal and able to serve in any capacity.

I am reading these interviews as examples of womanist ethical leadership because of this emphasis on equality and seeking holistic justice. I am also doing so to present new anchors or groundings for moral leadership. When ethicist David Gushee develops a list of leaders for his book on moral leadership, he discusses the discernment process of who counts as a moral leader. He rightly notes that societies decide who deserves to be remembered and that studying moral leaders teaches us about ourselves: whom we value.[16] I have been intentional about choosing leaders who represent everyday Black and queer people and who lead with the most marginalized societal members in mind. When I survey womanist ethicists whose scholarship I value, their cast of moral leaders tends to be either fictional characters or women from the late nineteenth or twentieth century. Certainly, their examples are all worthy candidates whose lives have stood the test of time and whose impact should be taught to subsequent generations. My choices are a bit riskier because I highlight those whose histories are still being recorded, who may, in fact, let us down, whose legacies may be deeply flawed. I turn to contemporary living agents because of the promise they offer to those reading the text: you, the reader, can reach out and access these women and ask questions, gain mentors, comrades, and even road maps for how your own lives can be lived. These women are able to influence our current age and empower you to do the same.

Cultivating Womanist Ethical Leadership Traits through
Formation/Training

So far, this book has presented three basic traits (authenticity, social justice consciousness, and spirituality) that demarcate a womanist ethical leader, and this chapter adds collaboration as a final trait. These traits are evident in the eighteen women I interviewed. Yet before I unpack the final trait, it is necessary to take a step back to learn about how these traits are cultivated and sustained in my subjects.

Each of my interviewees recounted how they were trained or formed early on in ways that were ultimately quite useful in their leadership roles. They learned the building blocks of responsibility and how to be accountable to someone other than themselves. For many, this first took place in their families, among both biological and chosen kin. For others, this formation occurred in institutions such as their schools or religious communities or secular organizations such as the Girl Scouts. Because I was conducting oral histories, every interview discussed family, and not all families were supportive of their queer relatives. Whether they were supportive or not, most expressed how their earliest lessons in communal responsibility came from their families. For example, in my 2011 interview with Bishop Flunder, she discussed her family as steeped in the Church of God in Christ and noted that as such they did not fraternize with many people outside of their family/faith tradition, for theologically they were taught to be insular, set apart from the world. She remembered singing her first solo in her grandfather's church and mentioned that this prepared her for her stint as a gospel singer. She also credits her training by family members who were church planters, church founders, and church administrators as reinforcing her seemingly natural ability to be a church leader. She has preached since she was sixteen, a task that required family support because she started preaching in a tradition that did not ordain women. Yet she learned from her mother the posturing and circumventing she would need to engage in order to be a religious leader, such as learning the language needed to get an audience to accept her: not calling it preaching, not standing in the pulpit, thanking the men for giving "this humble woman an opportunity," and so on. Her family training did not overcome her religious obstacles but gave her the skills to persevere in spite of those obstacles.

Likewise, Bishop Dr. Allyson Abrams also learned from her mother how to navigate patriarchal religious systems but still operate with her God-given gifts.

FIGURE 5.1. Bishop Dr. Allyson Abrams. Used by permission.

Bishop Dr. Allyson Abrams is founder and pastor of Empowerment Liberation Cathedral in Washington, DC, and is presiding bishop of Pneuma Christian Fellowship. Bishop Abrams was the youngest female called to a historic Black Baptist church in Detroit and served the Zion Progress Baptist congregation for five years until she resigned when she married Bishop Diana Williams. She is a published author and holds a mechanical engineering degree from Howard University and a masters and doctorate of divinity from United Theological Seminary in Dayton, Ohio. She was ordained in the Progressive and American Baptist tradition and performed the first Black same-sex wedding on a reality show on TVOne.[17]

Bishop Abrams was raised in Birmingham, Alabama, and remembered an early experience with God while accompanying her mother to a speaking event at a Baptist church. Because many Baptist churches do not license and ordain women, those who are gifted are chosen as "speakers," and she recalled God talking to her when she was seven or eight, telling her that she would speak before a congregation someday. She initially rejected the idea but accepted her family's view that one is committed to faith and is meant to use whatever gifts and talents one is given in the church. She joked with me that she was unaware of how much Bible she had absorbed living in the Bible Belt, but she just knew her worldview was shaped by the notion of "go[ing] with God." This teaching also corresponded with the lessons her family gave her to do right by others, whether she knew them or not, and to speak up for what's right, a capacity that reinforced her call to be an advocate. As in the opening epigraph, Bishop Abrams connects her contemporary advocacy to being groomed to help others.

In my conversation with Dean Emilie Townes, I learned that she too was taught by her family to speak up for others. She was primarily raised in a United Methodist church in Durham, North Carolina, where spirituality and social justice coincided, but she also received messages in her family which dictated that their family values and Christian values called them to greater accountability. As a future leader, these instructions were important to how she would lead, considering the connectedness she was to have with others. She recalled:

> I was raised to be a Christian woman. I don't often use that language, but that's how I was raised and that means you tell the truth, you do right by yourself, and you do righter by people you work with, you recognize that you don't get anywhere in life by yourself and that, for me, I can't think of a single first or a single second or third or any of those that I have achieved all by myself. I have always had people who were engaged in the process with me, guiding me, calling me . . . to account, telling me to back off.

This intertwining of religious and family values also merged with her educational training and affected how she speaks out. For instance, her English teachers made an indelible mark on her by training her to think through what she wants to say before she says it so that she truly has something articulate to contribute to public dialogue.

Cultivating through Education

Just as Dean Townes was formed by her family and her English teachers, so too did other interviewees recall being shaped by educational experiences. One such leader is Rev. Dr. Renee McCoy.

FIGURE 5.2. Reverend Dr. Renee McCoy. Used by permission.

Rev. Dr. Renee McCoy has a religiously eclectic background. She was raised Roman Catholic, joined the Metropolitan Community Churches (MCC) in 1976, chaired the MCC Racism Task Force as director of Race Relations, and became the founding pastor of Harlem MCC in 1981. She was also the founding pastor of the Full Truth Fellowship of Christ Church in Detroit in 1989 and retired from the Unity Fellowship Movement Church in 1995. She also recently served as interim pastor of the Eastgate Congregational United Church of Christ in Bellevue, Washington. She was a founding member of the National Coalition of Black Lesbians and Gays and the New York Third World Coalition. She had an extensive career focused on HIV *in the Black community and holds a doctorate in anthropology from Wayne State University. She currently resides in Seattle with her wife, Rev. Dr. Patricia Hunter.*[18]

Rev. Renee is one of four interviewees who has had a private religious education. Although her values were certainly shaped by her family, she also reflected on the imprint of her Roman Catholic education. She graduated at age sixteen, but the Catholic Church left an impression on her, specifically with regard to social justice activism. For example, during the civil rights movement she felt compelled to raise money for the Student Nonviolent Coordinating Committee because she was shocked by her parents' stories of living in the South and by witnessing television coverage of Black people having hoses and dogs turned on them. When she got to a school where she had a religious education course every day, she was constantly being told that that discrimination was not right and that as a Christian she had a responsibility to say "Enough!"—like Jesus did with oppression. She organized with Black Catholics in Action in high school because she was being taught that "life changes when you feed the hungry, clothe the naked, house the homeless. When you take care of each other, life changes." She felt compelled to deliver food baskets to families in need in Detroit because she believed that if her faith was real, she had to act. When she got to college at Wayne State University, she also attended the Catholic University Club as an outlet for her social justice concerns. She organized friends from the campus's Newman Catholic Center to ask the church for space to run a youth center for kids in their neighborhood, who she discovered did not have any outlets either, and from that site the group of friends provided health and other direct services for the community. She was again putting into practice what she had learned in her Catholic high school.

Another interviewee who also had a transformative educational experience is Mandy Carter. She was not shaped by her family, being raised in an orphanage for most of her childhood, but her experience with Quaker education changed her life.

*Mandy Carter is a cofounder of Southerners on New Ground (*SONG*) and the National Black Justice Coalition. She has more than fifty years of social justice organizing experience, having participated in the War Resisters League, the Poor People's Campaign, and various types of political activism as a campaign manager in North Carolina and Florida and as one of the five national cochairs of Obama Pride and Hillary Clinton's North Carolina* LGBT *Steering Committee. She was nominated for a Nobel Peace Prize in 2005 and*

FIGURE 5.3. Mandy Carter. Used by permission.

has received numerous awards, including a 2018 Peace Award from the War Resisters League, a 2015 Union Medal from Union Theological Seminary, and the 1995 Paul Anderson Stonewall Award from the National Gay and Lesbian Task Force. She is the coeditor of We Have Not Been Moved: Resisting Racism and Militarism in 21st Century America *and currently runs her own consultancy group.*

Unlike many of the other interviewees, Mandy Carter has had quite a bit written about her and has even donated her personal papers to two different libraries: Duke University and the Schomberg Center for Research in Black Culture. Although she has done many interviews and often shares publicly about herself, my interview was one of the first to connect her religious and spiritual background to her more than fifty years of activism. Because she was raised at both the Albany Children's Home and the Schenectady Children's Home, she was expected to attend a white Protestant church. She recalled that half of the time she did not attend church but that she did go to school.

She remembers being an active learner, and she had an experience in her high school that changed the trajectory of her life. Her high school social studies teacher brought in a guest speaker from the American Friends Service Committee who spoke about the Quakers and their stance on equality, peace, and justice. She was impressed by what she was told of the Quakers' solidarity with the civil rights movement, and she was particularly moved by the concept of the "power of one"—the idea that everyone has a moral compass and gets to decide whether to use their life to change the world positively or negatively. At the conclusion of the speaker's talk, he invited interested parties to attend the American Friends Service Committee Work Camp in the Pocono Mountains, which is where Ms. Carter was both formed as a Quaker and educated in the ways of nonviolent resistance. She attended the camp in 1965 and recalled that the camp brought in Guy and Candie Carawan from the Highlander Center. Although the camp was only a week long, it taught her about Bayard Rustin's work and gave her the opportunity to read about Gandhi and how his tactics had been used in the civil rights movement. She remembered doing a lot of reading that week, which really gave her a passion for nonviolent resistance. She was convinced to be a "Quaker or a pacifist until [someone could] give [her] some other reason why." Although she briefly attended services with Unitarians and even a Unity Fellowship church, she kept coming back to the Quaker community based primarily on her brief but compelling encounter with the group in high school.

This commitment to Quaker philosophy was also expanded at the work camp because of her introduction there to Joan Baez, who ran the Institute for the Study of Nonviolence in the Carmel Valley. Ms. Carter briefly attended community college but left to join Baez's peace initiatives out west. There she was formed again at the institute. She read more about Gandhi, learned about the significance of silent meditation, and had discussions on pacifism.[19] At the time, the institute was planning its very first civil disobedience actions against the war in Vietnam, and she and Baez protested and were arrested. While they were in prison, Martin Luther King Jr. visited Baez, and Ms. Carter remembers his visit's impact on the prisoners. She also realized the importance of the moral leadership she was learning from her time at the institute. In essence, she was being taught not to follow the pattern of leaders like Baez, Gandhi, Rustin, or King but to realize that social change was possible "not because of who they were but [because of] what they believed in."[20] At the institute and in her work with the War Resisters' League, she was learning the power of grassroots organizing for social justice.

Education also provided a type of formation for Bishop Flunder. Her family was influential in forming her moral character, but she also gives credit to her educational pursuits as providing her a moral grounding for her ministry and social justice commitments. Because she was so experienced in ministry and so talented musically, she did not always place primary value on education. She described herself as reluctant because she was already doing the work of serving the most marginalized, but it became clear to her that she needed a way to get through the theological conundrums she was having while doing the work. She sought out theological education to provide her a systematic way of working out some of the theological questions with which she had been wrestling. Ultimately, she went from one degree to another until she had earned a doctor of ministry degree from the San Francisco Theological Seminary (now University of the Redlands). She soon realized that she required the same experience for her congregation and for members of her fellowship. Bishop Flunder helped develop a certificate program that more than a hundred people from her community have now completed. She also secured funding from the Ford and Carpenter Foundations for Project Access, a program to help people with "remedial issues as it related to writing and research" receive access to the certificate program. Educational training is a staple in her leadership development of her community; she wants people to have no shame and not feel deficient in their leadership.

Cultivation through Honing Charisma

Bishop Flunder's congregation trusted her enough to risk their fears of academic rejection because she stressed the importance of education for their work as leaders and because they were largely drawn to follow her charismatic lead. By all accounts, she and many of the other women interviewed can be viewed as charismatic leaders. Here I am referencing *charisma* as a type of religious power that is perhaps uniquely linked to personal characteristics or abilities. But whether inherent or cultivated, such charisma has the ability to influence others to bestow authority and trust on a particular individual.[21] Much has been written about charisma and how and why people tend to follow certain individuals. This is not a central concern of this chapter. Here, I am simply highlighting charisma as a trait to be honed in pursuit of ethical leadership because many of my interviewees mentioned learning to use this power for the greater social good. It is also important to mention because charisma has been historically used to reference a gendered structure of authority where the attributes of an ideal leader typically belong to men, a structure that has tended to disregard or masculinize Black female leaders.[22] The charismatic leadership of Black lesbian religious leaders expands these contemporary leadership discussions by refusing to fit into narrow or even fictionalized assumptions of what charismatic leadership should be or is.

Bishop Flunder often talks about charisma when questioned about her leadership. In our interview she explained that some things had come naturally to her, among them charisma:

> I think the charisma, the leadership skills. As a little girl, I used to sit on the curb sometime, not by the house. Before very long, other little children would come and sit down next to me, And then it'd be some other little children, you know what I mean? And they would say, what are you doing today? And then I would have an idea, and they would say, well, I want to do that. That's the story of my life. I can't remember. I think there's a certain bees-to-honey charisma, you know, that has accompanied me most of my life as a leader, and I couldn't have fashioned it; I think I came here with that assignment, you know. So that part of it I think is natural.

In Ellen Lewin's *Filled with the Spirit*, Bishop Flunder repeated a similar statement, telling Lewin that charisma was part of the gift of her calling to gather people. Lewin refers to Flunder as a charismatic leader, and her book's entire second chapter is devoted to investigating Flunder as an example of unusual charisma. Lewin highlights sociologist Max Weber's theories of charisma as qualities not accessible to ordinary persons, and she goes on to laud Flunder's natural gifts as unique or, in Flunder's own words, as "anointing," which goes beyond skill.[23] Ultimately, the examples that Lewin provides from Flunder's members and partners in the Fellowship of Affirming Ministries demonstrate that Flunder goes out of her way to be "real" and an ordinary person. The author experiences the allure of charisma and seems to ignore the lesson shared by Ms. Carter: it's not the person but the cause that she believes in that is the truly unique gift.

One of the reasons that Ms. Carter was so cautious about charismatic leadership was that she had experienced firsthand its negative impact on a community. In her experiences in both the orphanages and in a foster home, she felt that she was on her own in developing moral guidelines. She had structure but not really a moral centering that she trusted. She described that the first time she realized she knew right from wrong was when she had been sent to the Schenectady Children's Home at the age of thirteen or fourteen:

One of the neat things people like[d] to do is just run away because if you ran away that was sort of a status, like a status kind of thing. And I organized our entire senior dorm, which is only what, fifty women, to run away, and I didn't. And the head of the thing brought me in and said Mandy, you just got a lot of people to run away and you didn't go; you might want to think about how you want to use your time and energy. And that was the first time I had someone question me—why you have something that you do and why would it be put toward having people run away from the home. In other words, if you have the ability to do something, why did you use it negatively?

And when he asked me that question, that was the first prick of kind of like yeah, so why did I do that? What was the point of it? And I'll never forget that, because then I thought maybe I really should think about how I want to utilize my energy. That's why I'm an organizer now, because if I can organize people to run away and I don't go, then. . . .

At an early age, Ms. Carter recognized that she had a gift to get others to follow her instructions and that with such a great gift came responsibility. It was a gift that certainly came to her without any divine call or religious or spiritual experience, for she had no personal connection to a faith community at the time. She also notes that this charismatic influence led her to social justice organizing as she learned to refine that talent for social good.

Ms. Carter is an example of how someone else observed her gift in operation and alerted her to it. Other interviewees had a similar experience of others "seeing something in them" worth following, a recognition that often surprised them. Elder Darlene Garner explained that "leadership was thrust upon her" after others saw that she was faithful in handling small things and felt she would be faithful also with larger tasks. Rev. McCoy recognized this gift of faithfulness too, but neither woman called their gift charisma.

Rev. Renee realized that this was God's gift to her that she demonstrated to others. She recalled almost whimsically that "people trusted me, and worked with me, and gave me a lot of support not because of who I was, but because of whose I was, because God used me to demonstrate faithfulness." Although she founded churches for gay and lesbian persons of African descent in two different cities, she did not have clout or a big name to draw an audience. She started churches during the worst years of the AIDS deaths affecting the Black community, and many found it hard to imagine a gay Black church.

Initially, they may not have trusted her as a religious leader, but they grew to trust her as a social activist. She was faithful in the community, providing assistance and direct services. In Harlem she did "street ministry with substance abusers," and in Detroit she did the same. She noted how God put the right people in her path, but she was also aware that those people saw something in her that made them show up for her in a consistent way.

Similarly Rabbi Lawson expressed her shock that others had nominated her as a leader of a community that she had only recently joined. She recalled being active and being on the board of the synagogue, but not until much later of having the "aha" moment when she realized that they regarded her as a leader:

> Now I'm on the board, and I'm part of the leadership of the community. And then at some point I become the executive vice president or the first vice president, which gives me more authority. Which is kind of weird because I never saw it that way. But other people did. And so like I'm now signing checks and have keys to things. It's sort of like . . . like I never saw, like I remember when I brought a question up about something that was a little problematic during the service, and I didn't realize how much weight my voice had because I was now one of the leadership, part of the leadership of the synagogue. And then I think that's when it sort of started to register that I'm now not just a member; I'm actually a leader in this community.

What started out simply as having a heart for the community developed into much more for her, and soon she realized that to be that community's best representative, she would need to attend rabbinical school. Rev. Renee and Rabbi Lawson are two examples of women whose work in their communities drew others to them, who then validated that work.

A final example of accidental awareness of their own charismatic leadership is Bishop Allyson Abrams. While she was not initially aware of it, she has since grown to take on quite a bit of pride and authority in her charisma. Like Rev. Renee, Bishop Abrams also founded two churches in two different cities, but in her case only one was predominantly gay and lesbian. She recognized a call to pastor early in her life and had to persevere to make that a reality. After receiving a call to pastor a Baptist congregation (which for a Black Baptist woman is no easy feat, given the denomination's polity), she realized that others were willing to be led by her. She was active in the city of Detroit, serving on the Detroit Council of Baptist Pastors, in the NAACP, as an elected school board official, and as a chaplain for the Detroit Public Schools. She also held a leadership position as coeditor of the Progressive National Baptist Convention magazine. Despite all of this leadership experience, she was unsure why other pastors would be soliciting her advice:

> I think probably around 2010 I had noticed that there were a lot of preachers calling me for different things, who were pastoring churches. And I was always kind of giving people advice and telling them what to do in their ministries and different things that I felt would possibly work. In 2011 I had a gentleman who was a bishop who called me and asked me to become a bishop as a part of his fellowship that he had. . . . I had been praying about it. . . . And I believed that it was [God's will for me]. I had seen so many needs that people had for training and for helping them with the different ministries that they were trying to accomplish.

She eventually created her own ecumenical body, Pneuma Christian Fellowship, and after getting her Baptist congregation on board, she was elected its presiding bishop. When she married her partner, Diana Williams, bishop emeritus of the Imani Temple African American Catholic Congregation, she resigned from her church and all her other roles rather than see the Christian community divided over her choice of partner. In subsequent interviews she is careful to note that she was not forced to resign and that she left to live her truth and to join Diana, who lived in Washington, DC. She faced another loss when the leaders of the Christian fellowship that she had founded refused to serve under her as a lesbian bishop. Years after this incident, she rejoiced that the call to pastor had not left her, nor had the calling to be a bishop.[24] She knew that the same charismatic preaching that had caused people to follow her ministry would encourage others to do the same.

The skills that Bishop Abrams learned in building her fellowship involved creating consensus, for she was bringing together pastors from various ecumenical bodies. Despite their collaboration, she did not have the ability to keep the original group anchored to her. She is currently seeking new pastors to mentor but has not given up on consensus as a way to bring the likely disparate members together. Learning from her painful experience, she has since added several questions to the membership application form, questions about whether the church/minister is affirming and how they demonstrate this belief, and this certainly decreases the possibility of a new set of members being unwilling to be led by her.

FIGURE 5.4. Dr. Imani Woody. Used by permission.

Cultivating Consensus-Building Skills

Donna Kate Rushin's 1981 poem "The Bridge" is about the difficulty of building consensus: the work involved in having to see both sides of an issue and constantly translate ideas and perspectives for others.[25] She encourages the reader to be the bridge to their own power, a bridge to their true selves, which is ultimately what Bishop Abrams is seeking to create as she reestablishes her Pneuma Christian Fellowship. Yet she is not the only interviewee who found consensus building to be necessary work. Rabbi Lawson experienced the lack of coalition building in her early organizing days in Atlanta with various minority populations. She discovered that her very being could create bridges to various communities. As a rabbi, she draws on her intersectional identities to reach across her campus to form coalitions. Another interviewee who likewise affirms the consensus leadership style is Dr. Imani Woody.

Dr. Imani Woody is the founding director and CEO of Mary's House for Older Adults. She is an active participant in the MCC Washington, DC, congregation, serving as a member of the board of directors and as a national MCC program officer for the Older Adults Advisory Council. She earned a PhD in Human Services from Capella University and is currently the principal of IWF Consulting, where she works as a diversity and inclusion consultant in the fields of health, aging, and issues affecting the LGBTQ and people-of-color communities.

She is also a life coach and a mayoral appointee to the Washington, DC, LGBTQ Advisory Council.[26]

Perhaps because my interviewees are outliers in society because of their being queer, the idea of building bridges across their various identities resonated with many of them. However, Dr. Imani's advocacy for collaboration came from a surprising place—a desire to avoid dictatorial authority. Her mother died when she was ten years old, her pastor father worked full-time, and this left her to care for herself and four small children, the youngest being a year old. Understandably, this eventually became too much for her, and she left home and ended up in an orphanage. Her pastor father had been quite strict and abusive, so she actually found the orphanage the "best place ever." Unfortunately, she learned to rule in the same manner as her father.

After she turned eighteen, she married a recent widower and proceeded to make a home in the fashion she had learned. She quickly had a son but realized that she was in another abusive relationship and divorced her husband. During our interview she described having started an independent school on Saturdays for her son that was attended by neighborhood children and their parents. This school's purpose was to teach Black history and culture to Black children. She taught in her house, supplementing what she knew with field trips and other classes. She told me that despite running this school on her own, she was still quite young and lacked all that she needed to lead:

> I had no supervisory skills. I had leadership skills but no real supervisory skills. You know, when you're the oldest of five, you can be a leader, and you can be a tyrant, too, I suppose. And so I was leading, doing that, using those skills. And I was very clear the teachers had to come in dressed this way. I was very Afrocentric. My whole house, my whole world, was Afrocentric. Women couldn't come in showing their boobs, and, you know, you just had to be right. And these were young people like me. [*Laughs.*] And so they rebelled, had a coup, said we're not doing this anymore. [*Laughs.*] So that was a very good lesson learned. Thank God I learned it later in life, you know. So now I supervise by consensus, usually, with the last, you know, the buck stops here as opposed to my way or the highway, so it's a different framing of the same thing.

Thus, her desire to lead by consensus was in fact the result of her trying to break the tyrannical cycle of her past. Having learned this lesson, she grew to understand the importance of working together for a common cause.

In her current efforts to raise funds to provide LGBTQ elders a safe place to live, she has to work with various organizations (health care, zoning/construction, LGBTQ advocacy, senior advocacy) to achieve her goal. She was gifted her father's home and hopes to break ground on its conversion in 2022 to turn it into the first LGBTQ communal senior home in Washington, DC. Beyond that one home, she and her board are doing the work to train and educate staff and residents of existing senior wellness centers, retirement facilities, and nursing homes to become more welcoming spaces for the LGBTQ elderly.[27] Her volunteer board of directors also uses the consensus leadership model she has learned to appreciate. Relatedly, she has been involved in numerous social justice endeavors that bridge communities. Among these are her work with the Mautner Project for Lesbians with Cancer, which she joined to bring attention to how cancer affects lesbians of color, and her work helping AARP integrate LGBTQ services in its national trainings and programs.

Ms. Mandy Carter is another interviewee who placed great value on being a bridge builder and leading through consensus. As one of the oldest interviewees, she has quite an extensive history as a social justice activist in varied arenas, from peace building to politics to LGBTQ organizing that spanned racial, geographic, gender, and age demographics. She recalled her experiences with predominantly white organizations:

> I didn't mind being what I would perceive to be like kind of the bridge builder. I can certainly step in and be a big part of being in the Black community. I love that, and I love that. . . . But then I also noticed that it was sometimes important, because a lot of the organizations around women, peace, others where you had to coordinate and collaborate with predominantly white organizations, I didn't mind being that bridge builder. And that's what Bayard did. And so, for me it was a role model.

Bayard Rustin was an apt model for Ms. Carter. The Quaker-meeting approach, which involved sitting in a room where any person has the ability to "stand up and speak truth to power," influenced his leadership style.[28] She also would have resonated with the Quaker notion of the power of one, or each human being's ability to effect change. Although as a teenager she was energized by the idea that she had the power to change her life and our world, she also recognized that everyone having the power to speak and act does not mean that coalition work is without risk.

In spite of her own bridge-building commitments, she acknowledged that at times consensus work can in fact be tokenizing, such that Black women are brought into organizations when the agenda is already set. She had worked for several years for the Human Rights Campaign, which at that time did not have Black women in its leadership or staff. She was criticized by her friends about working for a "predominantly white organization that doesn't even care about us." Her response to the critics was that she had "been a bridge builder all of my life who doesn't mind intentionally working with/in multiracial places." Yet despite this doubling down, the most effective consensus work happens when all participants work on a common cause: designing the bridge together or finding out who else needs to be in the room.

Cultivating Collaborative Leadership

Developing leadership through consensus building, through honing charisma, and through family/moral formation and education is how transformative and holistic justice can be achieved. Ultimately, that is the bridge each of the interviewees is seeking to build, yet they do so following what Debora Jackson regards as a womanist leadership approach, which "values the marginalized voices that are typically silenced because it understands the inherent complexities of intersectionality."[29] One method for ensuring vulnerable voices are at the center is by advocating for collaborative leadership.

Collaborative leadership stems from the leader's ability to share a vision with the community. For many of my interviewees, this shared goal is also a part of their sense of their calling or compulsion to pursue a certain purpose. A few participants were uncomfortable with the somewhat Christian language of "call" or vocation, but for those for whom it matched their realities, calling was never solely about what they were meant to do or be. Those persons felt compelled by a greater power to work toward holistic justice for all, and for them this negates the idea of call as individualistic and limiting. Stephen Lewis, Matthew Williams, and Dori Baker's leadership text, *Another Way*, posits that if a call centers around a single individual, this disconnects that person from the larger community.[30] Instead, it suggests conceiving of a calling as our shared purpose, for this helps persons think about how they are each meant to serve the common good. *Another Way* widens the concept of call and purpose by asserting that calling is contextual and communal. The authors believe that acknowledging this expanded understanding of calling is foundational for leadership.

An interviewee who reflected this expanded sense of calling in her leadership style is Bishop Tonyia Rawls. As founder and executive director of the

Freedom Center for Social Justice and pastor of the Sacred Souls Community Church, she led through collaboration, and this leadership style was animated by her spiritual calling. She spoke about learning to lead with compassion even the seemingly unforgivable because she believed God had given her the capacity as a bishop, pastor, and leader to "hear unthinkable things, to see things, and to feel things" and still be able to help move others through. One of the mechanisms that helped her to shepherd persons through dismal times was the realization that she was also specifically called to help other persons acknowledge their calling as religious leaders. When I asked her what that meant in daily practice, she explained:

> I focus a lot on calling. Again, all of my experiences . . . lead . . . up to this moment, [and] really prepared me for this kind of pastoring. . . . I genuinely believe everyone exits the womb with a call, with particular giftings for the ways we are called to serve the world. Anybody that ever came through our doors, I assumed they had a great call. It was just a general assumption, and [I assumed] that my job was not to give it to them but to help nurture it.

Bishop Rawls fundamentally believes that everyone has a call that must be discovered and nurtured. Nurturing the congregation's call meant connecting the community's needs to the congregation's abilities. She beamed with pride as she recounted how her members have excelled in leadership both in religious circles and in civic society as a result of having their calling cultivated in her church. For example, one of Charlotte's first out elected officials was a member of her church; her congregants helped start the South Carolina Black and Latino Pride and Charlotte's Black Pride weekends; and she has members "building bridges" in arenas to do with countering domestic violence, with education, with working with youths, and more. Watching her congregants thrive in these new roles is a testament to her belief that a church that is committed to social justice will raise up members who are called to work on behalf of social justice. She believes that our calling as religious leaders is for the world, and not just for our religious communities, so it is not surprising that her examples of raising religious leaders go beyond what is happening in the physical church.

Another interviewee whose focus on calling was similarly foundational to her collaborative leadership style is Rev. Darlene Franklin.

Rev. Darlene Franklin is an air force veteran and the former pastor of Full Truth Fellowship of Christ Church in Detroit. She is a radio show host and author

FIGURE 5.5. Reverend Darlene Franklin. Used by permission.

who is also a community activist working primarily in the arenas of domestic violence, substance abuse, Alzheimer's care, and HIV/AIDS *care. Rev. Franklin is not currently serving a religious community, but she and her wife have created a healing ministry outside of the confines of religious denominations.*[31]

My interview with Rev. Franklin happened at an interesting point in her life related to calling. She was just graduating from Wayne State University's Master of Social Work program, and she was starting a business called Live on Purpose Center for Creative Being, a creative counseling initiative. Personally, she was at a crossroads and reflecting on her leadership decisions and next steps. When she started in leadership at Full Truth, she was thrown into full-time ministry at a time when the community was reeling from AIDS deaths. She recounted that initially "it wasn't about you got a calling and now you go do seminary. That's not that type of ministry. That ministry was about literally saving people's lives." They were engaged in direct service, ministering to the physical needs of those who had been ostracized by their families, church, and medical communities. Thus, her first sense of calling to ministry was a response to the needs of her community. Eventually, she served that community as pastor, and during her tenure her calling and the church's purpose evolved beyond merely repeating and living by Unity Fellowship bishop Carl Bean's mantra that "God is love and love is for everybody." She wanted the congregation to realize that it was time for them to learn to be visible in their community, to lead by having members who went out into the places where they were not wanted, and to minister to the needs of the community.

In a way, her calling has always been outward facing and beyond the confines of a traditional church. Even in between religious positions, she has recognized that her religious leadership serves the purpose of helping herself and others tap into their purpose—hence the title of her counseling practice:

> Right now, my faith is about, especially at the age that I am, I have to work in what fulfills my destiny, if that makes sense. In other words, I can't just go and get a job, just because somebody's going to pay me. I have to be committed to, because I work with people, I can't just usher people in because the company's going to get so much. I have to really make an impact on people. I have to be about healing. I'm about healing. That comes in many ways. In a sentence, it is about, for my individual gifts are for people to get in contact with their purpose, as to why they are here at this time, breathing breath. What are you here to do?

Her consideration of her calling was intertwined with helping others discern their callings. Just like Bishop Rawls, she took for granted that God had endowed every person with a purpose to fulfill. Her mission was to help individuals acknowledge and live into their purpose. This sense of interdependence is also demonstrated in other interviewees' leadership styles.

Transformation and Holistic Justice via Collaborative Leadership Styles

Because this project's telos is the greater good and the holistic well-being of the planet and its inhabitants, this book amplifies collaborative leadership, which can be understood through various leadership styles. Ella Baker's style of community leadership is a worthy model. Because of her experiences with sexism and racism, she found leadership titles unnecessary and even a handicap. Instead, she argued that the "charismatic leader usually becomes a leader because he has found a spot in the public limelight."[32] She worried that acclaim would be persuasive enough to convince the leader that he was the movement without actually knowing and sharing the will of the people. Her own experiences battling men who were used to women in supportive but not leadership roles taught her that it was primarily the work of organizing people that mattered. During her work with the NAACP, SCLC, and SNCC, she promoted democratic and communal leadership by putting the organizations in the hands of their local constituents.

Baker's preference for group-centered leadership was well known. She believed that "what is needed is the development of people who are interested not in being leaders as much as in developing leadership among other people."[33] Although Baker eschewed the title *leader* and how it centralized power into one person, she was an advocate of teaching people to claim their own power, understanding that this taught self-sufficiency rather than dependence. The women I interviewed mirror the idea of teaching self-sufficiency and were all actively involved with teaching the next generation to find and live out their role in society. Learning self-sufficiency had also activated their ability to see how their personal struggles were interconnected.

In the examples of King and Thurman, Fluker presents another leadership style that is relevant to my understanding of womanist ethical leadership— that of the "relationist leader," who understands that humanity is interrelated and interdependent.[34] Fluker contends that our commitments to one another must be based on interdependence in community. Similarly, Toni King offers the term *communal leader* to describe someone who "contributes to a group's development and wholeness by assisting the group in valuing and drawing upon the talent of all its members to achieve an overarching vision."[35] Like Fluker, King highlights the symbiotic relationship of community members and reiterates that our communities have within them all that we need to pursue justice and freedom. The task of the communal leader is to help develop the group's talents and to develop new leadership from within. Part of the reason that my interviewees are able to risk collaborative leadership is because they have a deep belief in how our communities are connected and in how God has gifted each community with talented individuals who can serve the whole.

The model that comes closest to what I witnessed in my interviews and in researching the leadership of the eighteen Black lesbian religious leaders is the liberating leadership model espoused by Lewis, Williams, and Baker. Their chapter on liberating leadership shifts the focus to leadership that "seeks to dismantle the dominant forms of living and leading that reinforce the oppressive nature of empire." Such liberating leadership works within and beyond current structures to bring about transformation. It builds on the prior models discussed, with the emphasis on building the capacity of communities while moving beyond the imagined solo leader. Yet such liberating leadership also offers something new: it "creates space for *others* to speak their truths, to listen deeply to one another, and to determine the strategic direction that can best guide a community's collective action."[36] This new space relies on the gifts in the community and the community's vision, rejecting a messianic and charismatic leader in favor of trusted partnerships. Whereas this model most closely resembles the approaches of my interviewees, a major difference is that so many of the interviewees were in fact charismatic leaders to whom the community turned despite their best efforts to widen the leadership circle.

Leadership Style: Pluralistic and Entrepreneurial

Thus, collaborative leadership is a leadership style that emphasizes the role of the leader in helping shape the community's vision while valuing its input and investing in its sustainability. One leader of this type is Rabbi Sandra Lawson. When she joined a Reconstructionist synagogue in Atlanta, she landed in a lay-led community. She had been invited to attend by her friend and client Rabbi Josh Lesser, and she found a home within that community. The more at home she felt, the more leadership opportunities she accepted, which she later came to realize is part of what it means to belong to an active religious group, in this case within Judaism. But it is also the result of the type of congregation and the form of Judaism that she chose. As a Reconstructionist Jew in a synagogue that was initially not even led by a rabbi, she was joining a tradition that privileged lay leadership and the collaborative sharing of religious power. She recognized that her particular congregation "don't necessarily want to be led. They want to be guided, but not led from the top down." The congregation's comfort in sharing religious authority is also theologically oriented, for she contends that Reconstructionist seminaries do not train the rabbi to be the decision maker but rather that they are "more pluralistic and bring in other voices." Rabbi Lawson shares that because of Reconstructionist Judaism's focus on community, the group is accustomed to accepting, welcoming, and relying on the talents and gifts of its members. This is one of the reasons she is so adamant about claiming all of her identities in her religious authority because this means calling forth different gifts that are a part of her various identities. She also does this because in claiming all of her identities, she is demonstrating the need to expand and celebrate Jewish diversity. This religious training and prior experience created an alternative way for her to envisage her career path after attending rabbinical school.

As Rabbi Lawson contemplated what types of career options she might consider after rabbinical school, she was certain only that she wanted to be a "free-spirited rabbi who takes the Jewish imperative for *tikkun olam* seriously."[37] She leads from outside a traditional Jewish congregation, serving at the time of her interview as a chaplain at Elon University, and via her social media content. Often finding herself in uncharted territories for a rabbi, she depends on both physical and digital partnerships to make Judaism accessible to others. She calls herself an entrepreneurial rabbi who partners with nontraditional settings to connect wherever Jews are congregating. Her position at the Elon Hillel was to do outreach across her campus. The committee that hired her noted that what caught its attention was her "willingness to put others above herself," a trait that went beyond even the selection committee's criteria and expectations.[38] This sense of communal awareness is essential to her goal of creating a new type of rabbinate for herself.

Leadership Style: Empower the People

Rev. Darlene Franklin's sense of community leadership has propelled her into new definitions of her religious vocation. She rejects an individualistic calling because it does not fit with her leadership style. She described to me a variety of leadership experiences that she had had, from the military, to human services work, to her church. When pressed to define how she leads, she said, "I think I connect to people, if that's a leadership style. Anywhere I go, white, Black, Jewish community . . . I put people together, you know what I mean? My leadership style in my church was I don't have all the gifts." Rev. Franklin described a deliberative process of helping persons into leadership by discovering how they are particularly gifted, whether that meant ministry, singing, preaching, or some other area:

> If I had a church right now, I would not, like I see a lot of churches, the pastor on the pedestal, the pastor knows all. If I had a church right now, my congregation would be about, "What is God saying to you? I want you to get in touch with your inner voice. I want you to learn to trust your inner voice. What are you hearing? What are you feeling? What is your every day? Why are you here? Do you know that? Let's talk about that.

How do you feel about what's going on around you? Why are you here taking up space? What are you doing? What has God gifted you with?" That's what my church would be about, and that is the type of thing that I'm in the process of creating.

She felt especially called to help the most vulnerable societal members, those who had been silenced, to bring them into leadership in their communities:

That was what I was called to do and still am. I see something in you, and I'm going to give you the space to do it. That's my leadership style, if that's a style. If that's what you're looking for. That's my leadership style, empower the people. Everybody is worthy, everybody. I tell people, "You are not your circumstances." That's what I do now; I do substance abuse counseling. "You are not your circumstances. I don't care where you've been, you are not your circumstances. If you're still breathing, there's some life in there, there's some value in there, and there is some fire. We've got to get to it, so you can have a purpose for who you are."

She regarded this approach as a biblical mandate, following 1 Corinthians 12: 15–26, which discusses how various body parts learn that they are valued despite being differently gifted. She reiterates that the LGBTQ community should not throw away the Bible, for some of its lessons are edifying. In fact, her leadership style particularly emphasizes 1 Corinthians 12: 26, which states that "if one part suffers, every part suffers," and if one part flourishes, then so does the whole community. This reiterates her belief that because we are all interdependent, our communities thrive only if the most marginalized reach their full potential.

With time she realized that she was not creating the types of leaders at Full Truth that she desired and that she was losing herself in the process of being its pastor. She began to preach a unification message that was strangely similar to the other interviewees who had left Unity Fellowship Church Movement. In particular, she emphasized that Full Truth was not meant to be a traditional church and that it existed only because the Black community was oppressing its LGBTQ members. She noticed this same oppression and ostracization of other segments of the community. Rev. Franklin questioned how "in our fighting for equality as gay people, and justice or whatever, we turn around and we oppress those of our own? As a Black woman, lesbian, oppressed in all of those intersections, I began to think, 'Something's not right about this. Something is not feeling right about this for me. I've got to look at something else.'" She realized that she could not fulfill her leadership vision at Full Truth, and she resigned. Yet she does not see this as a personal failure but noted instead that this experience taught her that church is supposed to transform. After all, church is about a community, and communities change.

Similarly, Bishop Rawls reflected the perspective that attention to the community's needs means empowering them to engage their gifts. When she founded Unity Fellowship Church in Charlotte (UFC), she started with the assumption that everyone who joined had been called to be a leader. She admits that it took a great deal of patience to get persons who had been devalued by the church to find their place in its leadership team:

> We did a lot of things that weren't things that people would typically do for themselves or even see themselves as leaders. That was who they understood themselves to be. As leaders it was also important that we understand the points of how we also follow. In practice, what that looks like is enabling people to listen for their callings and then to also trust it and to be willing to have the support that's necessary to walk in the fullness of it.

Bishop Rawls notes that she was intent on molding persons of any age into leaders and that she expected and helped even children to grow into leadership by, for example, inviting them to preach and to count money with the church trustees. The congregation's novice leadership made great strides not only in learning to lead in their religious space; they also learned how to advocate in the greater community as persons of faith. She wrote in a book chapter about her UFC congregation that the "members of this congregation have helped transform this region. The empowerment they experienced in the church through simple acceptance led to empowerment in other areas of life."[39] She tried to model in her church leadership an openness that embraced the diversity in their changing church demographic and welcomed this diversity as a new infusion of talent.

When Bishop Rawls expanded her mission and left Unity Fellowship to create a new religious community called Sacred Souls Community Church, she continued her same leadership style of empowering others to lead. Her hope with her new church was to bring various communities together that spanned racial, national, and socioeconomic lines. She started by seeking an even broader ministry, for she felt God challenging her about leaving out non-LGBTQ communities.[40] She believed that being a true Christian meant caring for her neighbor. In Charlotte, for her and her community that meant stepping out of their comfort zones—even outside of the religious space.

Her commitment to collaborating across diverse perspectives is also reflected in her work with the Freedom Center for Social Justice, which accomplishes its mission through partnerships and advocacy with various groups. Although it had four main platforms (advocacy, community education, faith-based organizing, and campaigns), these are developed with some of the same principles expressed in her church and in her leadership style. For example, the Freedom Center's mission and vision statement delineates its organizational pillars as (1) belief in empowering each person to make significant lasting change as leaders in culture shift (the process of changing culture); (2) collaboration with other social justice organizations to advance the cause of justice for LGBTQ people and the marginalized; and (3) celebration of diversity, intentionally emphasizing the intersections of race, sexual orientation, gender identity, faith, age, and class.[41] The center achieves this vision through programming such as advancing the Equality Act through the North Carolina legislature; hosting the Transgender Faith and Action Retreat and Liberating Theologies Speaker series; the Yes, You Can Go restroom-safety campaign; and its national Do No Harm campaign, which asks clergy, public officials, and small-business owners not to use religion to create unsafe spaces. All of this programming is possible because the Freedom Center and its director really do rely on collaboration with partners, creating allies to promote transformational change. Acknowledging the value of effective partnerships has been a leadership skill since Bishop Rawls helped create the International Black Buyers and Manufacturers Expo and Conference in 1995. Although she has been criticized for seemingly cozying up to religious conservatives during her organizing in the South to fight for justice and LGBTQ rights, she speaks of their common ground around challenging such areas as education, poverty, homelessness, and health disparities as a means to address real issues harming entire communities, not just the LGBTQ community (though particularly pernicious for that community.)[42] Creating allies around issues of general justice is possible when collaborative leaders take the helm.

Leadership Style: Leading Up/Wagon-Wheel Leadership

One such quintessentially collaborative leader is Bishop Flunder. She relies on allies to tackle a host of social justice topics. In her particular advocacy on HIV/AIDS, she has worked with the Centers for Disease Control, the Congressional Black Caucus, the Department of Health and Human Services, the Gates Foundation, and numerous San Francisco and Oakland agencies. She has established a faith-based social justice 501c3 that promotes national networks offering education, training, and so forth to provide direct services such as medical case management, after-school programs, housing, meal support, and national and international advocacy for the social and moral inclusion of LGBTQ persons. She has also established The Fellowship of Affirming Ministries, an alliance of primarily Black-affirming churches and organizations in the United States, Africa, and Mexico. This commitment to shared responsibility when tackling large social issues is a result of her personal leadership philosophy that others can do the work and not be in competition with the other projects that she has undertaken. She sees herself as a "builder" who likes to "create new things and then hand them over." In handing over projects, she is not in the least bit afraid that her own work will be eclipsed or surpassed, and she is instead delighted to share in others' success. Having partners in the work for the common good is what makes it sustainable:

> I think that all those things have contributed to helping me to lead. So I think that that part of me that is a leader, it came with the package. I can believe I'm born with it. The thing is, the things that I've had to learn, and I'm still in the process of learning, have everything to do with what I'm called to, which is the third world in the United States, the inner city, and Third World of the world. . . . I think I'm pretty clear that I'm called to the inner city, and I'm constantly trying to find ways to make it affordable for our people to be their best and highest selves in the places that are the hardest and the most difficult places to do that. So in the literal sense, that means trying to find funding and find money to do the government's policy things that are necessary to make a literal success happen in the inner city. And the same was true, I think in the way that I, I work theologically trying to find theology that will enable people who have been kicked to the curb by virtue of their race, age, gender, gender expression, orientation, and all of that, to find ways for us to not only exist but to thrive.

She was clear that although the tools or partners she used to achieve her goals might vary, her commitment and trust in the partnerships to help her achieve her goals remain steady.

Bishop Flunder's confidence in the effectiveness of collaboration may have something to do with the scale of the ministries and enterprises for which she is responsible. A sensible leader in her position would realize the need for help. It also indicates a window into her leadership philosophy. She contends that by empowering others to flourish, she knows that they are happy with their roles and not in competition for her position. She is comforted by the fact that her coleaders are not somewhere waiting for her demise but are comfortable in their own leadership. She described the experience as one in which her coleaders "are mature people who have the graces that are needed to lead up . . . they critique me, they make recommendations to me. . . . They lead up [because] I don't know that I have the grace to do what a lot of the people who work with me and for me have the grace to do. And I'm grateful to God." She was grateful because she saw her leadership as the result of a bunch of people leading when others might not recognize them as being leaders.

Finally, Bishop Flunder's leadership and past experience and successes point to the effectiveness of collaboration. She has tested the leadership model in her own church. In the same way that Rev. Franklin used scripture to help her congregation recognize their value despite having different leadership roles, Bishop Flunder

> teach[es] a whole thing about changing or redesigning church from being a pyramid, where it's a top-down thing, to being a wagon-wheel concept, where we are all spokes, where we are all of our different ministry, including the worshipping community, that are equal distance between the hub and rim and they, each of these realities, one of them may be worshipping. The other one may be providing food, providing housing, providing public policy training. All of those things are necessary to have a faith-based organization in a city that we are called to. So that's a huge part of what I'm thinking about all the time and is on my mind in every major metropolis that we work in.

Her image of wagon-wheel spokes evokes a unified and strong community that works together to achieve the vision of justice. Leadership from the center of the wagon wheel ensures that the organization is headed toward a common goal.

Leadership Style: Lifting as We Climb/
Never the Last Leader

A final leadership style I found among my interviewees was the sense of duty to ensure that others are capable of leading. During my 2010 interview with Elder Darlene Garner, we talked quite a bit about her legacy in the

Metropolitan Community Churches. She was the highest-ranking African American in the denomination for some time and was close to being elected its moderator in 2016. She told me that she had felt called to MCC because of its commitment to diversity and human rights. She experienced it as "Heaven on Earth" because everyone was able to use their gifts and there was initially an integrity in collectively pursuing justice. When she was first elected to the Board of Elders in 1993, she was elected by a majority of the delegates of the entire church, persons she believed saw trustworthy leadership qualities in her. Over the course of time, they recognized that part of her responsibility as a leader was to lift others as she climbed the rungs of leadership. She recognized that "being the first spiritual leader of African descent in MCC [meant] a responsibility to make sure that [she] was not the last leader." Ironically, ten years later, she was essentially forced to retire from the church. Many of its Black leaders left in protest over her treatment. Despite this unforeseeable outcome, her legacy within the MCC is of promoting leadership, especially among more marginalized community members.

Likewise, Rabbi Sandra Lawson has taken as a personal mission the role of ambassador for the Jewish community in an effort to diversify the tradition. After her experience of serving as a representative for the Jewish community at an LGBTQ memorial service for Coretta Scott King, she realized that as a Black Jew she could bring several different communities together. Perhaps because she has been forced to defend her Jewishness in so many arenas, she noted that she "wants to get to a point where when I Google 'rabbi' I see someone other than a bearded white guy."[43] In our interview she noted that she tended to accept social media friend requests from strangers so that others are aware of the racial and ethnic diversity within the Jewish community and within Jewish leadership. Yet her push to acknowledge diversity is not just about image. She is intently interested in being involved with bridge building across identities. For the 2020 Juneteenth celebration, she participated in a Juneteenth Kabbalat Shabbat with another Black lesbian university rabbi, Isaama Goldstein-Stoll, that had seven thousand people watching via Facebook and Zoom.[44] This was a national service sponsored by Be'chol Lashon, a Jews-of-color organization. It highlighted the impact of diverse Jewish leadership for many new audiences, capitalizing on the growing public interest in race because of the Black Lives Matter movement and the 2020 summer of racial unrest. Her commitment to representation is also tied to the necessity of building relationships, a value she learned from her mentor. Rabbi Lawson's desire not to be the last such rabbi and to lift others into Jewish leadership is especially needed to advance social justice.

Leadership Development

None of these leaders assumed that their sterling examples would be enough to bring others into leadership. Each actively implemented structures of leadership development for their community. For example, Elder Darlene Garner created the MCC Conference for People of African Descent in 1997. The triennial conference was a manifestation of her desire to improve the spiritual life of people of faith who are of African descent:

> The reason that we do this conference is to . . . recogniz[e] that in many parts of the country, it is very easy for there to be only one person of African descent in a church, and so it can be a very isolating experience. So we do this conference as a way to empower and encourage people of African descent to make MCC their home, to make it look like them, feel like them, and just know that there is space, there is space for all of us in this thing that we call MCC.
>
> So we do a lot of focus on leadership development, on helping people to network with one another. We encourage people who are considering the possibility of answering a call to professional ministry. We always make sure that there are at least five seminaries [re]present[ed], seminaries that kind of have a track record of being relevant to LGBT people and LGBT people of African descent, in particular—being relevant and being open to our students succeeding in their academic setting.[45]

This conference is the second-largest one that the MCC hosts, and she was immensely proud of its reputation for providing practical resources for leadership and spiritual development.

Bishop Flunder's Fellowship of Affirming Ministries (TFAM) serves a similar social and leadership function for its participants. According to its website, TFAM supports religious leaders and laity in moving toward radical inclusivity. Bishop Flunder teaches that radical inclusivity is the "intentional inclusion of all persons; especially people who have traditionally lived at the margins of society," and that it requires a radical social ministry to serve those most marginalized.[46] Yet she rightly does not assume that the assembled congregations and organizations will have any clue about how to create this signature mission. Thus, TFAM serves as a network of "collaborative support" so that persons can learn from one another and be taught how to train others into a new more inclusive theology. They seek to be change agents, but they recognize that to do so, persons must have the tools to "lead up."

Bishop Flunder noted that she tries very hard to expose TFAM leaders and churches to some of the best cutting-edge theologies because knowledge is power. She contends that "lots of [their] training opportunities [are] conversations about cutting-edge issues to reframe our thinking and our work out there in the world. It's critically important that we see the intersections of the justice issue."[47] The organizational structure of TFAM is open because of its trans-denominational identity, so as people train, they also combine leadership skills and styles from a variety of sources. The approximately one hundred congregations and organizations over which she has oversight require some structure for things like ordinations, installations, and elevations, but she sees TFAM's conferences and meetings as opportunities for "leadership development, information dissemination and cross-pollination, worship, and as opportunities to showcase gifts and skills, choirs, and dancers, and preachers . . . for the work of liberation." Serving as presiding bishop of such a large enterprise demands that she use partners and her executive committee to train and lead others.

Another interviewee who incorporated educational training in how she developed others as leaders is Bishop Rawls. One of her Freedom Center's platforms is education; she believes that to shift culture requires a reeducation of communities. The Freedom Center has several initiatives devoted to faith-based education around transgender community concerns. One such initiative is its Trans Seminarian Cohort, a year-long leadership development program for transgender and genderqueer seminarians that is cosponsored by the National LGBTQ Task Force and the Center for LGBTQ and Gender Studies in Religion at the Pacific School of Religion. Its goals are to "encourage trans students during their training for religious leadership . . . to embrace the fact that their impact as faith leaders can and should extend beyond their chosen settings for ministry and service to include the welfare of the broader communities."[48] The Freedom Center encourages these cohort members to participate in its educational Transgender Faith and Action Retreat, at which they are trained and equipped to go out and teach others.

Similarly, Rev. Franklin encouraged her congregation at Full Truth to pursue education as a means of preparing them for leadership. She remembered telling congregants: "You want to minister; you want to be deacons.

We don't have any college education to move on into a seminary . . . [, but] we can start somewhere." She started them out with an evangelical school that allowed members to earn bachelor's degrees (albeit unaccredited ones), and she remarked how, more than just a degree, this gave the membership a sense of accomplishment. Within that same congregation, Rev. Renee McCoy also promoted education as a key tool for training persons for religious leadership. She started this process by earning her own doctorate, but the lack of educational training for leadership was a bone of contention between her and the Unity Fellowship structure. She felt that Unity should have required its leaders to go to seminary but that its reliance on the Holy Ghost instead left people unprepared in many avenues of ministry:

> People will criticize me, but I went back to school because I had done everything I could with what I had. I had done a lot. But I realized that what an education does in the trenches is that it enables you to crawl out of the trenches and begin to throw those tools back into those trenches so other people can crawl out. If you don't get that basic education, you are unable to throw back the tools that will keep people from . . . they can grab hold, but the tools won't grab hold, you know? And so for me, going back to school was my way of . . . be[coming] able to throw those tools back into the trenches.
>
> And if we're serious about ministry, that's what we do. We get the tools, and we help people not so that they can just say hallelujah and, you know, on Sunday, but so that they can have better lives, fuller lives, richer lives, so that they can raise families, so that they can have quality lives. It's not just about finding out you're all right 'cause you're gay. Shit, you knew that. Now what?

For Rev. Renee, education is the tool necessary for future leaders. Thus, it makes sense that Rev. Darlene Franklin, who had been trained by Rev. Renee, promoted the benefits of education during her tenure as pastor.

Achieving Transformational and Holistic Justice

This chapter has emphasized collaborative leadership as a primary model of womanist ethical leadership not because my interviewees preferred the term, because they needed the help for collaboration to become key, or because it was sustainable for them as they aged. Rather, collaborative leadership is an effective model because it is community inspired and led, which is how transformative and holistic justice is achieved. Yet holistic justice is a momentous task, and it is hard to measure its success.

In *Another Way* the authors observe that the typical determination of a leader's success is through products—achievements such as awards, budgets, honors—that decide whether a leader has achieved particular goals and objectives.[49] In the initial slate of interviewees, I also fell victim to this logic, privileging leaders who had amassed critical acclaim and were regarded as being at the pinnacle of their religious communities. When I began expanding my list to include younger and more religiously diverse Black lesbian leaders, I bristled at the privileging of institutional leaders over others. For example, one of my criticisms of Robert Franklin's depiction of moral leadership is his reliance on moral leaders as persons who "invest in the next generation by building enduring institutions."[50] As a former university president, his personal investment in institutions is understandable, and in a way each of my interviewees also demonstrated a commitment to the next generation, which sometimes included institutions, denominations, organizations, and so on. Yet more typically, my interviewees shared an ambivalence toward institutions that had at every turn blocked their access and thriving, as depicted in Dean Townes's view that everybody is expendable in an institution, so "don't ever cast your lot with an institution. Cast your lot with people."[51]

Instead, one could measure the leaders' success in terms of how the leaders were "built." *Another Way* is curious about what it would mean to focus on the process of leadership rather than its products. This requires attention to the hows of leadership—how we listen, engage in dialogue, organize time, receive and integrate feedback, convene and connect people, manage organizations, build leadership in others, motivate and mobilize collective action, and tend to our inner lives.[52] Achieving holistic justice may be a lifelong journey, so measuring the process as progress is a more transformative way to lead. Bishop Rawls would agree. She noted that this is the more difficult task—"to think about how we pastor, how we are bishops, how we are leaders"—but that taking the more difficult path was ultimately the way to help the most people.

This attention to people and places and favoring the process over products may in fact offer a more sustainable model leadership than the solitary-savior model of leadership that tends to be perpetuated. If one builds a better leader, that leader should take on the same process to build on their own success. As Bishop Flunder noted, she sees her collaborators' and mentees' success as her own personal success and considers this to be the way in which the work of holistic justice continues. It is also a more sustainable model because it anticipates leadership burnout—the point at which every leader needs to step away to preserve their own sanity and health. Most of my leaders had walked away from something that they had built, but I notice that they were able to do so because they had previously put into place provisions to continue the work. This is extremely important for helping institutions weather leadership transitions. For if they have already been trained to rely on the talents within their communities, then when it is time for new leadership, they can be confident that a new leader is probably already in their midst.

Collaborative leadership also offers a mechanism by which leaders can be present at any age or stage of life. Bishop Rawls trained children and teenagers for leadership so that they knew from an early age that great leadership is possible in people of all ages and stages of life, not only in mature adults. Bishop Flunder encourages leadership across denominational traditions and even races. Bishop Abrams's church started a wellness center that has created leaders in immigration reform because they shared a building and conversations with lots of immigrants. Leadership theorist Jean Lipman-Blumen terms this philosophy "connective leadership." It is a model in which many persons share the burdens of leadership and leaders all learn to be "equally comfortable members of the team, as behind-the-scenes helpers, or as facilitators and mentors."[53] Former Auburn Seminary president Kathleen Henderson notes that by highlighting the egalitarian nature of leadership as available to any and all, collaborative leadership can actually be more appealing and draw in a more diverse cast of potential leaders.

As much as this chapter advocates for collaborative leadership, I remain aware of the dangers of this leadership style. Collaboration and interdependence entail vulnerability. They mean that you may find yourself in partnership with someone who is not actually interested in sharing power but seeks to eclipse you. My interviewees did not hide the costs of their leadership decisions. Bishop Flunder spoke about the personal costs of leadership to her, and Bishop Rawls referenced the "high physical price in terms of weight and strength and health . . . [and the] high emotional prices" of doing the work. Not one leader hinted that collaboration meant less toil; in fact, they were aware of the added headaches that come from sharing a load.

Cooperation does not undo power inequities. In the ebbs and flows of shared leadership, some people are not going to rise to the challenge as quickly as needed or may rise and abuse their power. Although the leadership-development practices make access to leadership skills available to all, we are not equally talented. Rev. Franklin reminisced over her work with a minister at her church who was a talented musician but not as gifted as a minister. Sharing responsibilities meant encouraging him in ways that would be best for the congregation. She shared with him that "if you play the organ before you get up to preach, you will have just what you're looking for," but he was offended and never played the organ again, despite his gift being in music. She took the same philosophy about her activist engagement. In an article devoted to Black Pride, she suggested that rather than relying on private funders or the larger white gay and lesbian organizations, the Black LGBTQ people in Detroit needed to find their own voice.[54] On the surface this is not controversial and perhaps just ethnic pride, but in practice this means advocating for Pride without the infrastructures gifted by white funders, such as organizational connections useful for navigating the city's regulations. Cooperation does not guarantee that an event will be successful, but it does build better leadership capacity.

This is why when I interviewed Rev. Renee, she expressed that she was most proud of Full Truth. Although she considered it "a piece of shit right now," she was proud of the fact that "there are people [there] that know that God loves them, that God's not mad at them, and that God is faithful . . . that something in [her] life had empowered other people to believe in God's faithfulness and through [her] life God demonstrated love and compassion and caring." Both she and Rev. Franklin had real concerns with the stability of Full Truth as a congregation, but they had full confidence in it as a community. This is success, not whether they still own the building ten years from now.

Although Rev. Renee can find Full Truth's current state "shitty," the fact that it is logistically messy and sometimes even impractical is one of the risks of collaborative leadership. My favorite example of this is the case of Bishop Rawls splitting from Unity Fellowship Movement Church. When she decided to leave Unity for the United Church of Christ (UCC) denomination, she wanted to do so without causing a schism. At that time, she was vice president of the Unity national board and working with the day-to-day operations of the denomination. She knew that extracting herself would be tricky. In fact, the most complex task turned out to be related to her physical church. Unity Fellowship Church Charlotte had bought a building, and she and her coleaders' *verbal* agreement was that after a congregational vote, whichever leader had the most congregants would keep the church building. The majority of the congregation chose to come with her to form a new UCC church, but the ten people remaining in the Unity denomination would not relinquish ownership of the church. Ultimately, she admits she "hadn't done the stuff [she] should have done legally on the front end," and she had relied on their verbal agreement to protect the property. To make the transition, her new UCC congregation had to buy the church back from the ten members staying in Unity. She admits it was "extremely painful" (the building was almost paid off when they split), but the bittersweet lesson from "having to buy the same building twice" was that she "grew a lot as a leader through that process." One of her former co-pastors still leads the Unity Charlotte church, and as a result they have done the "work of healing between the two congregations" because they are still her family. This painful example of personal vulnerability, betrayed trust, and perhaps even naïveté in leadership demonstrates that there are potential land mines in undertaking this collaborative leadership approach but that if one is cautious and attentive, the process to transformative and holistic justice can be worthwhile.

Nonetheless, collaborative leadership as exemplified in the narratives of these ten interviewees is a means to study how we are making and sustaining leaders for the next generation. According to Phyllis Leffler's *Black Leaders on Leadership*, scholars tend to place less significance on the *individual* traits and attributes of Black leaders.[55] This chapter has done the opposite, choosing to examine *collective* leadership as a trait of a womanist ethical leader. This book dives deeply into the four traits (authenticity, social justice consciousness, spirituality, and collective leadership) because of the need to study Black women's leadership in a different way. As moral agents, these Black lesbian religious leaders demonstrate how these traits are available to all. Unlike the moral exemplars of Martin Luther King Jr. or Howard Thurman or even Sojourner Truth, these women's narratives illustrate that our society can use more than one leader at a time. Black America can have more than one spokesperson for justice. Our leaders do not have to fit a single mold—being male and Christian—nor do they have to represent any one age or other demographic. The book's conclusion considers the advances of queer leadership models for ethical leadership and sustained social change.

Conclusion

Leading from the Margins

All that you touch you change. All that you change changes you.
—OCTAVIA BUTLER, *Parable of the Sower*

I name myself "lesbian" because I want to be visible to other Black lesbians. I name myself "lesbian" because I do not subscribe to predatory/institutionalized heterosexuality. I name myself "lesbian" because I want to be with women (and they don't all have to call themselves "lesbians"). I name myself "lesbian" because being woman-identified has kept me sane. I call myself "Black," too because Black is my perspective, my aesthetic, my politics, my vision, my sanity.
—CHERYL CLARKE, "New Notes on Lesbianism"

When I first sat down with the hundreds of pages of transcripts from the oral histories, I was overwhelmed and not quite sure where to start. I had thoughts, but I did not yet have the road map to get my audience there. So I called a dear friend hoping to complain and then eventually recenter myself. Yet the conversation did more than recenter me; it also provided a new lens for thinking about the book. Albert Smith, my friend since my doctoral program in Nashville, was now a director of Diversity and Inclusion and the founder and principal consultant of a boutique consulting firm. Because he is a trusted, knowledgeable source and a Black gay man, I hoped he would understand my dilemma in trying to bring these diverse queer leaders' stories to light. He and I talked about the benefits of queer leaders in the marketplace, and he asked me why I was writing on leadership. As I stumbled for the impact I hoped to make, he pondered out loud: What if your contribution is a leadership book for queer leaders?

Immediately, I felt energized as he and I hypothesized how this book could provide a means of displaying queer leadership styles as models for others to emulate. What if my purpose was not to convince heterosexuals of the "morality" of these leaders but rather to demonstrate that queer leaders could become the standard for ethical leadership? His questions pushed me to reflect beyond prescriptive analysis to the utility of using frameworks oriented for heterosexual people. This meant I would need to focus on the particularities of Black lesbian religious identity to understand their queer leadership capacities. Yet as an ethicist, I had an obligation to avoid the trap that Audre Lorde warned us about when she posited that "lesbians and gay men are expected to educate the heterosexual world. The oppressors maintain their position and evade responsibility for their own actions."[1] Thus, this research could not be about just educating the dominant group; in fact, the goal should be to provide queer leaders with the tools they would need for sustained social change.

In this regard, I hoped to contribute to the scholarship on ethical leadership, moving beyond the Black women's club movement or civil rights movement for ethical leadership models. I agreed with womanist-activist Renee Hill, who contended that too often LGBTQ people are seen as a problem to be solved instead of persons worthy of dignity, respect, and liberation.[2] I wondered what it could mean to see this group of people as the solution rather than the problem. Thus, this chapter interrogates Black queer leadership and specifically Black lesbian models of religious leadership. It concludes with an overview of the promise of such leadership models for scholarship on ethical leadership.[3]

Defining Queer Leadership

Theorizing on queer leadership is a relatively modern concept that coincides with the adoption of *queer* as a positive identity for LGBTQ persons. Theologian Patrick Cheng discusses *queer* as an umbrella term that refers collectively to LGBTQ persons and those who identify with nonnormative sexualities and/or gender identities.[4] He also describes *queer* as transgressive action that disrupts the status quo. Taking this starting point, it should be noted that this chapter does not provide a genealogy of the reclaiming of the term or even provide more than a glancing reference to the academization of queer theory via Teresa de Lauretis and others. Instead, this chapter focuses on discussions of queer leadership within leadership literature in general and specifically within conversations on ethical leadership within Black religion.

Queer leadership is a burgeoning subfield of leadership scholarship that matches the growing research on the impact of queer experiences in the workplace. Organizational and workplace literature highlights discrimination experienced by LGBTQ persons and only recently began to investigate the "characteristics and perspectives that sexual minorities bring to the leadership process."[5] One interlocutor from education leadership scholarship who addresses this omission is Jonathan Pryor. He contends that queer leaders who identify as LGBTQ should not exclude the other pertinent social identities in their leadership because identity is an important aspect of grassroots leadership.[6] Thus, the queer leader centers her queer experiences as central to her leadership practice and efforts to disrupt the status quo. Pryor's subsequent work defines queer leadership as the "intentional process to advance equity for sexual and gender minoritized communities through grassroot leadership strategies," and he conceives of the queer leader as one who challenges hetero/cisnormative practices.[7] His definition is useful, but it is perhaps too narrow in its application, given his prior understanding of the various identity commitments that a leader might have. His queer lens acknowledges race and gender but presumes that these identities will be subsumed under lesbian identity in their efforts to disrupt heterosexism. The women in this study are equally Black lesbian religious leaders: they do not have the luxury of privileging one identity formation over another. As Cheryl Clarke alludes in the opening epigraph, it matters that they are Black queer women, for this shapes how their leadership has been formed and how it will be perceived.

Black Female Leadership

Womanist scholar-activist Melina Abdullah reminds us that for Black women, leadership has been a means of redesigning power structures to include their realities. She engages nineteenth-century Black women's leadership, positing that Black women's alternative leadership model has bridged theory with practice, proactively centered collaborative leadership, and used both traditional and nontraditional forms of activism.[8] Historically, Black female leadership has another vision beyond protests and political reforms, and Black female leaders are diverse yet indicative of their experiences in fighting intersectional oppressions. When sociologist Beverlyn Lundy Allen assesses more contemporary depictions of Black female leadership, she focuses on the survival techniques, the Black female networks, and the collective experience and action toward community empowerment that encompasses Black female leadership.[9] She points out their reluctant association with the term *leader*, preferring instead other terms that emphasize the collective efforts involved in community leadership while questioning if this difference accounts for their marginalization in leadership and sociological studies.

This difference in style and in terminology may account for the dearth of Black women's experiences accounted for in leadership studies. My research with Black lesbian religious leaders indicates that perhaps it is more than a classification issue. If queer and Black leadership theorizing is correct and identity constructions matter, the unique subjectivities of the women interviewed go beyond the burgeoning arena of queer leadership or Black female leadership literature. In fact, this is what Cherríe Moraga and Gloria Anzaldúa had in mind when they crafted their concept of "theory in the flesh" as an idea that deeply appreciates the diversity of one's life experience and sees this diversity as how we relate to the world and create justice in this world.[10] This method links theory with embodied resistance, noting the importance of their various identities. By our insisting on discussing the Black female, queer, feminist, religious experience and its impact on leadership decisions and followers, these interviewees' lives can expand and intersect into various subfields and disciplines.

One way this is done is through an explication of the term *leader* and its usefulness for Black lesbian religious subjects. Chapter 3 indicates some of the ambivalence reported around the term *activist*, and I expected to see a similar response to being seen as a leader. Despite the literature that abounds with women's aversion to the term *leader* (and Toni King and S. Alease Ferguson's discussion of Black women specifically distancing these writers from the term), only one of my interviewees reported discomfort with being called a leader.[11] This was surprising as even the one standout—Buddhist lay leader Dr. Pamela "Ayo" Yetunde—admitted that her ambivalence around being considered a Buddhist leader was the result of the projections that she felt that are placed on leaders, not an aversion to actually leading. She acknowledged that she had been "trained as a Buddhist lay leader. In chaplaincy settings, we are called to be leaders for the community. And interestingly, when it comes to doing leadership things, I did not have a problem with that." Her issues with the leadership title came from being expected to look a certain way or to be held at a higher standard than others. This matches the historical association of leader with elitist ideas of control or even egoism.[12]

Black Lesbian Religious Leadership

My interviewees were predominantly Christian, and perhaps religious background had more of an influence on leadership identity than I anticipated. Thus, the fact that the other seventeen women interviewed expressed no issues with being known as a leader made me ponder whether Black lesbian leadership in general had less tension than Black female leaders (or female leaders in general) had with the term. Again, this points to their unique subjectivities as Black lesbian religious leaders as worthy of study. Concurring with the work of Black feminist scientist Evelynn Hammonds, my research agrees that "Black lesbian sexualities are not simply identities. Rather, they represent discursive and material terrains where there exists the possibility for the active production of speech, desire, . . . agency," and leadership.[13]

Black lesbian religious leadership offers new possibilities both of imagining oneself as a leader and imagining what types of leadership roles that one inhabits. When interviewed regarding how she created a welcoming and affirming congregation, Rev. Deborah Johnson also alluded to her leadership as a space of queer possibilities. She recounted that part of her congregation's calling was to be "pioneers of possibility living in Oneness," and she embraces this value and propels it as leader, resulting in a congregation that has largely adjusted to living and teaching inclusion.[14]

Pioneering possibility did not always look like standard pastoral ministry, and it was perhaps the diversity of leadership possibilities expressed that was so intriguing about these interviewees. For example, almost half of them had served on boards, almost half were teaching or had taught in academic settings, and several had started their own 501c foundations. Six interviewees had even started their own consulting agencies and were actively serving the public, private, and nonprofit sectors. In essence, they were in charge of training future leaders. None of the interviewees' leadership was limited to just religious spaces, and this may be the reason that so many were accepting of the leadership mantle. They were recognized in so many varied spaces as leaders that they were apt to accept this identity.

Another reason why Black lesbian religious leadership led to generative community possibilities is because of their connection to their religious communities. They were not just appointed leaders, but they arose as leaders in their particular religious spaces. Ethicist Victor Anderson speaks about this generativity in overwhelmingly positive ways because he attributes the presence of same-sex-loving members as ironically keeping Black churches open to the "newness of life and the creativity it fosters and flourishes."[15] He contends that Black same-sex-loving members keep the Black church sexually honest because as members they have buy-in to the community. Their presence in these spaces confirms and perhaps normalizes sexual difference, and because they are community members, they remain connected in ways that can create lasting change. This is possible in the case of my interviewees because they live their authenticity as lesbians.

Highlighting their Black lesbian religious leadership as defined by creative opportunities is also meant to shine a light on the distinctiveness of their style of queer leadership. Not only are they eager to accept the leader label; they are also willing to remain tied to a religious community, unlike what is reflected in studies done with lesbians of other races. Sociologist Melissa Wilcox conducted an important book-length study of queer women in the Los Angeles area and concurred with other congregational studies that lesbian, bisexual, and transgendered women were largely absent from religious spaces. She queried the explanation for the dearth of women in the studies conducted and found that sampling bias accounted for some of the eliding of lesbian women in current studies: the data polling from LGBTQ congregations or mainline Protestant denominations misses participants who are sporadic attendees or are attending alternative religions. This is significant because it may explain why both E. Patrick Johnson and Horace Griffin's studies indicated an absence of Black lesbian women in traditional religious spaces. Although this remains baffling to me, given my research and my experiences in Black churches, Wilcox's book does offer some additional answers that were missing from the previously mentioned studies. She reasoned that race, ethnicity, and culture do make a huge difference in the frequency and importance of religious affiliation for lesbian women. For example, all three of the Black women from her study were regular religious attendees, and more than three-fifths of the women of color in her study were regular attendees versus just one-third of white women.[16]

Another persuasive observation that Wilcox presented is that gendered leadership also makes a difference in lesbian religious attendance: typically, when lesbian women held the senior leadership position in a religious community, the congregation's gender balance tipped significantly in favor of women.[17] Because the qualitative studies that have been conducted on the

LGBTQ religious community tend to highlight religious spaces with larger numbers of male and/or and white leaders, it then follows that the resulting data pool is skewed to have fewer women and thus fewer Black women. This also helps explain why my experiences with Black lesbian religious leaders were so strikingly different: I attended several of their worship services and found not surprisingly larger numbers of Black lesbian women attendees.

Their identities as Black lesbian religious leaders most certainly provided a difference in how their queer leadership should be interpreted. For example, when examining what Rev. Irene Monroe calls the "homosexual patriarchy" of LGBTQ communities that maintain men in religious power, one should pay attention to how women leaders are followed.[18] It is not enough to just increase the number of female attendees in religious or even secular communities. The genius of queer leadership is that it points the way to a restructuring of patriarchal norms to provide new possibilities for communities. Yet the steps involved with liberating communities is more than just who gets to be in charge. For instance, in Rev. Deborah's leadership role she is quick to point out that despite being in a community that is favorable regarding racial diversity and LGBTQ issues, the challenge for her space was in "assisting new members in adjusting to the more inclusive environment. Most lack skills in interacting with such levels of diversity, especially with lesbians of color in positions of authority."[19] She leads with compassion and the awareness that for many, the learning curve will be steep. She also provides concrete trainings and conflict resolution to help persons unlearn the supremacist fallacies that have held up their lives.

Likewise, Bishop Flunder acknowledges that this work of unlearning is just as necessary in LGBTQ communities because of the need to resist internalized homophobia. She started with in-depth trainings of human sexuality as a means of helping those who followed her come to an understanding of a positive sexual theology. Then she worked to connect social justice to their understanding of what it means to be a follower of Christ. She is determined about her goal to support radically inclusive congregations, which means that her supporters must also support the vision that is descriptively laid out on the Fellowship website.

Bishop Tonyia Rawls is also aware that sidestepping the obstacles put into place for queer leadership requires deliberate planning, both spiritual and physical. She remarked that pastors and faith leaders of welcoming congregations must lead while knowing that the followers may be hesitant to follow a new type of leader or ministry. She advised having confidence in what God had called one to do but also seeking buy-in from one's leadership team via sharing the message/vision. One of her practical steps was to "give people permission to journey," understanding that although the Holy Spirit does not have communication problems, people may need space to accept and understand a new way of being.[20] Another interesting practical step that she advocated was to avoid careerism or to avoid making decisions based on how it will affect church attendance or standing within the larger community. Her queer leadership vision was bold but also compassionate; she acknowledged that sometimes not everyone will stay on the justice journey but that the good work still continues.

One of the greatest benefits of queer leadership is its dogged pursuit of holistic justice. This was evident for each of my interviewees, who accepted the perhaps never-ending journey while continuing to train others for authentically, spiritual, communal, justice-oriented lives. Angela Davis advocates the comprehensive nature of queer leadership as effective leadership, positing that the "most effective Black leadership will be leadership not simply for Black people but leadership for all people . . . and rather than go backwards and talk in terms that excluded people of color, that excluded women, that excluded transgender people, that excluded LGBTQ communities, then we have to find a language that is all embracing."[21] Even though queer leadership is a burgeoning category and its attributes are still being fully developed and acknowledged, it has the potential to be the new, all-embracing language that Davis is calling for.

In chapter 5's focus on collaborative leadership styles, I highlight ways this emphasis on wholeness for their communities is paramount to all-embracing leadership and point out that this often means seeking the multiple roots of oppression or doing justice work from an intersectional framework. Renee Hill described this as the multiplicity of oppression, which demands leadership that addresses wide-ranging oppressions and identities. She talked about how as a leader she had to be transparent about how she perpetuated certain oppressions and work to end her contributions by acknowledging her privilege. Hill asserted this awareness is a "unique role for leadership" because of the "incredible resistance all the way around for people to be guided by that leadership."[22] She contends that there is a unique leadership role for lesbians and gay men of color but that their leadership must be distinctive because of their commitments to holistic justice, not just because of their multiple identities. Thus, when Rev. Renee McCoy jokingly tells me that as a Black lesbian she never had the luxury to not work on multiple things or when Rabbi Lawson cannot even remember a queer friend who was not involved in multiple arenas of social justice advocacy, they are both working from an intersectional frame.

Learning from History and Creating New Agendas

Although scholarship may be taking its time to theorize from the perspectives of queer leaders, queer leaders' lives theorize miles ahead of scholarly analysis. A simple genealogy of queer leaders' historical accomplishments should make this point, and my interviewees were present for each of these moments. They were on the ground at Stonewall and other protests for gay liberation; they fought both in and outside of the military for the demise of Don't Ask Don't Tell; they labored on the front lines for marriage equality (while simultaneously working to inform the media and lesbian/gay organizers that liberation required more than marriage); they campaigned and served the first Black president, who also happened to support LGBT concerns; they supported those initially dying (and now living longer lives) because of HIV/AIDS; they taught students during the seismic shift when sizable numbers of LGBTQ students and nonqueer allies could be trained by out lesbian educators; and they advocated for antidiscrimination policies to protect transgender people.[23] The interviewees who were sixty or seventy years old were particularly active in founding national organizations for Black LGBTQ persons during a time when such institutions did not exist. Several were cofounders of the National Coalition of Black Lesbians and Gays in 1978 (Mandy Carter, Renee McCoy, and Darlene Garner), and two were founders of the National Black Gay and Lesbian Leadership Forum in 1987 and the National Black Justice Coalition in 2003 (Sylvia Rhue and Mandy Carter). Their organizing made room for others, but these senior interviewees did not stop organizing just because a younger generation was on the scene. On the contrary, each of these women was taking part in contemporary organizations as mentors and activists.

This multigenerational work is encouraging because they are still participating in the long arc of justice, recognizing that this is a requirement for committing to social change. Because the ultimate goal is holistic justice and liberation for the planet and its inhabitants, the emphasis is not on individuals but on the social movements that are bringing about a restructuring of society. Whether the interviewee is seventy-three or thirty-seven, her participation reflects a similar drive to work toward making liberation possible here on Earth. None has let their spirituality relieve them from a responsibility to advocate on the behalf of the most marginalized. Yes, they believe in God's working in the world, but they all approach this work from a humanistic standpoint—people must manifest paradise and peace without waiting for these to be gifted by supernatural fiat.

Both Black and LGBT history had shown my interviewees that they could neither afford to wait until they were adults to act nor rest on their laurels as seniors in these movements. Bishop Flunder's interview indicated that the intergenerational mentoring in which she participated was to show the next generation a pathway forward but also to make her living not be in vain. They tended to participate in nonhierarchal leadership like collaborative efforts rather than apprentice models because collaboration made space for younger activists to take ownership and action now, instead of waiting for elders to die or move out of the movement. The younger interviewees also tended to participate in nonhierarchal leadership in organizations led by other younger activists who share leadership.

In addition to being intergenerational, nonhierarchal/collaborative, and female-led, another marker of queer leadership represented in my interviewees' lives is their para-institutional orientation toward leadership. The previous chapters detailed how many of these women were purposely left outside of societal hierarchies, but another reason that Black lesbian religious leaders turn toward para-institutional leadership is because it gives them the opportunity to work with numerous partners/organizations to address their multiplicity of oppressions. In their interviews they shared the desire to avoid going to various places to advocate for their various identities and wanting to work from one platform on a multitude of issues. Their lives confirmed Black feminist poet Audre Lorde's comments that "there is no hierarchy of oppression," such that when they are within the lesbian community, they are still Black, and within the Black community, they are still lesbian, so any attack against LGBTQ persons is also an attack on Black persons and vice versa.[24] My interviewees knew like Sister Audre that they could not afford to fight only one oppression at a time. Intersectional frameworks required attention to their race, religious, and sexual identities. This is the promise of queer religious leadership, which I view as womanist in its orientation.

Black Queer Leadership as Womanist Ethical Leadership

My interviewees represent a womanist leadership style that is shaped by their intersectional identities. Building on the various theories of womanism such as Black feminism, being concerned about women's culture and faith, and maintaining a communal anti-oppression orientation, their womanist leadership styles can teach such values as survival, liberation, wholeness, justice, and reciprocity. However, clearly this is just my interpretation of their leadership style because only six of the interviewees chose to identify as womanist; thus, I had to question whether I was doing rhetorical harm by giving them an identity or framework that they had not chosen for themselves. Examining the disciplinary record of oral history writings led me to believe that I could fairly do so because feminist oral historians had argued that "women's oral history, then, is a feminist encounter, even if the interviewee is not herself a feminist [because] it is the creation of a new type of material on women; it is the validation of women's experiences; it is the communication among women of different generations."[25] Their narratives fit this rubric, but this book proceeds from my interpretation with awareness that my ethical commitments were to present their life stories as they presented them to me and to not subsume their lives to the whims of my understanding.

I was first led to read their leadership as womanist after conducting one of my interviews with Bishop Flunder. She had published some writings and identified as a womanist, which allowed me to ask about her womanist identity during our interview. Her vision of womanism was captivating, and listening to her words showed me the potential for the womanist framework outside of the academy. She describes womanism at length:

> There is a nurturing and a need for a womanist hand. Not a fragile womanist hand but a womanist hand in Alice Walker's concept of womanist and womanist theology womanist ecclesiology. That, that we are not designed to weaponize religion. It's supposed to gather us. Yeah, it's supposed to nourish us. That's why I said we need to put some breath on it. You know, there's a nourishing that is supposed to come from faith and [the] whole business of weaponizing faith to spend time talking about who cannot be inclusive. I don't think seeks the heart of God at all. And womanist notions [are] to dignify and lift us those who are most marginalized.
>
> And, and not to suggest that just be an all-woman church, but when there's a womanist hand on it, I believe that what happens is the whole family is welcome. It's like almost all of the Black movies that are about conflict when you get to the end of the movie, right? The mothers, the aunties, the grandmothers they start cooking, right, and there's a big old meal that happened. That gets everybody straightened out. Now that's the table that I'm talking about now. They've been fighting since the movie started, but by the time they get to the end it's amazing what some chicken

and greens, black-eyed peas and sweet potato pie can do! To get people sitting down. I think the womanist ecclesiology or the womanist table is holy greens and chicken and black-eyed peas and sweet potato pie. In a spiritual sense, a way to bring us all together with a common table and a common balm to heal us. That's what I mean when I say I'm womanist and unapologetically womanist.

This depiction of womanist leadership is of bridge building and collaboration. It signals free exchange, dialogue, and hope. Her understanding offered holistic healing to all in the community because to be a womanist is expansive and inclusive, which fits her mission of creating radically inclusive spaces here on Earth. This also resonated because as a womanist scholar, my goal is to promote liberation and to bring religious communities into conversation with media and societal influences. Examining this project from this lens, the future is bright not because we are fulfilling Alice Walker's prophetic definition and unsilencing the lesbian voice but because we are doing the work of holistic justice and tending to needs within the community.

This book's presentation of Black lesbian religious leadership as the model for future generations to follow is the result of a determined commitment to seek the thriving of all. Yet there are limitations to this study's blueprint, namely, the overrepresentation of cisgender Christian women as exemplars. Future studies that examine transgender Black lesbian religious leaders or a larger sample of non-Christian Black lesbian religious leaders may indicate other leadership styles in the pursuit of holistic justice. I have acknowledged how womanism perhaps overdetermined the book's agenda: future research may point to other modes of activism that are not oriented toward social justice. If womanist ethical leadership is marked by deliberately resisting oppression that prevents holistic well-being, then all forms of resistance must be taken seriously.

Bishop Rawls told me this can occur only when the needs of the most marginalized in society are met, and the expectations from Black queer leadership that holistic justice be pursued are a path toward that goal. The eighteen individuals who shared their life experiences with me did so hopeful, as theologian Mark Jordan attests, that I would read their archives not as narratives about the past but rather as more "adequate language for more hopeful futures."[26] These women's lives have been about transformative social change, and it was my goal to amplify their narratives as ways that everyday people could transform the world. Taking my cue from Dean Emilie Townes, the purpose of analyzing these oral histories was not to create a legendary, larger-than-life figure; instead, the goal was to highlight how these women came to their authenticity, activism, spirituality, and communal awareness.[27] By emulating these practical steps in leadership, an interested change agent would have the skills needed to become an ethical leader, which in this framework predisposes her to holistic justice.

This project pursued three questions: How are Black lesbian religious leaders incubators for social justice activism? How does spirituality animate their social justice activism? And how can these leaders function as models of ethical leadership for future generations? Thus, the book started with several assumptions: social justice activism can lead to societal reform, Black lesbian religious leadership is a worthy model exemplar, and transformative social change is possible in our lifetimes. Although these women have extraordinary accomplishments, each one is an individual who saw a societal wrong and tried to make it right. Their lives are inspiring because of their insistence on dismantling the multivalent oppression threatening all of our survival. My interviews offered me answers to my research questions, and they demonstrated that "we can create the conditions which lead to our flourishing—and we can bring others along."[28] They are proof of the validity of Octavia Butler's opening epigraph that we are changed by our connections to others that and we should seek to change the world for their benefit.

This is one of the many reasons why the book presents these women as ways forward for the next generation of ethical leaders. According to Judy Alston and Patrice McClellan's *Herstories: Leading with the Lessons of the Lives of Black Women Activists*, Black women's historical transformative leadership has been grounded in morality, and current transformational leadership literature has missed the opportunity to examine "spirit-filled resistance" as motivation for social change.[29] This exploration of Black lesbian religious leadership fills the void in scholarship as well as presents activists with strategies and living examples of how one works to usurp oppression. The text also presents an intervention to my chosen guild—womanism—offering it a way to live out its fullest potential.

Finally, this text is my attempt to respond to a question I received from an African exchange student, Angelina Amoako Yeboah, who asked me what US womanists have built that lasts. She had given me the example of African feminists who had built dormitories for female students in an institution that had not previously housed female students as evidence of the concrete impact of African feminism. When I answered this question, I initially spoke about US womanists documenting narratives of survival, but I realize that the Black lesbian religious leaders I interviewed were also architects of building a new way of being in the world. They have built institutions, but they have also built a legacy of resistance and flourishing that I am proud to share with others.

Epilogue

Online Archives

Just put a little dab on your lips to speak truth to power or on your hands to write authentically. And as you become more in tune with the frequency of your truth, the other uses will be revealed to you. You have the gift of gab. That was your birthright as a southerner. Now you have been given the gift of others' stories. Your burden is to hold them.

—E. PATRICK JOHNSON, *Honeypot*

When an elder dies, a library is burned. . . . I've gained an understanding of how documenting the spoken stories of a people is a way to preserve culture. To take these stories and present them on an academic level—that gives more power to the individuals I've interviewed. There is power in this project. I know that now.

—PENDARVIS HARSHAW, "OG Told Me"

As I returned to write the closing sentences of the manuscript, I hear my grandmother's stories echoing in my memory. Mildred Carter was a master storyteller and always instilled the importance of carefully listening to someone's story to understand their lives. She was raised by extended family in an economically depressed bootlegging home where she heard many customers' tales, and in true southern fashion she knew the privilege of sharing, expanding, and even exploiting stories to eke out a means to survive. She was a religious leader in her own right, and she was fully aware that "if it wasn't for the women," many of our traditions would not have survived. As I finished this manuscript, she transitioned into the ancestral realm, and I was left pondering journalist Pendarvis Harshaw's opening epigraph that notes that with the passing of an elder we lose parts of our culture. I was led back to the point of my initial gathering of these Black lesbian religious leaders' oral histories— telling the story so that others might learn from their visionary leadership.

What this decade of interviews with queer women illuminated was that queer leadership paves the way for not just religious communities but for secular society as well. Initially, I hoped that amplifying these women's stories would offer resources for other queer women and road maps for future possibilities. This was one of the reasons that I partnered with LGBTQ-RAN to create profiles and conduct oral histories so that the scope of this work could be magnified. I know that this has been accomplished, but along the way I realized that this process also gave other gifts: the expansion of online archives for representing Black lives and the ability to promote a queer leadership for a social justice model that could be useful beyond just its impact on the Black LGBTQ community. This epilogue addresses each of these gifts and concludes with the impact that these women's stories can have beyond this text.

The expansion of Black lesbian archival collections is a gift to current and future generations because it adds the diversity of religion, race, age, and social justice to these queer collections. The scarcity of archives was mentioned in the introduction, but it is worth explicating how the most notable existing archives—the Lesbian Herstory Archives in Brooklyn, the ONE National Gay and Lesbian Archives at the University of Southern California, and New York's Schomburg Black Gay and Lesbian Archive Project—all neglect the categories gathered by these oral histories. If media historian Kate Eichhorn is accurate that the queer archive has come to "stand for something missing—a home, center, nation, or stable notion of community," then the work of preserving the culture of Black lesbian religious leaders is a means of reifying homes within and beyond religious communities.[1] These archival spaces are necessary, and the medium I chose was an online or virtual means of preserving stories via oral histories.

Conducting these oral histories offered me a window into the multidimensional lives of my subjects, but my curation of these archival records was not without ethical consideration. I learned to prod about their lives but not circumvent their privacy. I learned to respect the choices they made of what to share and what would not be a part of public record. I often left with more information than what the archive would reflect because of personal and political decisions they made when reviewing their transcripts to excise from the audio and written transcript something they had shared. They had trusted me with not only their stories but in some instances with their secrets. Harshaw noted that in his interviews with older Black men he was cognizant of the need to record these "living people . . . in an honest and dignified fashion."[2] Likewise, I had a moral responsibility to hold their stories and to represent them in the most dignified manner I could while honoring their personal decisions to represent themselves in ways that may have run counter to my politics of respectability. When using oral history as a means of sustaining memory and history, I was constantly reminded that this medium, when led by "people directly affected by oppression who are trying to use oral history to change their lives," is a transformative tool.[3]

Ultimately, I was writing for change, and they were donating their papers, pictures, and stories to ensure that change was swiftly coming. We found the internet to be a great democratizer that allowed greater access to and visibility for these efforts. Perhaps because I had chosen for their oral histories to be housed virtually within the LGBTQ-RAN website, I had inadvertently helped create a community archive of Black lesbian religious leaders, thus making them more visible than within larger archives focused on just one component of their identities. This amplification is one solution, but another is to continue to expand the linkages between these subjects and these other archives. For example, Mandy Carter expressed concern about the accessibility of her materials; thus, she placed her records in multiple places (community spaces, Black spaces, and LGBTQ spaces) to increase access. She saw technology as another means of increasing visibility, for she was intent on creating mechanisms for people who wouldn't necessarily know where to look to "bump into our history" and have easy access to it.[4] A promise of these oral histories is that these persons light the path to recover other names and stories that we do not already know. By choosing an online format whose only barrier is the privilege of internet access, their stories are highlighted not just in their community spheres but in perhaps the most public manner. Additionally, this offers security and safety to those seeking inspiration and who may not feel at home at or have access to academic institutions, where archives tend to be housed. It also offers "cover" to those who are exploring the contours of their sexual identities and may not have yet publicly come out, but who need evidence that it is possible to live and tell their truth.

I "bumped" into their history and realized that my life would not be the same. Their stories helped me recognize both as a womanist ethicist and an ally that queer leadership was the solution to sustaining social justice movements. The text has implicitly assumed that queer leadership was analogous to social justice leadership, which can be defined as leadership models that "make issues of race, class, gender, disability, sexual orientation, and other historically and currently marginalizing conditions in the United States central to their advocacy, leadership practice, and vision."[5] Because Black queer leaders operate in similar marginalized conditions, their intersectional analyses make possible leadership structures that see the bigger picture. At its core, the text hoped to present these women's leadership as living embodiments of the promise of womanist thought. I hoped that by examining their stories, the link to womanism's theoretical positioning that advocated for the thriving of all would be realized. My womanist frame has perhaps been overdetermined in this project, but this concern for those marginalized comes from these leaders' intersectional life experiences. It also represents a new possibility of leadership that is indicative of their life as queer, Black, and religious women.

E. Patrick Johnson wrote of this possibility as a "quare" performance in embodied resistance, where *quare* represented someone both Black and queer who was committed to intersectional struggle against oppression.[6] My text is in many ways indebted to Johnson's intervention into queer historiography, and although he is clear on the point that he enters as a performance theorist and how that shapes his depiction of Black queer women's stories, I must also be equally clear that this project is shaped by my approach as a womanist ethicist. I read, hear, and think analytically with justice issues in mind, and this reverberated in the types of questions that I asked the interviewees and in the ready connections I made to them as social justice ambassadors. In many ways, this rendering of Black lesbian leaders brings womanist theorizing to the concrete example of multifaceted LGBTQ rights.

This book also contends that queer leadership *can* produce different possibilities for our world. Ms. Carter believes that future LGBTQ-of-color leaders can and will redefine leadership by thinking creatively in ways that empower people and give equal ownership of justice.[7] Black queer leadership provides many of the progressive solutions that our society requires, such as attention to environmental racism while discussing climate change; eliminating student loan debt and advocating for living wages; increasing access to equitable health care; and advocating for racial, gender, and sexual justice. Black queer leadership is rooted in black freedom and justice, and Black lesbian religious leaders imbue their activism with deep theological beliefs that support this sense of full thriving for humanity. What interviewing queer religious leaders and studying their leadership showed me was that they are the future—our means of becoming a "more perfect union."

Thus, my role as interviewer was to offer space and potentially an amplification for their lives and leadership model. As the opening epigraph indicates, I had been gifted with their stories, and my ethical commitments required that I use them responsibly.[8] I was transformed into a disciple, changing not only my religious community (as I now virtually attend a Christian church pastored by a queer leader) but also my academic focus. Whereas my prior research has centered on Black women's private sexual desires, in this work I asked no such questions. I did not pry into their private relationships and pursuits of sexual pleasure because to write about their lives authentically meant to honor their boundaries. Although they gave me access to deeply personal and private stories, I respected their right to hold some things for just themselves: their leadership was public, but their intimate connections and private family life belonged to just them. Many interviewees provided me with pictures that included their family, partners, and wives, and these are housed on the LGBTQ-RAN website alongside their transcript and audios of their interviews, but when they did not offer, I did not request. Through the deeply personal work of conducting oral histories, I came to realize that although my scholarship is centered on Black women's sexual freedom, this project reiterated how intertwined this freedom is with our material realities. It remained my joy to gather these stories, but the work is only partially done because as Harshaw's epigraph notes, there is power in this project. My next move and phase of scholarly and social activism is to continue to use my voice to point toward their leadership as our path forward and to acknowledge that they are in fact the leaders that we have been looking for.

General Questions Asked in Oral History Interviews

Personal Information

1 Can you tell me about your early life? Did you have siblings or an extended family?

2 What did you do as a child for fun?

3 What messages/values were you given about social justice or activism as you were growing up?

4 What were your high school/teenage years like?

5 After high school, what did you do next? College/job—where and why? What was your college major or career position?

6 Do you define yourself as a womanist?

7 What identities are important to you? How did you learn to merge these identities?

8 When and how were you aware of your sexuality? Describe your coming-out process.

9 Where do you find joy and fulfillment?

10 What are you most proud of?

Spiritual/Religious Information

1 Describe your religious upbringing. What spiritual practices remained as an adult?

2 How did your spirituality or religious commitment grow/change over time?

3 What pulled you into your particular religious community?

4 When and how did you move into leadership in that community?

5 How does your faith intertwine with your activist work?

Leadership/Activism Information

1   What were the motivations for your organizing/leadership/activism?

2   How were you involved in social justice organizations—e.g., in what roles?

3   Describe your career choices.

4   What led you to organize in religious or secular spaces? How do you choose which causes to prioritize?

5   Do you see yourself as a leader? What does that mean to you?

6   What leadership skills were you honing? What are the markers of your leadership?

7   How is your scholarship activism?

8   What sustains you in social justice activism/leadership?

9   Discuss how you make inroads in white spaces for conversations about people of color. Discuss how you make inroads in Black spaces for conversations about LGBTQ concerns.

10 What are your retirement goals/plans?

NOTES

Introduction

1 "Are the Gods Afraid of Black Sexuality: Religion and the Burdens of Black Sexual Politics" Conference, Columbia University Center on African-American Religion, Sexual Politics, and Social Justice, October 23–24, 2014, www.carss .columbia.edu/blog/are-gods-afraid-Black-sexuality-conference-re-cap.

2 Leffler, *Black Leaders on Leadership*, 12; King and Ferguson, "Introduction," 11.

3 This speaks to the issue about using materials from archives because some types of relationships are left out of official public documentation. According to archivist Brittany Bennett Parris, massive archives such as the Schlesinger Library avoid "assigning lesbian-related subject headings to materials unless the women in the documents in question are indeed 'forthright lesbians,'" instead using a term like *friendship*. See Parris, "Creating, Reconstructing, and Protecting Historical Narratives," 18.

4 Johnson, *Black.Queer.Southern.Women*, 165.

5 I am aware that my sample is too small to make any generalizable statements. I wanted to provide an in-depth exploration of Black lesbian religious leaders' lives and to diversify historical records on Black women's leadership. My "dream list" was compiled by looking for religious diversity and variety in leadership experiences, and factoring in whether I could reach these women to conduct the interview in person.

6 The use of titles by Black women has a history tied to the denigrations of white supremacy, which denied our ancestors the ability to be referenced with respect. Black culture teaches younger Black women to show deference to older Black women and never to call an older woman by her first name. As the interviewer, this logic prevented me from being at ease referring to any of the participants who were older than me by anything other than their titles. As they reviewed their transcripts to approve them for my use, many of them corrected the transcribers' use of just their first names.

7 Collins, *Black Feminist Thought*, 11–13.

8 Johnson, *Black.Queer.Southern.Women*, 9.

9 Laura Micham, quoted in DiVeglia, "Accessibility, Accountability, and Activism," 85.

10 Leffler, *Black Leaders on Leadership*, 3.

11 Oral History Association, "Oral History Defined."

12 Leffler, *Black Leaders on Leadership*, 19.

13 Hine, "Rape and the Inner Lives of Black Women in the Middle West," 915.

14 Etter-Lewis, "Black Women's Life Stories," 43.

15 Historian Gary Okihiro determined that oral history thus acted as a tool for recovering history, but specifically a more complete history that included the "common folk and the dispossessed." See Okihiro, "Oral History and the Writing of Ethnic History," 209.

16 Voice of Witness, "History on a Human Scale," 13.

17 Boyd and Ramírez, "Introduction: Close Encounters," 7.

18 Cannon, "Structured Academic Amnesia," 21.

19 See the 2015 US Department of Health and Human Services recommendation that oral histories be excluded from institutional review boards because oral history already had its own code of ethics involving informed consent. www .oralhistory.org/2018/07/06/institutional-review-boards-and-oral-history-an -update.

20 Salazar, "Third World Women's Text," 98.

21 Townes, "Ethics as an Art of Doing the Work Our Souls Must Have," 36.

22 Walker, *In Search of Our Mothers' Gardens*, xi–xii.

23 Maparyan, *Womanist Idea*, xx, xxvi.

24 There are varieties of womanist methodological frameworks employed by different disciplines. Womanist theologian and anthropologist of religion Linda Thomas's analysis of womanist theology and ethics reports that their sources include fiction, poetry, and historical narratives but that there has been a historical lack of research engaging the lives of poor Black women. This critique of womanist theology and ethics was also waged by Patricia Hill Collins, who noted that there is a relative mismatch between what privileged Black women in the academy and everyday Black women identify as important themes. Daphne Wiggins's ethnographic study of everyday Black church women also reveals a mismatch of cultural values in that the lived concrete realities of these Black women's lives did not seem to match the language or theory of womanist theology and ethics. See Thomas, "Womanist Theology"; Collins, "What's in a Name?," 15; and Wiggins, *Righteous Content*.

25 Cannon, "Emancipatory Historiography," 81. Womanist emancipatory historiography takes its definition from ethicist Beverly Harrison's "dance of redemption," which asserted that the methods for human liberation must be historical

and therefore acknowledge human agency and resistance. See Harrison, *Making the Connections*, 249.

26 Gluck, "What's So Special about Women?," 217.

27 Jackson, *Meant for Good*, 17.

1. Shattering Stained-Glass Ceilings

1 Talvacchia, *Embracing Disruptive Coherence*, 7.

2 Arguably, one could search for early markers of intersectional analysis in the work of Sojourner Truth, Anna Julia Cooper, Frances Beal, and Patricia Hill Collins.

3 "Combahee River Collective Statement," 22–23.

4 Crenshaw, "Demarginalizing the Intersection of Race and Sex," 140.

5 Flunder, *Where the Edge Gathers*, 5.

6 Black Protestantism or the Black church is widely understood to include seven majority Black Protestant denominations: the National Baptist Convention, the National Baptist Convention of America, the Progressive National Convention, the African Methodist Episcopal Church, the African Methodist Episcopal Zion Church, the Christian Methodist Episcopal Church, and the Church of God in Christ. See Lincoln and Mamiya, *Black Church in the African American Experience*, 1.

7 Collier-Thomas, *Daughters of Thunder*, 18.

8 Collier-Thomas, *Daughters of Thunder*, 24.

9 Collier-Thomas, *Daughters of Thunder*, 26–28.

10 Lyons, "Breaking through the Extra-Thick Stained-Glass Ceiling," 79.

11 Collier-Thomas, *Daughters of Thunder*, 29.

12 Gilkes, *If It Wasn't for the Women*, 46.

13 Wiggins, *Righteous Content*, 113.

14 Dickerson, *African Methodist Episcopal Church*, 526.

15 Human Rights Campaign, "Stances of Faiths on LGBTQ Issues"; "Response to Criticism of Faith in Human Rights Declaration." Church of God in Christ, "General Assembly Declaration and Apologetic of Marriage." Accessed February 28, 2022. www.cogic.org/wp-content/uploads/2012/09/FINAL-DRAFT -OF-RESPONSE-TO-CRITICISM-OF-FAITH-IN-HUMAN-RIGHTS -DECLARATION.pdf

16 Brown Douglas, "Heterosexism and the Black American Church Community," 184.

17 Hammonds, "Black (W)holes and the Geometry of Black Female Sexuality," 136–37. Hammonds notes that the historical narrative about Black female sexuality has tended to avoid discussion of the lesbian or queer subject, often deeming her dangerous and potentially even traitorous to the Black race.

18   Brown Douglas, "Heterosexism and the Black American Church Community," 190.

19   These passages include Genesis 19:1–29; Judges 19; Leviticus 18:22; Leviticus 20:13; Romans 1:18–32; 1 Corinthians 6:9–11; and 1 Timothy 1:8–11.

20   Anderson, "Deadly Silence," 191.

21   Smith, *Towards a Black Feminist Criticism*, 17.

22   Griffin, *Their Own Receive Them Not*, 129.

23   Moore, "Lipstick or Timberlands?," 114–39.

24   Johnson, *Black.Queer.Southern.Women*, 166–67.

25   Jones, "The Will to Adorn," 229.

26   Battle, Pastrana Jr., and Harris, *Examination of Black LGBT Populations across the United States*, 43.

27   According to a 2016 Pew Research Center survey, the acceptance of gays and lesbians was up to 50 percent for Black Protestants, with white mainline Protestant acceptance at 76 percent but white evangelical Protestant acceptance at only 34 percent. See Fingerhut, "Support Steady for Same-Sex Marriage and Acceptance of Homosexuality."

28   Robert Jones et al., "Emerging Consensus on LGBT Issues."

29   Monroe, quoted in Comstock, *A Whosoever Church*, 69.

30   Battle, Pastrana Jr., and Harris, *Examination of Black LGBT Populations across the United States*, 36. See also Jones and Cox, "America's Changing Religious Identity."

31   Chapter 4 discusses those who did leave Christianity to pursue alternative religions or spiritualities.

32   Bishop Yvette Flunder, oral history interview conducted by author, 2011.

33   Carpenter, *A Time for Honor*, 139–40.

34   Campbell-Reed, "State of Clergywomen in the U.S. Report," 8.

35   Perry, *Lord Is My Shepherd and He Knows I'm Gay*, 116.

36   "MCC Fact Sheet." Pew Research Center data classify MCC as a Protestant denomination, categorizing it as an Other/Protestant nonspecific in the mainline tradition. See www.pewforum.org/2015/05/12/appendix-b-classification-of-protestant-denominations.

37   McQueeney, "We Are God's Children Ya'll," 154.

38   Lewin, *Filled with the Spirit*, 47.

39   Griffin, *Their Own Receive Them Not*, 188.

40   Unity Fellowship Church Movement, "History."

41   Lanoix, quoted in Wilcox, *Queer Women and Religious Individualism*, 39.

42   Leong, *Religion, Flesh, and Blood*, 19.

43   Abrams, "Black Lesbian Bishop's Journey in Ministry."

44   Abrams, "Black Lesbian Bishop's Journey in Ministry."

45   Lewin, *Filled with the Spirit*, 59.

46 City of Refuge UCC, "About."

47 Lewin, *Filled with the Spirit*, 51, 59.

48 Fellowship of Affirming Ministries, "About Us."

49 hooks, *Talking Back*, 8.

50 hooks, *Talking Back*, 14.

51 Lu and Steele, "Joy Is Resistance," 825.

52 Smith, quoted in Flunder, *Where the Edge Gathers*, 35.

53 hooks, *Talking Back*, 9.

2. *Going to Hell for My Authenticity*

1 Hammonds, "Black (W)holes and the Geometry of Black Female Sexuality," 136–37. Hammonds provides a notable historical critique of the coinage of queer theory in addressing white lesbian Teresa de Lauretis's failure to theorize queer theory in such a way that would include Black lesbians. Hammonds asserts that in its early stages, queer theory was structured to doubly silence or erase Black lesbian sexualities.

2 American studies scholar and novelist Lashonda Barnett and historian Eric Garber have written about the religious autonomy of Black lesbians during the Harlem Renaissance, Irene Monroe writes about the religious ideologies of Black lesbians supporting the past and current civil rights movements, and Yvette Flunder is documenting the religious activism of lesbian and transgender persons participating in her international fellowship of fifty-six primarily African American Christian churches that practice radically inclusive Christianity. Even as this list of scholarly attention to Black lesbian leaders is sparse, it in no way diminishes the impact of white and Black feminist attention to the formation of Black lesbian identity, which is much more nuanced and employed among those studying black lesbians and religion.

3 Moultrie, *Passionate and Pious*, 88.

4 Jackson and Scott, "Sexual Skirmishes and Feminist Factions," 13.

5 Rich, "Compulsory Heterosexuality and Lesbian Existence," 135–36.

6 Clarke, "Lesbianism," 159, 155.

7 Lorde, "An Interview," 99.

8 Rev. Dr. Deborah L. Johnson, oral history conducted by author, 2017.

9 Moultrie, *Passionate and Pious*, 88.

10 Elder Darlene Garner, oral history interview conducted by author, 2010.

11 In October 2017 Elder Garner's position was "restructured" out of the church that she so loved. Despite being the first Black person to be elected to the Council of Elders and to serve on the Senior Leadership team and despite her four decades of leadership within MCC, she was passed over as the next moderator for the denomination in 2016. She eventually signed a separation agreement from MCC and then retired her active clergy credentials on January 1, 2018.

12 Rev. Candy Holmes, oral history interview conducted by author, 2017.

13 Proposition 8 refers to the November 2008 California state ballot initiative which added to the constitution that only marriage between a man or woman was valid or recognized in California. Proposition 8 was legislative backlash from the May 2008 appealing of the 2000 California Proposition 22 ballot initiative which defined marriage as between one man and one woman.

14 Maparyan, *Womanist Idea*, 70–71.

15 Holmes, "Rev. Candy Holmes' Resignation from MCC Leadership."

16 Bishop Tonyia Rawls, oral history interview conducted by the author, 2018.

17 Rev. Dr. Cari Jackson, oral history interview conducted by author, 2018.

18 Jackson, "Her Story."

19 Rev. Naomi Washington-Leapheart, oral history interview conducted by author, 2019.

20 Taylor, *Ethics of Authenticity*, 66.

21 Taylor, *Ethics of Authenticity*, 27.

22 Rev. Kentina Washington-Leapheart, oral history interview conducted by author, 2019.

23 Washington-Leapheart, "The Ordination I Never Could Have Imagined."

24 Washington-Leapheart, "Center for the Church and the Black Experience Celebrating 45 Outstanding Black Alums."

25 Taylor, *Ethics of Authenticity*, 33.

26 Hill, "Who Are We for Each Other?," 348–49.

27 Collins, *Black Feminist Thought*, 252. I acknowledge Michel Foucault's original use of the term *subjugated knowledge* to indicate disqualified or naive knowledge that merely reacts to oppressive scenarios, but here I am referencing Collins's use of the term as knowledge that seeks to outwit and outmaneuver social systems.

28 Clarke, "Lesbianism," 160.

29 Walker, *In Search of Our Mothers' Gardens*, xi–xii.

30 Floyd-Thomas, "Radical Subjectivity," 16.

31 Cannon, "Structured Academic Amnesia," 21.

3. Justice Is Spiritual

1 "Combahee River Collective Statement," quoted in Keeanga-Yamahtta Taylor, *How We Get Free*, 9.

2 Bostic, *African American Female Mystical Activism*.

3 Giddings, *When and Where I Enter*.

4 Ross, *Witnessing and Testifying*.

5 For example, in studies of the civil rights movement, notice the absence of attention to religion in Collier-Thomas and Franklin, eds., *Sisters in the Struggle*;

Allen, *Black Women Leaders of the Civil Rights Movement*; and Robnett, *How Long? How Long?*

6 See Gibson, *Frederick Douglass*; Blum, *W. E. B. Du Bois*; Raboteau, *American Prophets*; and Baldwin and Anderson, *Revives My Soul Again.*

7 Townes, "Finding the Legacy," 36.

8 Collier-Thomas, *Jesus, Jobs, and Justice*, xviii–xix.

9 Collins, "Learning from the Outsider Within," 114–15.

10 Dr. Sylvia Rhue, oral history interview conducted by author, 2011.

11 Ross, "Lessons and Treasures in Our Mothers' Witness," 115.

12 Lee, "Excommunicate Me from the Church of Social Justice."

13 Rev. Dr. Emilie Townes, oral history interview conducted by author, 2018.

14 Johnson, *Black.Queer.Southern.Women*, 352.

15 For example, see the special (March 16, 2016: https://www.christiancentury.org/magazine/2016) *Christian Century* edition devoted to Black Lives Matter; Vesely-Flad, *Racial Purity and Dangerous Bodies*; Brown Douglas, *Stand Your Ground*; and Francis, *Ferguson and Faith.*

16 Farrag, "Spirit in Black Lives Matter."

17 Moultrie, "#BlackBabiesMatter," 255.

18 Rev. Dr. Pamela Lightsey, oral history interview conducted by author, 2017.

19 Lightsey, quoted in Barlow, "Eyewitness to the Turmoil in Ferguson." This was her mechanism for supporting the protest for justice by moving outside of mainstream media. She claims that close to two million people viewed her amateur videos. Livestream's mission is to "enable organizations to share experiences through live video, unlocking a world where every event is available live online." See https://livestream.com/about.

20 "Combahee River Collective Statement," in *How We Get Free*, 18.

21 At the time of this writing, the United Methodist Church had voted in its April 2019 Special Session of General Conference to uphold restrictions on ordination and same-sex weddings. Due to growing resistance there have been calls to separate the denomination before the next General Conference in 2024. In May 2022, the Wesleyan Covenant Association launched a new denomination, the Global Methodist Church as a more conservative alternative.

22 Lightsey, *Our Lives Matter*, 88.

23 Bryant-Davis and Adams, "Psychocultural Exploration of Womanism, Activism, and Social Justice," 220.

24 Walker, *In Search of Our Mothers' Gardens*, xi.

25 Given that most of my interviewees are Christian, their discussion of spirituality relates to the concept of the Holy Spirit, so the following scholarship seems applicable. See the literature explored in Hayes, *No Crystal Stair*; Townes, *In a Blaze of Glory*; and Baker-Fletcher, *Sisters of Dust, Sisters of Spirit*. There are also notable discussions of womanist spirituality that do not presume a connection

to Christianity, such as Smith, "Green Lap, Brown Embrace, Blue Body"; Harris, *Gifts of Virtue, Alice Walker, and Womanist Ethics*; Harris, *Ecowomanism*; Coleman, *Making a Way out of No Way*; and Coleman, *Ain't I a Womanist, Too*?

26 Maparyan also posits that womanist spirituality has six identifying characteristics: it is eclectic, synthetic, holistic, personal, visionary, and pragmatic. Maparyan, *Womanist Idea*, 90–102.

27 Maparyan, *Womanist Idea*, 141.

28 Rev. Dr. Yvette Flunder, oral history interview conducted by author, 2011.

29 Coleman, *Making a Way out of No Way*, 93, 97.

30 Black feminist poet June Jordan speaks of this as the "paralysis of identity politics," which makes available a "moral attachment to a concept beyond gender and race" that she refers to as justice. See Jordan, "Waiting on a Taxi," 302.

31 Collins, "Searching for Sojourner Truth," 241.

32 Hernandez and Rehman, *Colonize This!*, xxi.

33 Maparyan, *Womanist Idea*, 141.

4. Mighty Causes Are Calling Us

1 Asanti, "Living with Dual Spirits," 61.

2 Rev. Dr. Cari Cari Jackson, oral history interview conducted by author, 2018.

3 Bishop Dr. Yvette Flunder, oral history interview conducted by author, 2019.

4 Martin, *Beyond Christianity*, 9.

5 Martin, *Beyond Christianity*, 25.

6 Rev. Dr. Deborah L. Johnson, oral history conducted by author, 2017.

7 Martin, *Beyond Christianity*, 10, 62, 146.

8 Johnson, *Sacred Yes*, 363.

9 Johnson, *Sacred Yes*, 321–29.

10 Wilcox, "Same-Sex Eroticism and Gender Fluidity in New and Alternative Religions," 247–56.

11 Moore, "Black and Gay in L.A.," 207–8.

12 Hull, *Soul Talk*, 1.

13 Harris, "Womanist Spirituality," 148.

14 Rabbi Sandra Lawson, oral history interview conducted by author, 2018.

15 American Jewish Population Project, "Race and Ethnicity of American Jews."

16 Lawson, "Rabbi, Musician, and Activist."

17 Elwell and Alpert, "Introduction," 2, 12.

18 Eger, "Ten Years . . . and Counting," 163.

19 Sales, "Sandra Lawson."

20 Pamela "Ayo" Yetunde, oral history interview conducted by the author, 2019.

21 Yetunde, *Object Relations*, 5, 27.

22 Cadge, "Lesbian, Gay, and Bisexual Buddhist Practitioners," 149.

23 Frederick, *Between Sundays*, 4, 10, 14.

24 Williams, "Engaging Womanist Spirituality in African American Christian Worship," 100.

25 Edwards, "'Let's Imagine Something Different,'" 5.

26 Townes, *In a Blaze of Glory*, 13, 49, 123.

27 Harris, "Buddhist Meditation," 68, 70.

28 Harris also maintains that discomfort around the fluid spirituality of Alice Walker and an overdetermination of Christian spirituality for womanists have stymied their ability to take seriously the religious plurality of Black women.

29 Maparyan, *Womanist Idea*, 93, 117.

30 Alexander and Yescavage, "Bi, Buddhist, Activist," 176.

31 Leath, "Canada and Pure Land, a New Field and Buddha-Land," 61.

32 Eger, "Ten Years," 165.

33 Guillory, *Spiritual and Social Transformation in African American Spiritual Churches*, 68, 74.

34 Association for Global New Thought, "Welcome."

35 Rankow, "Toward the Prophetic."

36 Johnson says in the book created from these letters that she is not channeling an entity and that the messages come directly to her in the first-person voice of Spirit. She remains conscious and receives the letters or songs through known and unknown senses. She transcribes the letters into a recorder but says that the recorded voice does not sound like her own as the speech patterns, tonality, voice and inflections are unique. See Johnson, *Sacred Yes, xxii.*

37 Johnson, *Your Deepest Intent*, 155.

38 Johnson, *Your Deepest Intent*, 350.

39 Townes, *In a Blaze of Glory*, 11.

40 Walker, *In Search of Our Mothers' Gardens*, xi.

41 Lawson, "My Vision."

42 Yetunde, *Object Relations*, 24. This comes from Ayo's self-definition of *womanist*, which involved learning from Black lesbians and taking the risk to share this wisdom with oppressors in order to help the oppressor to awaken from ignorance.

43 Johnson, *Sacred Yes*, xxiv.

5. Doing the Work Their Souls Must Have

Epigraph: Angela Davis quoted in Leffler, *Black Leaders on Leadership*, 196.

1 Lee, quoted in Houchins, *Spiritual Narratives*, 23.

2 They are not presented as straw men for my own argument: both have served as mentors and teachers during my own studies. They are representative of the

genre of Black leadership studies that emphasizes historical male leaders as examples of racial progress.

3   Fluker, *Ethical Leadership*, 33, 62.

4   Fluker, *Stones That the Builders Rejected*, 11.

5   Fluker, *Ethical Leadership*, 32.

6   Franklin, *Moral Leadership*, xxvii.

7   Franklin, *Moral Leadership*, 95.

8   Collins, "Learning from the Outsider Within," 121. Collins's work reiterates that there is no homogenous Black women's standpoint and that it is more accurate to say a Black woman's collective standpoint exists only in her differing responses to common challenges. When I reference a Black lesbian religious standpoint, Collins's perspective also holds true. See Collins, *Black Feminist Thought*, 28.

9   Rhode, *Women and Leadership*, 5.

10   Rosser-Mims, "Black Feminism," 7.

11   Fluker, *Ethical Leadership*, 129.

12   My understanding of womanist ethical leadership is also in conversation with the growing scholarship on womanist ethical leadership, notably the works of Toni King, S. Alease Ferguson, Deborah Jackson, Marcia Riggs, and Emilie Townes. My theorizing does not adopt King and S. Alease Ferguson's connection of womanist leadership to the motherline or transmission via feminine lineage, but I accept their articulation that leadership should reflect the "desire, ability, and efforts to influence the world around us, based upon an ethic of care for self and other and fueled by a vision that sustains over time." See King and Ferguson, "Introduction," 11.

13   Walker, *In Search of Our Mothers' Gardens*, xi–xii.

14   Ella Baker criticizes the leadership style favored by men such as Martin Luther King Jr., who is quoted as stating that "leadership never ascends from the pew to the pulpit . . . but descends from the pulpit to the pew." See Fairclough, *Martin Luther King Jr.*, 19.

15   Payne, "Ella Baker and Models of Social Change," 893.

16   Gushee and Holtz, *Moral Leadership for a Divided Age*, 346–47.

17   Bishop Dr. Allyson Abrams, oral history interview conducted by author, 2019.

18   Rev. Dr. Renee McCoy, oral history interview conducted by author, 2017.

19   Doyle, *Radical Chapters*, 234.

20   Carter, "Nonviolent Activism and Santa Rita Prison."

21   Jackson, *For the Souls of Black Folks*, 9.

22   Edwards, *Charisma and the Fictions of Black Leadership*, 21. A notable counterpoint to this argument is Wessinger, "Charismatic Leaders in New Religious Movements," 80–96.

23   Lewin, *Filled with the Spirit*, 54–55, 66, 77.

24 Abrams, "A Black Lesbian Bishop's Journey in Ministry."

25 Rushin, "This Bridge," xxi–xxii.

26 Dr. Imani Woody, oral history interview conducted by author, 2017.

27 Woody, "Why Mary's House? (Again.)."

28 Leffler, *Black Leaders on Leadership*, 182.

29 Jackson, *Meant for Good*, 19.

30 Lewis, Williams, and Baker, *Another Way*, 55.

31 Rev. Darlene Franklin, oral history interview conducted by author, 2018.

32 Baker, "Developing Community Leadership," 351.

33 Baker, "Developing Community Leadership," 352.

34 Fluker, *Ethical Leadership*, 48.

35 King, "Don't Waste Your Breath," 87.

36 Lewis, Williams, and Baker, *Another Way*, 129, 133.

37 Lauren Markoe, "She's Black, Gay and Soon You Can Call Her 'Rabbi,'" *Washington Post*, May 28, 2015, www.washingtonpost.com/national/religion /shes-black-gay-and-soon-you-can-call-her-rabbi-correction/2015/05/28 /54d9e186–0578–11e5–93f4-f24d4af7f97d_story.html.

38 Gibbs, "Rabbi Redefines Religion."

39 Rawls, "Yes, Jesus Loves Me," 331.

40 Matt Comer, "Lesbian Bishop Tonyia Rawls Founds New Church," *Creative Loafing Charlotte*, February 26, 2014, https://clclt.com/charlotte/lesbian -bishop-tonyia-rawls-founds-new-church/Content?oid=3339368.

41 Freedom Center for Social Justice, "Mission, Vision, Values."

42 Weekes-Laidlow and Rawls, "Facing Race: Stories and Voices."

43 Sales, "Sandra Lawson, Black Lesbian Vegan Rabbinical Student."

44 Ben-Moche, "Rabbi Sandra Lawson Opens Up on Finding Connection in Unprecedented Times."

45 Elder Darlene Garner, oral history interview conducted by author, 2010.

46 Fellowship of Affirming Ministries, "About Us."

47 *Filled with the Spirit*, Lewin's book-length study of Flunder and TFAM, confirms this philosophy, but Lewin bases it on Flunder's refusal to be classified as a "para-preacher." My interview with Bishop Flunder felt less related to her ego and more as if she had realized that doing transformational and holistic justice work requires broad training and skill sets.

48 Freedom Center for Social Justice, "Partner Programming."

49 Lewis, Williams, and Baker, *Another Way*, 139.

50 Franklin, *Moral Leadership*, 67.

51 Quoted in Johnson, *Black.Queer.Southern.Women*, 352.

52 Lewis, Williams, and Baker, *Another Way*, 140.

53 Lipman-Blumen, quoted in Henderson, *God's Troublemakers*, 91.

54 Barlett, "Black and Proud."

55 Leffler, *Black Leaders on Leadership*, 13.

Conclusion

1 Lorde, "Age, Race, Class, and Sex," 115.

2 Hill, "Human Sexuality," 185.

3 Ethicist Roger Sneed advocates for a tempering of placing such a moralizing function on Black gays and lesbians; thus, I intend to highlight potential opportunities offered, not prescriptive claims that constrain Black queers into the already predetermined and heterosexual field of ethical leadership studies. See Sneed, *Representations of Homosexuality*, 104.

4 Cheng, *Radical Love*, 3.

5 Chang and Bowring, "Perceived Impact of Sexual Orientation," 288.

6 Pryor, "Queer Activist Leadership," 3.

7 Pryor, "Queer Advocacy Leadership."

8 Abdullah, "Emergence of a Black Feminist Leadership Model," 328–29.

9 Allen, "Re-articulation of Black Female Community Leadership," 62.

10 Moraga and Anzaldúa, *This Bridge Called My Back*, 23.

11 King and Ferguson's research identified several barriers to Black women laying claim to leadership identities, among them gendered projections of leaders as masculine, cultural and racial projections of female leaders being associated with caretaking, negative perceptions of leaders as militant or uppity, socialization to deny or downplay one's contributions, and contradictions between terminology and action. See King and Ferguson, "Introduction," 5–6.

12 Allen, "Re-articulation of Black Female Community Leadership," 62.

13 Hammonds, "Toward a Genealogy of Black Female Sexuality," 102.

14 "Rev. Deborah L. Johnson: Inner Light Ministries."

15 Anderson, *Creative Exchange*, 160. Anderson acknowledges the role that gay and lesbian religious leaders play in the flourishing of the Black community, yet I concur with Sneed in worrying that Anderson veers close to making gay and lesbians' presence heroic or salvific. See also Sneed, *Representations of Homosexuality*, 102.

16 Wilcox, *Queer Women and Religious Individualism*, 134–36, 140–41.

17 Wilcox, *Queer Women and Religious Individualism*, 148.

18 "Rev. Irene Monroe," 70.

19 "Rev. Deborah L. Johnson: Inner Light Ministries."

20 "Bishop Tonyia Rawls: Unity Fellowship Church Movement."

21 Davis, quoted in Leffler, *Black Leaders on Leadership*, 196–97.

22 "Rev. Dr. Renee L. Hill," 197.

23 Johnson, "Introduction," 3.

24 Lorde, "There Is No Hierarchy of Oppression," 220.

25 Gluck, "What's So Special about Women?," 219. This viewpoint is also weighed against the views of feminists such as folklorist Katherine Borland who recounted a conflict with interpretative authority when interviewing her grandmother. Her grandmother rejected Borland's analysis of her oral history and particularly being called a feminist, which made Borland question the field's exchange with its informants. See Borland, "'That's Not What I Said,'" 63–76.

26 Jordan, "Spiritual, Sexual, and Religious?," 24.

27 Townes, *Womanist Justice, Womanist Hope*, 20.

28 Lewis, Williams, and Baker, *Another Way*, 183.

29 Alston and McClellan, *Herstories*, 98.

Epilogue

1 Eichhorn, "Queer Archives," 132.

2 Harshaw, "OG Told Me," 89.

3 Loose, with Starecheski, "Oral History for Building Social Movements," 236.

4 See DiVeglia, "Accessibility, Accountability, and Activism," 81.

5 Theoharris, "Social Justice Educational Leaders and Resistance," 223.

6 Johnson, "'Quare' Studies," 125, 127.

7 See Pastrana, "Intersectional Imagination," 230.

8 Johnson, *Honeypot*, 217.

Appendix: Interview Guide

Individual oral histories are transcribed and catalogued on the Lesbian, Gay, Bisexual, Transgender, Queer Religious Archives Network website, https://lgbtqreligiousarchives.org/oral-histories.

Abdullah, Melina. "The Emergence of a Black Feminist Leadership Model: African American Women and Political Activism in the Nineteenth Century." In *Black Women's Intellectual Traditions: Speaking Their Minds*, edited by Kristin Waters and Carol B. Conway, 328–45. Burlington: University of Vermont Press, 2007.

Abrams, Allyson. "A Black Lesbian Bishop's Journey in Ministry." Believe Out Loud. Accessed February 28, 2022. https://www.believeoutloud.com/voices/article/a-black-lesbian-bishops-journey-in-ministry.

Abrams, Bishop Allyson. Oral history interview conducted by author, 2019. LGBTQ-RAN Oral History transcript. https://lgbtqreligiousarchives.org/media/oral-history/allyson-nelson-abrams/Allyson%20Abrams%202020-01-18%20transcript.pdf.

Alexander, Jonathan, and Karen Yescavage. "Bi, Buddhist, Activist: Refusing Intolerance, but Not Refusing Each Other." In *Sexuality, Religion, and the Sacred*, edited by Loraine Hutchins and H. Sharif Williams, 176–82. New York: Routledge, 2014.

Allen, Beverlyn Lundy. "Re-Articulation of Black Female Community Leadership: Processes, Networks, and a Culture of Resistance." *African American Research Perspectives* 3, no. 2 (Spring 1997): 61–67.

Allen, Zita. *Black Women Leaders of the Civil Rights Movement*. London: Franklin Watts, 1996.

Alston, Judy, and Patrice McClellan. *Herstories: Leading with the Lessons of the Lives of Black Women Activists*. New York: Peter Lang, 2011.

American Jewish Population Project. "Race and Ethnicity of American Jews." Brandeis University. Accessed February 28, 2022. https://ajpp.brandeis.edu/publications.php#section2&gid=null&pid=3.

Anderson, Victor. *Creative Exchange: A Construction of African American Religious Experience*. Minneapolis: Fortress, 2008.

Anderson, Victor. "Deadly Silence: Reflection on Homosexuality and Human Rights." In *Sexual Orientation and Human Rights in American Religious Discourse*, edited by Saul Olyan and Martha Nussbaum, 185–200. New York: Oxford University Press, 1998.

"Are the Gods Afraid of Black Sexuality: Religion and the Burdens of Black Sexual Politics" Conference. Columbia University Center on African-American Religion,

Sexual Politics, and Social Justice, October 23–24, 2014. https://carss.columbia.edu
/events/are-gods-afraid-black-sexuality-religion-and-burdens-black-sexual-politics.

Asanti, Ifalade T. "Living with Dual Spirits: Spirituality, Sexuality and Healing in the
African Diaspora." In *Sexuality, Religion, and the Sacred: Bisexual, Pansexual, and
Polysexual Perspectives*, edited by Loraine Hutchins and H. Sharif Williams, 54–62.
New York: Routledge, 2012.

Association for Global New Thought. "Welcome." Accessed February 28, 2022. www
.agnt.today.

Baker, Ella. "Developing Community Leadership." In *Black Women in White America:
A Documentary History*, edited by Gerda Lerner, 345–51. New York: Vintage, 1973.

Baker-Fletcher, Karen. *Sisters of Dust, Sisters of Spirit: Womanist Wordings on God and
Creation*. Minneapolis: Fortress, 1998.

Baldwin, Lewis V., and Victor Anderson, eds. *Revives My Soul Again: The Spirituality of
Martin Luther King Jr.* Minneapolis: Fortress, 2018.

Barlett, Jackson. "Black and Proud: Putting Community Back into Queer Organizing."
Critical Moment, July 8, 2011. https://critical-moment.org/2011/07/08/black-and
-proud-putting-community-back-into-queer-organizing.

Barlow, Rich. "Eyewitness to the Turmoil in Ferguson." *BU Today*, August 26, 2014.
www.bu.edu/today/2014/eyewitness-to-the-turmoil-in-ferguson.

Battle, Juan, Antonio Pastrana Jr., and Angelique Harris. *An Examination of Black LGBT
Populations across the United States: Intersections of Race and Sexuality*. New York:
Palgrave Macmillan, 2017.

Ben-Moche, Erin. "Rabbi Sandra Lawson Opens Up on Finding Connection in Unprecedented Times." *Jewish Journal*, July 9, 2020. https://jewishjournal.com/culture
/318616/rabbi-sandra-lawson-on-findingconnection-in-unprecedented-times.

Blum, Edward J. *W. E. B. Du Bois, American Prophet*. Philadelphia: University of Pennsylvania Press, 2007.

Borland, Katherine. "That's Not What I Said: Interpretive Conflict in Oral Narrative
Research." *In Women's Words: The Feminist Practice of Oral History*, edited by Sherna
Gluck and Daphne Patai, 63–76. New York: Routledge, 1991.

Bostic, Joy. *African American Female Mystical Activism: Nineteenth-Century Religious
Activism*. New York: Palgrave Macmillan, 2013.

Boyd, Nan, and Horacio Roque Ramírez. "Introduction: Close Encounters." In *Bodies
of Evidence: The Practice of Queer Oral History*, edited by Boyd and Ramírez, 1–22.
New York: Oxford University Press, 2012.

Brown Douglas, Kelly. "Heterosexism and the Black American Church Community."
In *Heterosexism in Contemporary World Religion: Problem and Prospect*, edited by
Marvin Ellison and Judith Plaskow, 177–200. Cleveland: Pilgrim, 2007.

Brown Douglas, Kelly. *Stand Your Ground: Black Bodies and the Justice of God*. Maryknoll, NY: Orbis, 2015.

Bryant-Davis, Thema, and Tyonna Adams. "A Psychocultural Exploration of Womanism, Activism, and Social Justice." In *Womanism and Mujerista Psychologies: Voices
of Fire and Acts of Courage*, 219–36. Washington: American Psychological Association, 2016.

Butler, Octavia. *Parable of the Sower.* New York: Grand Central, 2000.

Cadge, Wendy. "Lesbian, Gay, and Bisexual Buddhist Practitioners." In *Gay Religion,* edited by Scott Thumma and Edward R. Gray, 134–51. Walnut Creek, CA: AltaMira, 2005.

Campbell-Reed, Eileen. "State of Clergywomen in the US Report." www.StateofClergy women.org, 2018. Accessed February 28, 2022.

Cannon, Katie. "Emancipatory Historiography." In *Dictionary of Feminist Theologies,* edited by Letty Russell and J. Shannon Clarkson, 81. Louisville: Westminster John Knox, 1996.

Cannon, Katie. "Structured Academic Amnesia: As If This True Womanist Story Never Happened." In *Deeper Shades of Purple: Womanism in Religion and Society,* edited by Stacey Floyd-Thomas, 19–28. New York: New York University Press, 2006.

Carpenter, Delores. *A Time for Honor: A Portrait of African American Clergywomen.* St. Louis: Chalice, 2001.

Carter, Mandy. "Nonviolent Activism and Santa Rita Prison." YouTube, February 9, 2018. Accessed February 28, 2022. www.youtube.com/watch?v=-ww3AEzxDxI.

Chang, Jerome, and Michèle A. Bowring, "The Perceived Impact of Sexual Orientation on the Ability of Queer Leaders to Relate to Followers." *Leadership* 13, no. 3 (2017): 285–300.

Cheng, Patrick. *Radical Love: An Introduction to Queer Theology.* New York: Seabury, 2011.

Christian Century edition devoted to Black Lives Matter; Rima Vesely-Flad, Racial Purity and Dangerous Bodies: Moral Pollution, Black Lives and the Struggle for Justice; Kelly Brown Douglas, Stand Your Ground: Black Bodies and the Justice of God and Leah Gunning Francis, Ferguson & Faith: Sparking Leadership and Awakening Community

Church of God in Christ. "General Assembly Declaration and Apologetic of Marriage." Accessed February 28, 2022. www.cogic.org/wp-content/uploads/2012/09/FINAL -DRAFT-OF-RESPONSE-TO-CRITICISM-OF-FAITH-IN-HUMAN-RIGHTS -DECLARATION.pdf.

"City of Refuge History." City of Refuge. Accessed February 28, 2022. https:// cityofrefugeucc.org/about.

Clarke, Cheryl. "Lesbianism: An Act of Resistance." In *Feminism and Sexuality: A Reader,* edited by Stevi Jackson and Sue Scott, 155–61. New York: Columbia University Press, 1996.

Clarke, Cheryl. "New Notes on Lesbianism." *The Days of Good Looks: The Prose and Poetry of Cheryl Clarke, 1980–2005,* 81–88. New York: Carroll & Graf, 2006.

Coleman, Monica A. *Ain't I a Womanist, Too? Third Wave Womanist Religious Thought.* Minneapolis: Fortress, 2013.

Coleman, Monica A. *Making a Way out of No Way: A Womanist Theology.* Minneapolis: Fortress, 2006.

Collier-Thomas, Bettye. *Daughters of Thunder: Black Women Preachers and Their Sermons, 1850–1979.* San Francisco: Jossey-Bass, 1998.

Collier-Thomas, Bettye. *Jesus, Jobs, and Justice: African American Women and Religion.* New York: Alfred A. Knopf, 2010.

Collier-Thomas, Bettye, and V. P. Franklin, eds. *Sisters in the Struggle: African American Women in the Civil Rights–Black Power Movement*. New York: New York University Press, 2001.

Collins, Patricia Hill. *Black Feminist Thought: Knowledge, Consciousness, and the Politics of Empowerment*. New York: Routledge, 2000.

Collins, Patricia Hill. "Learning from the Outsider Within: The Sociological Significance of Black Feminist Thought." In *The Feminist Standpoint Theory Reader: Intellectual and Political Controversies*, edited by Sandra Harding, 103–26. New York: Routledge, 2004.

Collins, Patricia Hill. "Searching for Sojourner Truth: Toward an Epistemology of Empowerment." *Fighting Words: Black Women and the Search for Justice*, 229–52. Minneapolis: University of Minnesota Press, 1998.

Collins, Patricia Hill. "What's in a Name? Womanism, Black Feminism, and Beyond." *Black Scholar* 26 (1996): 9–17.

Combahee River Collective. "Combahee River Collective Statement." In *How We Get Free: Black Feminism and the Combahee River Collective*, edited by Keeanga-Yamahtta Taylor, 15–27. Chicago: Haymarket, 2017.

Crenshaw, Kimberle. "Demarginalizing the Intersection of Race and Sex: A Black Feminist Critique of Antidiscrimination Doctrine, Feminist Theory and Antiracist Politics." *University of Chicago Legal Forum* 1989, Issue 1, Article 8, 139–67.

Dickerson, Dennis. *The African Methodist Episcopal Church: A History*. Cambridge: Cambridge University Press, 2020.

DiVeglia, Angela L. "Accessibility, Accountability, and Activism: Models for LGBT Archives." In *Make Your Own History: Documenting Feminist and Queer Activism in the 21st Century*, edited by Lyz Bly and Kelly Wooten, 69–88. Los Angeles: Litwin, 2012.

Doyle, Michael. *Radical Chapters: Pacifist Bookseller Roy Kepler and the Paperback Revolution*. Syracuse, NY: Syracuse University Press, 2012.

Du Bois, W. E. B. *Prayers for Dark People*. Amherst: University of Massachusetts Press, 1980.

Edwards, Elise. "'Let's Imagine Something Different': Spiritual Principles in Contemporary African American Justice Movements and Their Implications for the Built Environment." *Religions* 8 (2017). https://doi.org/10.3390/rel8120256.

Edwards, Erica. *Charisma and the Fictions of Black Leadership*. Minneapolis: University of Minnesota Press, 2012.

Eger, Denise. "Ten Years . . . and Counting." In *Lesbian Rabbis: The First Generation*, edited by Rebecca Alpert, Shirley Idelson, and Sue Levi Elwell. 161–72. New Brunswick, NJ: Rutgers University Press, 2001.

Eichhorn, Kate. "Queer Archives: From Collections to Conceptual Framework." In *The Routledge History of Queer America*, edited by Don Romesburg, 123–34. New York: Routledge, 2018.

Elwell, Sue L., and Rebecca T. Alpert. "Introduction: Why a Book on Lesbian Rabbis." In *Lesbian Rabbis: The First Generation*, edited by Rebecca T. Alpert, Sue Levi Elwell, and Shirley Idelson, 1–38. New Brunswick, NJ: Rutgers University Press, 2001.

Etter-Lewis, Gwendolyn. "Black Women's Life Stories: Reclaiming Self in Narrative Texts." In *Women's Words: The Feminist Practice of Oral History*, edited by Sherna Berger Gluck and Daphne Patai, 43–58. New York: Routledge, 1991.

Fairclough, Adam. *Martin Luther King Jr.* Athens: University of Georgia Press, 1995.

Farrag, Hebah. "The Spirit in Black Lives Matter: New Spiritual Community." *Black Radical Organizing Transition* 125 (2017): 76–88.

The Fellowship of Affirming Ministries. "About Us." Accessed February 28, 2022. www.radicallyinclusive.org/about-us.

Fingerhut, Hannah. "Support Steady for Same-Sex Marriage and Acceptance of Homosexuality." May 12, 2016. Pew Research Center. www.pewresearch.org/fact-tank/2016/05/12/support-steady-for-same-sex-marriage-and-acceptance-of-homosexuality.

Floyd-Thomas, Stacey. "Radical Subjectivity." In *Deeper Shades of Purple: Womanism in Religion and Society*, edited by Floyd-Thomas, 16. New York: New York University Press, 2006.

Fluker, Walter E. *Ethical Leadership: The Quest for Character, Civility, and Community*. Minneapolis: Fortress, 2009.

Fluker, Walter E. *The Stones That the Builders Rejected: The Development of Ethical Leadership from the Black Church Tradition*. Harrisburg, PA: Trinity Press International, 1998.

Flunder, Bishop Yvette. Oral history interview conducted by author, 2011. LGBTQ-RAN Oral History transcript. Accessed February 28, 2022. https://lgbtqreligiousarchives.org/media/oral-history/vette-flunder/Yflunder.pdf.

Flunder, Yvette. Oral history interview conducted by author, 2019.

Flunder, Yvette. *Where the Edge Gathers: Building a Community of Radical Inclusion*. Cleveland: Pilgrim, 2005.

Francis, Leah Gunning. *Ferguson and Faith: Sparking Leadership and Awakening Community*. St. Louis: Chalice, 2015.

Franklin, Darlene Rev. Oral History interview conducted by author, 2018. LGBTQ-RAN Oral History transcript. Accessed February 28, 2022. https://lgbtqreligiousarchives.org/media/oral-history/darlene-franklin/Darlene%20Franklin%202018-06-09%20transcript.pdf.

Franklin, Robert M. *Moral Leadership: Integrity, Courage, Imagination*. Maryknoll, NY: Orbis, 2020.

Frederick, Marla. *Between Sundays: Black Women and Everyday Struggles of Faith*. Berkeley: University of California Press, 2003.

Freedom Center for Social Justice. "Partner Programming." Accessed February 28, 2022. https://www.fcsj.org/partner-programs.

Freedom Center for Social Justice. "Mission, Vision, Values." Accessed February 28, 2022. https://www.fcsj.org/our-story.

Garner, Elder Darlene. Oral History interview conducted by author, 2010. LGBTQ-RAN Oral History transcript. Accessed February 28, 2022. https://lgbtqreligiousarchives.org/media/oral-history/darlene-garner/DGarner.pdf.

Gibbs, Abby. "Rabbi Redefines Religion." Elon News Network, March 15, 2019. http://projects.elonnewsnetwork.com/elonrabbi.

Gibson, Danjuma G. *Frederick Douglass, a Psychobiography: Rethinking Subjectivity in the Western Experiment of Democracy*. Cham, Switzerland: Palgrave Macmillan, 2018.

Giddings, Paula. *When and Where I Enter: The Impact of Black Women on Race and Sex in America*. New York: William Morrow, 1984.

Gilkes, Cheryl Townsend. *If It Wasn't for the Women: Black Women's Experience and Womanist Culture in Church and Community*. Maryknoll, NY: Orbis, 2001.

Gluck, Sherna. "What's So Special about Women? Women's Oral History." In *Oral History: An Interdisciplinary Anthology*, edited by David Dunaway and Willa Baum, 215–30. Walnut Creek, CA: AltaMira, 1996.

Griffin, Horace. *Their Own Receive Them Not: African American Lesbians & Gays in Black* Churches. Cleveland: Pilgrim, 2006.

Guillory, Margarita S. *Spiritual and Social Transformation in African American Spiritual Churches: More Than Conjurers*. New York: Routledge, 2018.

Gushee, David, and Colin Holtz. *Moral Leadership for a Divided Age: Fourteen People Who Dared to Change Our World*. Grand Rapids, MI: Brazos, 2018.

Hammonds, Evelynn. "Black (W)holes and the Geometry of Black Female Sexuality." *Differences: A Journal of Feminist Cultural Studies* 6, nos. 2–3 (1994): 126–45.

Hammonds, Evelynn. "Toward a Genealogy of Black Female Sexuality: The Problematic of Silence." In *Feminist Theory and the Body: A Reader*, edited by Janet Price and Margrit Shildrick, 93–104. New York: Routledge, 1999.

Harris, Melanie L. "Buddhist Meditation for the Recovery of the Womanist Self, or Sitting on the Mat Self-Love Realized." *Buddhist-Christian Studies* 52 (2012): 67–72.

Harris, Melanie L. *Ecowomanism: African American Women and Earth-Honoring Faiths*. Maryknoll, NY: Orbis, 2017.

Harris, Melanie L. *Gifts of Virtue, Alice Walker, and Womanist Ethics*. New York: Palgrave Macmillan, 2010.

Harris, Melanie L. "Womanist Spirituality: Legacies of Freedom." In *Contemporary Perspectives on Religions in Africa and the African Diaspora*, edited by Ibigbolade S. Aderibigbe and Carolyn M. Jones Medine, 147–63. New York: Palgrave Macmillan, 2015.

Harrison, Beverly Wildung. *Making the Connections: Essays in Feminist Social Ethics*, edited by Carol S. Robb, Boston: Beacon, 1985.

Harshaw, Pendarvis. "OG Told Me." In *Say It Forward: A Guide to Social Justice Storytelling*, edited by Cliff Mayotte and Claire Kiefer, 77–90. Chicago: Haymarket, 2018.

Hayes, Diana L. *No Crystal Stair: Womanist Spirituality*. Maryknoll, NY: Orbis, 2016.

Henderson, Katharine R. *God's Troublemakers: How Women of Faith Are Changing the World*. New York: Continuum, 2006.

Hernandez, Daisy, and Bushra Rehman. *Colonize This! Young Women of Color on Today's Feminism*. New York: Seal, 2002.

Hill, Renee L. "Human Sexuality—The Rest of the Story." In *Walk Together Children: Black and Womanist Theologies, Church, and Theological Education*, edited by Dwight N. Hopkins and Linda E. Thomas, 183–92. Eugene, OR: Cascade, 2010.

Hill, Renee L. In *A Whosoever Church: Welcoming Lesbians and Gay Men into African American Congregations*, edited by Gary Comstock, 189–201. Louisville: Westminster John Knox, 2001.

Hill, Renee L. "Who Are We for Each Other? Sexism, Sexuality and Womanist Theology." In *Black Theology: A Documentary History*, vol. 2: 1980–1992, edited by James Cone and Gayraud Wilmore, 345–54. Maryknoll, NY: Orbis, 1993.

Hine, Darlene Clark. "Rape and the Inner Lives of Black Women in the Middle West: Preliminary Thoughts on the Culture of Dissemblance." *Signs* 14, no. 1 (1989): 912–20.

Holmes, Rev. Candy. Oral History interview conducted by author, 2017. LGBTQ-RAN Oral History transcript. Accessed February 28, 2022. https://lgbtqreligiousarchives .org/media/oral-history/candy-holmes/CHolmes.pdf.

Holmes, Candy. "Rev. Candy Holmes' Resignation from MCC Leadership." Accessed February 28, 2022. www.believeoutloud.com/voices/article/rev-candy-holmes -resignation-from-mcc-leadership-roles.

hooks, bell. *Talking Back: Thinking Feminist, Thinking Black*. Boston: South End, 1989.

Hoover, Theressa. "Black Women and the Churches: Triple Jeopardy." In *Black Theology: A Documentary History*, vol. 1: 1966–1979, edited by James Cone and Gayraud Wilmore, 293–303. Maryknoll, NY: Orbis, 1993.

Houchins, Sue. *Spiritual Narratives*. New York: Oxford University Press, 1998.

Hull, Akasha G. *Soul Talk: The New Spirituality of African American Women*. Rochester, VT: Inner Traditions, 2001.

Human Rights Campaign. "Stances of Faiths on LGBTQ Issues: Church of God in Christ." Accessed February 28, 2022. www.hrc.org/resources/stances-of-faiths-on -lgbt-issues-church-of-god-in-christ.

Jackson, Cari. *For the Souls of Black Folks: Reimagining Black Preaching for 21st Century Liberation*. Eugene, OR: Pickwick, 2013.

Jackson, Cari. "Her Story." Accessed February 28, 2022. www.drcarijackson.com/her -story.html.

Jackson, Rev. Dr. Cari. Oral History interview conducted by author, 2018. Accessed February 28, 2022. https://lgbtqreligiousarchives.org/oral-histories/cari-jackson.

Jackson, Debora. *Meant for Good: Fundamentals of Womanist Leadership*. Valley Forge, PA: Judson, 2019.

Jackson, Stevi, and Sue Scott. "Sexual Skirmishes and Feminist Factions: Twenty-Five Years of Debate on Women and Sexuality." In *Feminism and Sexuality: A Reader*, edited by Jackson and Scott, 1–31. New York: Columbia University Press, 1996.

Johnson, Rev. Deborah L. "Inner Light Ministries." In *Creating Welcoming Congregations in the African American Tradition*, by National Black Justice Coalition. https:// nbjc.org/wp-content/uploads/2020/11/welcoming-congregations-in-the-african -american-tradition.pdf

Johnson, Rev. Dr. Deborah L. Oral history interview conducted by author, 2017. LGBTQ-RAN Oral History transcript. Accessed February 28, 2022. https:// lgbtqreligiousarchives.org/media/oral-history/deborah-johnson/DJohnson.pdf.

Johnson, Deborah L. *Sacred Yes: Letters from the Infinite*, vol. 1. Boulder, CO: Sounds True, 2006.

Johnson, Deborah L. *Your Deepest Intent: Letters from the Infinite*. Boulder, CO: Sounds True, 2007.

Johnson, E. Patrick. *Black.Queer.Southern.Women: An Oral History*. Chapel Hill: University of North Carolina Press, 2018.

Johnson, E. Patrick. *Honeypot: Black Southern Women Who Love Women*. Durham, NC: Duke University Press, 2019.

Johnson, E. Patrick. "Introduction." In *No Tea, No Shade: New Writings in Black Queer Studies*, edited by Johnson, 1–26. Durham, NC: Duke University Press, 2016.

Johnson, E. Patrick. "'Quare' Studies, or (Almost) Everything I Know about Queer Studies I Learned from My Grandmother." In *Black Queer Studies*, edited by E. Patrick Johnson and Mae G. Henderson, 124–57. Durham, NC: Duke University Press, 2005.

Jones, Melanie. "The Will to Adorn: Beyond Self-Surveillance, Toward a Womanist Ethic of Redemptive Self-Love." *Black Theology* 16, no. 3 (2018): 218–30.

Jones, Robert, and Daniel Cox. "America's Changing Religious Identity." PRRI, 2017. www.prri.org/research/american-religious-landscape-christian-religiously-unaffiliated.

Jones, Robert, Daniel Cox, Robert Griffin, Molly Fisch-Friedman, and Alex Vandermaas-Peeler. "Emerging Consensus on LGBT Issues: Findings from the 2017 American Values Atlas." PRRI, 2018. www.prri.org/research/emerging-consensus-on-lgbt-issues-findings-from-the-2017-american-values-atlas.

Jordan, June. "Waiting on a Taxi." In *Names We Call Home: Autobiography on Racial Identity*, 299–301. New York: Routledge, 1996.

Jordan, Mark. "Spiritual, Sexual, and Religious?" *Harvard Divinity Bulletin*, Autumn/Winter (2019). Accessed February 28, 2022. https://bulletin.hds.harvard.edu/spiritual-sexual-and-religious.

King, Toni C. "Don't Waste Your Breath: The Dialectics of Communal Leadership Development." In *Black Womanist Leadership: Tracing the Motherline*, edited by Toni C. King and S. Alease Ferguson, 87–108. Albany: State University of New York Press, 2011.

King, Toni C., and S. Alease Ferguson. "Introduction: Looking to the Motherline." In *Black Womanist Leadership: Tracing the Motherline*, edited by King and Ferguson, 1–22. Albany: State University of New York Press, 2011.

Lanoix, Alfreda Elder quoted in Melissa Wilcox. *Queer Women and Religious Individualism*. Bloomington: Indiana University Press, 2009.

Lawson, Rabbi Sandra. "My Vision." Accessed February 28, 2022. www.rabbisandralawson.com/support.

Lawson, Rabbi Sandra. Oral history interview conducted by author, 2018. LGBTQ-RAN Oral History transcript. Accessed February 28, 2022. https://lgbtqreligiousarchives.org/media/oral-history/sandra-lawson/Sandra%20Lawson%20oral%20history%20transcript.pdf.

Lawson, Rabbi Sandra. "Rabbi, Musician, and Activist." www.rabbisandralawson.com/whoiam.

Leath, Jennifer. "Canada and Pure Land, a New Field and Buddha-Land: Womanists and Buddhists Reading Together." *Buddhist-Christian Relations* 32 (2012): 57–65.

Lee, Frances. "Excommunicate Me from the Church of Social Justice." Autostraddle, July 13, 2017. Accessed February 28, 2022. www.autostraddle.com/kin-aesthetics-excommunicate-me-from-the-church-of-social-justice-386640.

Lee, Jarena quoted in Sue Houchins, *Spiritual Narratives.*

Leffler, Phyllis. *Black Leaders on Leadership: Conversations with Julian Bond.* New York: Palgrave Macmillan, 2014.

Leong, Pamela. *Religion, Flesh, and Blood: The Convergence of HIV/AIDS, Black Sexual Expression, and Therapeutic Religion.* Lanham, MD: Lexington, 2015.

Lewin, Ellen. *Filled with the Spirit: Sexuality, Gender, and Radical Inclusivity in a Black Pentecostal Church Coalition.* Chicago: University of Chicago Press, 2018.

Lewis, Stephen, Matthew Williams, and Dori Baker. *Another Way: Living and Leading Change on Purpose.* St. Louis: Chalice, 2020.

Lightsey, Rev. Dr. Pamela. Oral history interview conducted by author, 2017. LGBTQ-RAN Oral History transcript. Accessed February 28, 2022. https://lgbtqreligiousarchives.org/media/oral-history/pamela-lightsey/PLightsey.pdf.

Lightsey, Pamela. *Our Lives Matter: A Womanist Queer Theology.* Eugene, OR: Pickwick, 2015.

Lincoln, C. Eric., and Lawrence Mamiya. *The Black Church in the African American Experience.* Durham, NC: Duke University Press, 1990.

Lorde, Audre. "Age, Race, Class, and Sex: Women Redefine Difference." In *Sister Outsider*, 114–23. Berkeley, CA: Crossing Press, 1984.

Lorde, Audre. "An Interview: Audre Lorde and Adrienne Rich." In *Sister Outsider*, 81–113. Berkeley, CA: Crossing Press, 1984.

Loose, Sarah K., with Amy Starecheski. "Oral History for Building Social Movements, Then and Now." In *Beyond Women's Words: Feminisms and the Practices of Oral History in the Twenty-First Century*, ed. Katrina Srigley, Stacey Zembrzycki, and Franca Iacovetta, 236–43. New York: Routledge, 2018.

Lorde, Audre. *Sister Outsider.* Berkeley, CA: Crossing Press, 1984.

Lorde, Audre. "There Is No Hierarchy of Oppression." In *I Am Your Sister: Collective and Unpublished Writings of Audre Lorde*, edited by Rudolph P. Byrd, Johnnetta Betsch Cole, and Beverly Guy-Sheftall, 219–20. New York: Oxford University Press, 2009.

Lu, Jessica H., and Catherine Knight Steele. "Joy Is Resistance: Cross-Platform Resilience and (Re)invention of Black Oral Culture Online." *Information, Communication, and Society* 22, no. 6 (2019): 823–37.

Lyons, Courtney. "Breaking through the Extra-Thick Stained-Glass Ceiling: African American Baptist Women in Ministry." *Review and Expositor* 110, no. 1 (2013): 77–91.

Maparyan, Layli. *The Womanist Idea.* New York: Routledge, 2012.

Markoe, Lauren. "She's Black, Gay, and Soon You Can Call Her 'Rabbi.'" *The Washington Post*, May 28, 2015.

Martin, Darnise. *Beyond Christianity: African Americans in a New Thought Church.* New York: New York University Press, 2005.

Martinez, Elizabeth Betita, Mandy Carter, and Matt Meyer. *We Have Not Been Moved: Resisting Racism and Militarism in 21st Century America*. Oakland, CA: PM Press, 2012.

"MCC Fact Sheet." MCC Core Documents, 2019. www.mccchurch.org/overview.

McCoy, Rev. Dr. Renee. Oral history interview conducted by the author, 2017. LGBTQ-RAN Oral History transcript. Accessed February 28, 2022. https://lgbtqreligiousarchives.org/media/oral-history/renee-mccoy/RMcCoy.pdf.

McQueeney, Krista. "We Are God's Children Ya'll: Race, Gender, and Sexuality in Lesbian and Gay-Affirming Congregations." *Social Problems* 56, no. 1 (2009): 151–73.

Micham, Laura quoted in Angela L. DiVeglia, "Accessibility, Accountability, and Activism: Models for LGBT Archives." In *Make Your Own History: Documenting Feminist and Queer Activism in the 21st Century*, edited by Lyz Bly and Kelly Wooten, 69–104. Los Angeles: Litwin, 2012.

Monroe, Rev. Irene. In *A Whosoever Church: Welcoming Lesbians and Gay Men into African American Congregations*, edited by Gary Comstock, 59–71. Louisville: Westminster John Knox, 2001.

Moore, Mignon. "Black and Gay in L.A.: The Relationships Black Lesbians and Gay Men Have to Their Racial and Religious Communities." In *Black Los Angeles: American Dreams and Racial Realities*, edited by Darnell Hunt and Ana-Christina Ramon, 188–212. New York: New York University Press, 2010.

Moore, Mignon. "Lipstick or Timberlands? Meanings of Gender Presentation in Black Lesbian Communities." *Signs: Journals of Women in Culture and Society* 32, no. 1 (2006): 113–39.

Moraga, Cherríe, and Gloria Anzaldúa, eds. *This Bridge Called My Back: Writings by Radical Women of Color*. New York: Kitchen Table, 1983.

Moultrie, Monique. "#BlackBabiesMatter: Analyzing Black Religious Media in Conservative and Progressive Evangelical Communities." *Religions* 8 (2017). https://doi.org/10.3390/rel8110255.

Moultrie, Monique. *Passionate and Pious: Religious Media and Black Women's Sexuality*. Durham, NC: Duke University Press, 2017.

Okihiro, Gary. "Oral History and the Writing of Ethnic History." In *Oral History: An Interdisciplinary Anthology*, edited by David Dunaway and Willa Baum, 199–214. Walnut Creek, CA: AltaMira, 1996.

Oral History Association. "Oral History Defined." Accessed February 28, 2022. www.oralhistory.org/about/do-oral-history.

Parris, Brittany Bennett. "Creating, Reconstructing, and Protecting Historical Narratives: Archives and the LGBT Community." *Current Studies in Librarianship* (Spring/Fall 2005): 5–25.

Pastrana, Antonio Jr. "The Intersectional Imagination: What Do Lesbian and Gay Leaders of Color Have to Do with It?" *Race, Gender, & Class* 13, no. 3 (2006): 218–38.

Payne, Charles. "Ella Baker and Models of Social Change." *Signs* 14, no. 4 (1989): 885–99.

Perry, Troy. *The Lord Is My Shepherd and He Knows I'm Gay: The Autobiography of Rev. Troy D. Perry as Told to Charles L. Lucas*. Los Angeles: Nash, 1972.

Phillips, Layli. *The Womanist Reader*. New York: Routledge, 2006.

Pryor, Jonathan T. "Queer Activist Leadership: An Exploration of Queer Leadership in Higher Education." *Journal of Diversity in Higher Education*. 14, no.3 (2021): 303–315.

Pryor, Jonathan T. "Queer Advocacy Leadership: A Queer Leadership Model for Higher Education." *Journal of Leadership Education*. Research Manuscript, 70. January 2020. https://journalofleadershiped.org/jole_articles/queer-advocacy-leadership-a-queer-leadership-model-for-higher-education. Accessed February 28, 2022.

Raboteau, Albert J. *American Prophets: Seven Religious Radicals and Their Struggles for Social and Political Justice*. Princeton, NJ: Princeton University Press, 2016.

Rankow, Liza. "Toward the Prophetic: A New Direction in the Practice of New Thought." *Religion Online*. Accessed February 28, 2022. www.religion-online.org/article/toward-the-prophetic-a-new-direction-in-the-practice-of-new-thought.

Rawls, Bishop Tonyia. Oral history interview conducted by the author, 2018.

Rawls, Tonyia. "Bishop Tonyia Rawls: Unity Fellowship Church Movement." *Creating Welcoming Congregations in the African American Tradition*. National Black Justice Coalition. Accessed February 28, 2022. https://nbjc.org/wp-content/uploads/2020/11/welcoming-congregations-in-the-african-american-tradition.pdf.

Rawls, Tonyia. "Yes, Jesus Loves Me: The Liberating Power of Spiritual Acceptance for Black Lesbian, Gay, Bisexual, and Transgender Christians." In *Black Sexualities: Probing Powers, Passions, Practices, and Policies*, edited by Juan Battle and Sandra L. Barnes, 327–52. New Brunswick, NJ: Rutgers University Press, 2010.

Rhode, Deborah. *Women and Leadership*. New York: Oxford University Press, 2017.

Rhue, Dr. Sylvia. Oral history interview conducted by author, 2011. LGBTQ-RAN Oral History transcript. Accessed February 28, 2022. https://lgbtqreligiousarchives.org/media/oral-history/sylvia-rhue/Rhue.pdf.

Rich, Adrienne. "Compulsory Heterosexuality and Lesbian Existence." In *Feminism and Sexuality: A Reader,* edited by Stevi Jackson and Sue Scott, 130–43. New York: Columbia University Press, 1996.

Robnett, Belinda. *How Long? How Long? African American Women in the Struggle for Civil Rights*. Rev. ed. New York: Oxford University Press, 2000.

Rose, Tricia. *Longing to Tell: Black Women Talk about Sexuality and Intimacy*. New York: Farrar, Straus and Giroux, 2003.

Ross, Rosetta E. "Lessons and Treasures in Our Mothers' Witness: Why I Write about Black Women's Activism." In *Deeper Shades of Purple: Womanism in Religion and Society*, edited by Stacey Floyd-Thomas, 115–27. New York: New York University Press, 2006.

Ross, Rosetta E. *Witnessing and Testifying: Black Women, Religion, and Civil Rights*. Minneapolis: Fortress, 2003.

Rosser-Mims, Dionne. "Black Feminism: An Epistemological Framework for Exploring How Race and Gender Impact Black Women's Leadership Development." *Advancing Women in Leadership Journal* 30, no. 15 (2010): 1–10.

Rushin, Donna Kate. "This Bridge." In *This Bridge Called My Back: Writings by Radical Women of Color*, edited by Cherríe Moraga and Gloria Anzaldúa, xxi–xxii. New York: Kitchen Table, 1983.

Salazar, Claudia. "A Third World Women's Text: Between the Politics of Criticism and Cultural Politics." In *Women's Words: The Feminist Practice of Oral History*, edited by Sherna Berger Gluck and Daphne Patai, 93–106. New York: Routledge, 1991.

Sales, Ben. "Sandra Lawson, Black Lesbian Vegan Rabbinical Student, Hopes to Redefine Where Judaism Happens." Jewish Telegraphic Agency, June 19, 2016. www .jta.org/2016/06/19/united-states/sandra-lawson-black-lesbian-vegan-rabbinical -student-hopes-to-redefine-where-judaism-happens.

Smith, Barbara. *Towards a Black Feminist Criticism*. Freedom, CA: Out and Out, 1977.

Smith, Barbara, and Beverly Smith. "I Am Not Meant to Be Alone and Without You Who Understand: Letters from Black Feminists, 1972–1978." *Conditions: Four* 2, no. 1 (1979): 62–77.

Smith, Pamela A. "Green Lap, Brown Embrace, Blue Body: The Ecospirituality of Alice Walker." *CrossCurrents* 48, no. 4 (Winter 1998–1999): 471–87.

Sneed, Roger. *Representations of Homosexuality: Black Liberation Theology and Cultural Criticism*. New York: Palgrave Macmillan, 2010.

Talvacchia, Kathleen. *Embracing Disruptive Coherence: Coming Out as Erotic Ethical Practice*. Eugene, OR: Cascade, 2019.

Taylor, Charles. *The Ethics of Authenticity*. Cambridge. MA: Harvard University Press, 2018.

Theoharris, George. "Social Justice Educational Leaders and Resistance: Toward a Theory of Social Justice Leadership." *Educational Administration Quarterly* 43, no. 2 (2007): 221–58.

Thomas, Linda. "Womanist Theology, Epistemology, and a New Anthropological Paradigm." In *Living Stones in the Household of God: The Legacy and Future of Black Theology,* edited by Thomas, 37–50. Minneapolis: Fortress, 2004.

Townes, Emilie M. "Ethics as an Art of Doing the Work Our Souls Must Have." In *Womanist Theological Ethics: A Reader*, edited by Katie Geneva Cannon, Emilie M. Townes, and Angela D. Sims, 35–50. Louisville: Westminster John Knox, 2011.

Townes, Emilie M. "Finding the Legacy: Nineteenth-Century African American Women's Spirituality and Social Reform." In *In a Blaze of Glory: Womanist Spirituality as Social Witness*, 30–43. Nashville, TN: Abingdon, 1995.

Townes, Rev. Dr. Emilie. Oral history interview conducted by author, 2018. LGBTQ-RAN Oral History transcript. Accessed February 28, 2022. https://lgbtqreligiousar-chives.org/media/oral-history/emilie-m-townes/Emilie%20Townes%202018-05 -31%20transcript.pdf.

Townes, Emilie M. *Womanist Justice, Womanist Hope*. Atlanta: Scholars Press, 1993.

Unity Fellowship Church Movement. "History." Accessed February 28, 2022. https:// ufcmlife.org.

Vesely-Flad, Rima. *Racial Purity and Dangerous Bodies: Moral Pollution, Black Lives, and the Struggle for Justice*. Minneapolis: Fortress, 2017.

Voice of Witness. "History on a Human Scale." In *Say It Forward: A Guide to Social Justice Storytelling*, edited by Cliff Mayotte and Claire Kiefer, 10–13. Chicago: Haymarket, 2018.

Walker, Alice. *In Search of Our Mothers' Gardens: Womanist Prose*. New York: Harcourt, 1983.

Washington-Leapheart, Kentina. "The Center for the Church and the Black Experience Celebrating 45 Outstanding Black Alums." Accessed February 28, 2022. https://cbe45.com/2016/04/14/chaplain-kentina-washington.

Washington-Leapheart, Rev. Kentina. Oral history conducted by author, 2019. LGBTQ-RAN Oral History transcript. Accessed February 28, 2022. https://lgbtqreligiousarchives.org/media/oral-history/kentina-washington-leapheart/Kentina%20Washington%20Leapheart%202019-10-20.1%20transcript.pdf.

Washington-Leapheart, Kentina. "The Ordination I Never Could Have Imagined." Religious Institute, August 29, 2018. https://medium.com/@ReligiousInst/the-ordination-i-never-could-have-imagined-691b5b0247cf.

Washington-Leapheart, Rev. Naomi. Oral history interview conducted by author, 2019. LGBTQ-RAN Oral History transcript. Accessed February 28, 2022. https://lgbtqreligiousarchives.org/oral-histories/naomi-washington-leapheart.

Walker, Alice. *In Search of Our Mother's Gardens*. Womanist Prose, New York: Harcourt, 1983.

Weekes-Laidlow, Melinda, and Bishop Tonyia Rawls. "Facing Race: Stories and Voices." SoundCloud audio, 7:21, 2017. Accessed February 28, 2022. https://soundcloud.com/facingracestories/bishop-tonyia-rawls-on-working-with-the-black-church-for-lgbtq-justice.

Wessinger, Catherine. "Charismatic Leaders in New Religious Movements." In *The Cambridge Companion to New Religious Movements*, edited by Olav Hammer and Mikael Rothstein, 80–96. Cambridge: Cambridge University Press, 2012.

Wiggins, Daphne. *Righteous Content: Black Women's Perspectives of Church and Faith*. New York: New York University Press, 2005.

Wilcox, Melissa. *Queer Women and Religious Individualism*. Bloomington: Indiana University Press, 2009.

Wilcox, Melissa. "Same-Sex Eroticism and Gender Fluidity in New and Alternative Religions." In *Introduction to New and Alternative Religions in America*, edited by Eugene Gallagher and Michael Ashcraft, 247–56. Westport, CT: Greenwood, 2006.

Williams, Khalia Jelks. "Engaging Womanist Spirituality in African American Christian Worship." *Proceedings of the North American Academy of Liturgy* (August 2013): 95–109.

Woody, Dr. Imani. Oral history interview conducted by author, 2017. LGBTQ-RAN Oral History transcript. Accessed February 28, 2022. https://lgbtqreligiousarchives.org/media/oral-history/imani-woody/IWoody.pdf.

Woody, Imani. "Why Mary's House? (Again.)." Diverse Elders Coalition, September 29, 2016. www.diverseelders.org/2016/09/29/why-marys-house-again.

Yetunde, Pamela A. *Object Relations, Buddhism, and Relationality in Womanist Practical Theology*. New York: Palgrave Macmillan, 2018.

Yetunde, Dr. Pamela A. Oral history interview conducted by author, 2019. LGBTQ-RAN Oral History transcript. Accessed February 28, 2022. https://lgbtqreligiousarchives.org/media/oral-history/pamela-ayo-yetunde/Pamela%20Ayo%20Yetunde%202019-11-24%20transcript.pdf.

Abdullah, Melina, 170–71
Abrams, Bishop Allyson, 34–35, 128, 130–31, 133–35, 143–45, 165; biography, 134
academia, 81–82, 178–79, 184, 190n24. *See also* education
access, accessibility, 10–11, 184
activism, 14, 50–51; Black women's participation in, 69–70, 73–74; collective, 69–70, 82–83, 87, 93–96, 99–101, 121–23; digital, 69–70; and consensus, 147; against enslavement, 69–70; everyday, 68–69, 72–77; grassroots, 60–61, 87–89, 120, 139, 170; holistic, 98–100; as intersectional, 89–91, 101; and Judaism, 120–21; and leadership, 142–43; LGBTQ, 82–83, 87–91, 94; performing, 78–79; and religion, 2–5, 70–71, 77–78, 81–83, 86–89, 92, 98–105, 137–39; scholarship as, 81–82; spiritual, 92–94, 101; teaching as, 87–89; and trauma 73; and womanism, 91–92. *See also* justice; leadership; organizing; resistance
Adams, Tyonna, 91
advocacy, 64–65, 72–73, 77–79, 87–90, 134–35, 146–47, 157–58. *See also* activism
African feminism, 180–81. *See also* Black feminism
African Methodist Episcopal Church, 126–27, 191n6
African Methodist Episcopal Zion (AME Zion) church, 20–22, 191n6

Agape International Spiritual Center, 40–42, 107–8. *See also* Johnson, Rev. Dr. Deborah L.
agency, 1–2, 6, 21, 65, 69–70, 109, 190n25; moral, 13, 71, 129; and oral history, 10–11
aging, 145–47, 165, 177, 182
Allen, Beverlyn Lundy, 170–71
allyship, 8–9, 184–85
Alpert, Rebecca, 112
Alston, Judy, 180
American Academy of Religion, 80
American Baptist church, 30, 80
American Friends Service Committee (AFSC), 30, 138–39
American Jewish Population Project, 111–12
American Psychiatric Association, 42–43
Anabaptist church, 27
ancestors, 97, 105–6, 124–25, 189n6; ancestor worship, 83
Anderson, Victor, 22–23, 172–73, 200n15
Anti-Defamation League, 120
Anzaldúa, Gloria, 171
Apostolic church, 32–33, 49
archive: Black lesbian, 183; ethics of, 183–84, 189n3. *See also* history; interviewing
Association for Global New Thought, 122
Association of Welcoming and Affirming Baptists, 21–22
attire, 24–25. *See also* respectability

authenticity, 14, 38–40, 46–47, 56–62, 172–73; as dialogical, 64–67; ethics of, 61; and social justice, 42, 51–58, 66; and womanism, 65–67. *See also* identity; self

Baez, Joan, 139
Baker, Dori, 148, 152–53, 164
Baker, Ella, 69–70, 129, 132, 151–52, 198n14
Baptist church, 1, 20–21, 27, 34–35. *See also* individual denominations by name
Be'chol Lashon, 160–61
Bean, Archbishop Carl, 33–34, 54, 150–51
Beckwith, Rev. Michael, 107–8, 122
Bethune, Mary McLeod, 69–70
bible, biblical worldview, 1, 20–23
biomythography, 66–67
Black church, 191n6; and attire, 24–25; and gender, 23–25; historical leadership structures of, 17–18; and homophobia, 23–25, 29, 33–34; and oppression, 19–20, 23; and protest leader model of Black male preacher, 83; and same-sex marriage, 22; and sexuality, 21–26, 172–73, 192n27; and social justice, 25; and upward mobility, 19–20; and women in leadership roles, 20–21. *See also* religion; individual denominations by name
Black feminism, 36–37, 101, 177–78, 193n2, 198n8; and Black women's faith experiences, 109–10; and social justice activism, 86–87; standpoint theory, 73–74. *See also* womanism
Black Gay and Lesbian Leadership Forum, 74
Black Lives Matter movement, 69–70, 82–83, 85–89, 104, 119–21, 160–61
Black Power movement, 18
Boyd, Nan, 10–11
Brown, Michael, 85–89, 121. *See also* Black Lives Matter movement; Ferguson protests
Brown Douglas, Kelly, 22–23
Bryant-Davis, Thema, 91
Buddhism, 83, 105, 113–15; and Black women, 117; and spiritual activism, 119; and womanism, 117. *See also* Lawson, Rabbi Sandra
Butler, Octavia, 180

Cadge, Wendy, 115–16
Campbell-Reed, Eileen, 27
Candomblé, 105–6
Cannon, Katie, 13, 67, 127
Carpenter, Delores, 27
Carter, Mandy, 30, 137–39, 141–42, 147–48, 176, 184–85; biography, 137–38
Carter, Mildred, 182
Center for Spiritual Light, 55–56, 104–5, 118–19. *See also* Jackson, Rev. Dr. Cari
Centers for Disease Control, 157–58
Centers for Spiritual Living, 106. *See also* metaphysical communities
charisma, 140–44, 151–53. *See also under* leadership
Cheng, Patrick, 169–70
Christian Methodist Episcopal church, 20–22, 191n6
Christianity. *See* religion; *see also* individual denominations by name
Church in God in Christ (COGIC), 20–22, 27–29, 95–96, 133, 191n6
City of Refuge United Church of Christ, 35–36, 74, 94–97, 101, 106
civil rights movement, 69–70, 73, 83–85, 138–39, 193n2, 194n5
Clark, Septima, 69–70
Clarke, Cheryl, 40, 66, 170
class: and Black church, 19–20; and classism, 8–9, 80–81, 119
club movement, 69–74, 169
coalition building, 86–87, 101, 120, 145–48. *See also* community; leadership
Coleman, Monica, 97–98, 101
collaboration. *See under* leadership
Collier-Thomas, Bettye, 20, 71
Collins, Patricia Hill, 65–66, 68–69, 73–74, 101, 129, 190n24, 191n2, 194n27, 198n8
Combahee River Collective, 18, 69, 89–90
community, 3, 25–26; and authenticity, 61; empowering, 154–59; and ethical leadership, 131–32, 151–56, 163–64, 172–75; and identity, 61–62; and justice, 120–23; and noncommunity members, 8–9; and religion, 111; and shared goals, 148–49; and social justice activism, 93–96, 147; and spirituality, 117; and testimony,

9–10; and wholeness, 175; and womanism, 178–79. *See also under* leadership
Congressional Black Caucus, 157–58
consensus, 127, 144–48. *See also* leadership
conservatism, 1, 21–25, 83, 126–27. *See also* Black church; sexuality
Cooper, Anna Julia, 69–70, 191n2
COVID-19 pandemic, 104, 119
Crenshaw, Kimberle, 18–19
Cullors, Patrisse, 83
curation, 183–84. *See also* archive; history

Davis, Angela, 175
de Lauretis, Teresa, 169–70, 193n1
dignity, 114–17, 169
Disciples of Christ, 27
dissemblance, culture of, 9–10
Douglass, Frederick, 70–71
Du Bois, W. E. B., 70–71, 124

education, 135–41, 146, 162–63. *See also* academia; leadership
Edwards, Elise, 116–17
Eger, Rabbi Denise, 112–13, 120
Eichhorn, Kate, 183
elder (position), 20–21, 29, 32, 83, 90–91. *See also* ordination
elderly. *See* aging
embodiment, 10–11, 66, 109, 116–17, 171, 184–85
empowerment, 154–57. *See also* leadership
Empowerment Liberation Cathedral, 34–35, 134–35
enslavement, 19, 69–70
Episcopal Church, 26–27, 30–32
ethics: of archival curation, 183–84; of authenticity, 61; everyday, 13–14; of interviewing, 8–9, 185–86; of truth telling, 18; of womanism, 13
ethical leadership, 1–3, 13–14, 127–35, 140–42, 152, 163–64, 167, 169, 198n12, 200n3;
Etter-Lewis, Gwendolyn, 9–10
evangelist (position), 20–21
Evans, Dr. Mary, 5–6
Excellent Way Consulting, 55–56. *See also* Jackson, Rev. Dr. Cari
exile, 26–27, 32–36, 94, 105–6

experience: everyday, 12–13, 92, 179–80; learning from, 14; lived, 38–39, 66–67, 176, 180–81, 182–84, 190n24; and spirituality, 105–6; validating, 13–14

family, 77–79; and leadership formation, 133–35, 140
Fellowship of Affirming Ministries, The (TFAM), 30–31, 35–36, 58, 61–62, 118–19, 141, 157–58, 161–62, 174, 199n47
feminism, 12–14; and historiography, 70–71, 177–78, 201n25; movement, 18. *See also* Black feminism; womanism
Ferguson protests, 85–89, 121. *See also* Black Lives Matter movement
Ferguson, S. Alease, 171–72, 198n12, 200n11
First African Methodist Church, 29
Floyd-Thomas, Stacey, 66–67
Fluker, Walter, 128–29, 152
Flunder, Bishop Rev. Dr. Yvette, 8–9, 74–77, 94–97, 118–19, 130–31, 133, 158–59, 164–65, 174, 177–79, 193n2, 199n47; advocacy, 94–97, 101–2, 157–58; and alternative spiritualities, 118–19, 124–25; biography, 94; on education, 140–41; on oppression sickness, 19, 23; on radical inclusion, 29, 35–36, 161–62; religious exile, 26–27, 105–7
fragmentation, 44, 50, 61–63. *See also* identity; self
Franklin, Rev. Darlene, 34, 154–56, 159, 162–66; biography, 149–50
Franklin, Robert, 128–29, 164
Frederick, Marla, 116
Free Indeed, 89–90
Freedom Center for Social Justice, 52, 100–101, 148–49, 157, 162. *See also* Rawls, Bishop Tonyia
Full Truth Fellowship of Christ Church, 28, 34, 136–37, 149–51, 155–56, 162–63, 166. *See also* McCoy, Rev. Dr. Renee or Rev. Darlene Franklin
future, 179–80, 185

Gandhi, Mahatma, 138–39
Garner, Elder Darlene, 32, 47, 142, 159–61; biography, 44–46; forced retirement, 51, 193n11

Garrett-Evangelical Theological Seminary, 63. *See also* Washington-Leapheart, Rev. Kentina

Garza, Alicia, 83

Gates Foundation, 157–58

Gay and Lesbian Alliance against Defamation (GLAAD), 47–49

gender: and gender identity, 5, 23–25, 162; and leadership, 3, 5–6, 19–21, 27, 32, 126–31, 140–41, 170, 173–74, 200n11; and oral history, 13–14; and religion, 1–2, 126–27; and sexism, 3–4, 17–18, 20–21, 34–37, 54, 83–87; and sexuality, 174; and sexual violence, 69–70; and titles, 189n6. *See also* Black feminism; trans community; womanism

General Social Survey, 25

Gilkes, Cheryl Townsend, 21

Glide United Methodist Church, 114–15

glossolalia, 105

Gluck, Sherna, 13–14

God, Self, Neighbor Ministries (GSN Ministries), 97–98

Goldstein-Stoll, Rabbi Isaama, 160–61

Green, Miles, 87–89

Griffin, Horace, 6–7, 23–26, 33, 173

griot tradition, 9–10. *See also* history, oral; storytelling

Guillory, Margarita, 121–22

Gushee, David, 132

Haley, Alex, *Roots*, 10–11

Hamer, Fannie Lou, 69–70

Hammonds, Evelyn, 39, 172, 191n17, 193n1

Harlem Renaissance, 193n2

Harris, Melanie, 109–10, 117

Harshaw, Pendarvis, 182–86

Hawkins, Bishop Walter, 35–36

healing, 11–12, 115–17, 120–23, 151, 178–79

Henderson, Kathleen, 165

heteronormativity, heterosexism. *See* sexuality

Hill, Rev. Dr. Renee, 65–66, 169, 175

Hinduism, 105

history: and Black women's sexuality, 40, 191n17; and feminism, 70–71; and historiography, 5–6, 12–14, 70–71, 185, 190n25, 201n25; and inclusion, 10–12;

oral, 1–3, 7–14, 36–39, 124, 177–86, 190n15, 190n19, 201n25; and personal lives, 36–37; and queer studies, 185; recovering, 39, 71; and "structured amnesia," 11

HIV/AIDS, 33–34, 43–44, 83–85, 90–91, 94–97, 101, 114–15, 129–30, 136–37, 142–43, 149–51, 157–58. *See also* sexuality

Holland, Bishop Jacqueline, 54

Holmes, Ernest, 106–7, 121–22

Holmes, Rev. Candy, 32–33, 47–51, 68, 72–73, 92–93; biography, 47–49

hooks, bell, 36–37

Hoover, Theressa, 17–20

Huerta, Dolores, 129

Hull, Akasha Gloria, 109–10

Human Rights Campaign, 47–49, 147–48

Hyde Park Union Church, 30

identity, 2, 5–6; and authenticity, 5, 44–47, 51–64; and coalition-building, 146, 160–61; and community, 61–67; and diversity of experiences, 10–11; as embodied resistance, 171; as fluid, 66–67; identity politics, 18, 69, 196n30; and integration, 19, 46–51, 54–58, 61–66, 116, 153–54; intersectional, 6, 13–14, 18–19, 44, 145, 155–56, 171, 175–78; and leadership models, 170–71, 175; and oral history, 10–11; and "outsider/within," 8–9; and sexuality, 2, 5–6, 39–40, 44; and spirituality, 93; and value, 19. *See also* intersectionality; leadership; wholeness

Ifá rituals, 83

immigration reform, 165

IMPACT program, 123

incarceration, 23–24, 42–43, 62, 87–90, 93–94, 101, 123, 139

inclusion, inclusivity: in history, 10–11; radical, 29, 35–36, 94, 161–62, 174, 178–79, 193n2; and sexuality, 25, 90–91, 157–58, 172

Inner Light Ministries, 40–42, 107, 123. *See also* Johnson, Rev. Dr. Deborah L.

Insight Meditation, 113–16

Institute for the Study of Nonviolence, 139

Interdenominational Theological Seminary, 83–85

International Black Buyers and Manufacturers Expo and Conference, 157
intersectionality, 3–4, 13–14, 17–19, 52, 89–90, 101, 145, 148, 155–57, 162, 170–71, 175–78, 184–85, 191n2. *See also* activism; identity; justice
interviewing, 7–9, 12. *See also* history, oral
IWF Consulting, 145–46. *See also* Woody, Dr. Imani

Jackson, Debora, 14, 198n12
Jackson, Rebecca Cox, 5–6, 69–70
Jackson, Rev. Dr. Cari, 27–28, 55–58, 93–94, 103–5, 118–19, 124–25, 148; biography, 55–56;
Johnson, E. Patrick, 6–9, 24–26, 173, 182, 185
Johnson, Rev. Dr. Deborah L., 40–44, 66, 107–9, 122–25, 172, 174, 197n36; biography, 40–42
Jones, Melanie, 24–25
Jordan, Mark, 179–80
joy, 6–7, 42–44, 58
Judaism, 110–13; and diversity, 160–61; Reconstructionist, 153–54; and *tikkum olam* (repairing and healing the world through acts of justice and reconciliation), 120–21, 154
justice, 1–5, 14, 33–37, 38–39, 44–49, 77–83, 95–96, 99–101, 120–21, 124–25, 157–58, 174, 183–85, 196n30; and activism, 50–51, 56–60, 68–69, 72–73, 77–79, 85–89, 92–93, 98, 103–4, 122–24, 137–39, 147–49; and advocacy, 64–65; and authenticity, 42; and Black church, 25; and family, 77–79; holistic, 36, 132, 148, 162–65, 175–80; in Judaism, 120; and leadership, 132; racial, 30; and religion, 71; reproductive, 54–63, 74, 78–79, 93–94; and salvation, 97–98. *See also* activism; advocacy; intersectionality; leadership

King, Coretta Scott, 160–61
King, Martin Luther, Jr., 70–71, 73–76, 98–100, 128–29, 139, 152, 167, 198n14
King, Toni, 152, 171–72, 198n12, 200n11
knowledge, 65–66, 129, 194n27

Lancaster Theological Seminary, 28, 87–89
Lawson, Rabbi Sandra, 110–12, 118–21, 124–25, 143, 145, 153–54, 160–61, 175; biography, 110–11. *See also* Judaism
leadership, 5; and activism, 69–70, 142–43, 170–71; across ages and stages of life, 165; and autonomy, 36; as "calling," 130, 148–51; charismatic, 140–44, 151–53; Christian models of, 18; and collaboration, 2–3, 14, 131–33, 144, 148–54, 157–67, 175–79; and community, 3, 131–32, 147–57, 163–64, 172–75; and consensus, 145–48; costs of, 165–67; development, 133–40, 161–66; as egalitarian, 165; and empowerment, 154–55, 158–59; beyond established power structures, 3, 14, 18, 126–27, 130–31, 149–53, 164, 172, 177; ethical, 1–3, 13–14, 127–35, 140–42, 152, 163–64, 167, 169, 198n12, 200n3; and expansiveness, 112–13; and gender, 5–6, 19–21, 27, 126–31, 140–41, 170, 173–74, 197n2, 200n11; heteronormative structures of, 6, 17–18; and identity, 170; and institutional hierarchies, 130–35; and intergenerational mentoring, 176–77; and justice, 132, 175, 183–85; liberating, 152–53; and lifting others, 159–61, 164–65, 176–77; and marginality, 131–32; models of, 1–3, 164, 167, 171–73, 179–81, 183; and moral wisdom of Black women, 124–25; beyond pastorate, 21; and power, 170–71; in predominantly white institutions, 27–32, 56–58, 147–48; queer models of, 168–70, 174–81, 183–86, 200n3; and race, 5–6, 128–29, 167, 170, 200n11; and relationality, 152; and religion, 172, 180; and sexuality, 5–6, 129–31, 173, 200n15; and storytelling, 37; success of, 163–67; and womanism, 13–14, 127, 131–35, 163–64, 167, 178–79, 198n12. *See also under* queer, queerness; race; womanism
Leadership Council of Association of Global New Thought, 40–42. *See also* Johnson, Rev. Dr. Deborah L.
Leath, Jennifer, 119–20
Lee, Frances, 78–79
Lee, Jarena, 69–70

Lee, Rev. Jarena, 126–27
Leffler, Phyllis, 167
Lesbian Herstory Archives, 183
Lesbian, Gay, Bisexual, Transgender, Queer
    Religious Archives Network (LGBTQ-
    RAN), 3, 5, 7–8, 10–11, 38–39, 127, 183–86
Lesser, Rabbi Josh, 111, 153–54
Lewin, Ellen, 141, 199n47
Lewis, Stephen, 148, 152–53, 164
liberation, 18, 176–79; and leadership,
    152–53; theology, 33–34, 66–67, 83–86,
    97, 114–15; and resistance narratives,
    66–67
Lightsey, Rev. Dr. Pamela, 29, 83–87, 90–91,
    195n19; biography, 83
Lipman-Blumen, Jean, 165
listening, 9–10, 77–78
Live on Purpose Center for Creative Being,
    150–51
Lorde, Audre, 1, 6, 37, 40, 169, 177
Love Center Ministries, 35–36, 94
Lutheran church, 27
lynching, 69–70

Many Voices, 47–49
Maparyan, Layli Phillips, 12–13, 51, 68–69,
    92, 101, 118–19, 196n26; The Womanist
    Idea, 92. See also womanism
marginalization, 10–14, 17–18; and empow-
    erment, 155, 159–60; and justice, 36;
    and leadership, 131–32; and oppression
    sickness, 23; and radical inclusion,
    161–62, 179–80; and respect, 19. See also
    oppression
marriage equality, same-sex marriage,
    21–22, 47–51, 72–73, 123, 195n21. See also
    sexuality
Martin, Denise, 106–7
Martin, Rev. Dr. Kathi, 97–98
Martin, Trayvon, 69–70, 83, 87–89
Mary's House for Older Adults, 145–46.
    See also Woody, Dr. Imani
McClellan, Patrice, 180
McCoy, Rev. Dr. Renee, 28, 34, 135–37,
    142–43, 162–63, 166, 175; biography,
    136–37
metaphysical communities, 106–10, 121–23
Methodist church, 20–22

Metropolitan Community Church (MCC),
    26–28, 31, 44–49, 105, 159–60; au-
    tonomous structure, 33; Conference for
    People of African Descent, Our Friends,
    and Allies, 32–33, 44–49, 161; Older
    Adults Advisory Council, 145–46;
    Racism Task Force, 136–37
Micham, Laura, 8–9
Minority AIDS Project (MAP), 34
missionaries, 28–29, 52–54
Monroe, Rev. Irene, 25–26, 174, 193n2
Moore, Mignon, 109
Moraga, Cherríe, 171
morality: and agency, 13, 129; and leadership,
    128–29, 132, 164; moral wisdom, 124–25
Motivational Institute, 40–42. See also
    Johnson, Rev. Dr. Deborah L.
Murray, Pauli, 5–6
Murray, Rev. Cecil, 29
mutual aid, 69–70
myths, 1–2, 9, 25, 66–67. See also stereotypes

Nash, Diane, 69–70
National Association for the Advancement
    of Colored People (NAACP), 143–44
National Association of Colored Women,
    69–70
National Baptist Convention, 71, 191n6
National Baptist Convention of America,
    20–21, 191n6
National Baptist Convention, USA, 20–21
National Black Gay and Lesbian Leadership
    Forum, 176
National Black Justice Coalition, 47–49, 74,
    137–38, 176
National Coalition of Black Lesbians and
    Gays, 46–47, 136–37, 176
National Council of Churches (USA), 31
National LGBTQ Task Force, 47–49, 58, 61,
    89–90, 162
New Thought community, 32–33, 106–8,
    121–22
New York Third World Coalition, 136–37
Nhat Hanh, Thich, 119

Obama, President Barack, 47–51, 73
Obergefell v. Hodges (2015), 22. See also
    marriage equality

Omnifaith, 107. *See also* Johnson, Rev. Dr. Deborah L.

ONE National Gay and Lesbian Archives, 183

oppression, 6; and history, 11–12; internalized, 19; as intersectional, 18–19, 44; multiplicity of, 175, 177; oppression sickness, 19, 23; and radical subjectivity, 38–39, 66–67; resisting, 184–85; in sacred spaces, 17–18; and subjugated knowledge, 65–66, 129; and "talking back," 36–37. *See also* activism; intersectionality; justice; marginalization

Oral History Association, 9

ordination, 20–21, 49, 52–54, 195n21

organizing, 18, 30, 34, 52, 58–61, 69–71, 74, 82–90, 98–101, 120, 137–39, 141–42, 145–48, 157, 176. *See also* activism

pacifism, 138–39

panopticon, 24–25

Pentecostal church, 20–21, 27–29, 83–85, 93–96, 104–6

Pentecostal Church of God in Christ, 35–36

Perry, Rev. Elder Troy, 31

Philadelphia Commission on Human Relations, 44–46

Philadelphia Mayor's Commission on Sexual Minorities, 44–46

Pneuma Christian Fellowship, 34–35, 134–35, 144–45. *See also* Abrams, Bishop Allyson

politics: and engagement, 77–78; of identity, 18, 69, 196n30; of respectability, 183–84

Poor People's Campaign, 137–38

POWER Interfaith, 58

Presbyterian church, 27–28, 30, 55–56

Presbyterian Homes (retirement community), 63

Progressive National Baptist Convention, 20–21, 143–44, 191n6

Proposition 8, 50–51, 72–73, 194n13. *See also* marriage equality

Pryor, Jonathan, 170

Public Religion Research Institute, *American Values Atlas* (2017), 25

Pulse Nightclub massacre, 60, 89–90

Quakers (Friends), 26–27, 30, 137–39, 147

queer, queerness, 6, 39–40, 169–70; historiography, 185; leadership models, 168–81, 183–86, 200n3; queer theory, 193n1. *See also* sexuality

race: among Jewish population, 111–12; and Buddhism, 115–17; and Christianity, 1–2; and consensus work, 147–48; and homophobia, 83–85, 90–91; and indigenous spiritualities, 116–17; and leadership models, 128–29, 170, 200n11; and metaphysical communities, 106–10, 121–22; and police violence, 83, 85, 87–89, 104, 119, 160–61; and predominantly white institutions, 26–29, 32–33, 108, 147–48; and racism, 3–4, 17–18, 27–29, 33, 37, 104, 115–16, 119; and religion, 25; and respectability, 22–23; and sexism, 86–87; and sexuality, 3, 6–7, 40, 46–47, 50, 155–56, 172–73, 191n17, 193n1; and titles, 189n6; and worship styles, 33

Racial Diversity, Equity, and Inclusion for Reconstructing Judaism, 110–11

Radicallesbians, 39–40

Ramírez, Horacio Roque, 10–11

Rawls, Bishop Tonyia, 8–9, 28–29, 38, 52–55, 98–101, 148–49, 156–57, 162, 164–67, 174–75, 179–80; biography, 52

Reconciling Ministries Network, 85

Reformed Church, 27

Regional Center for the Developmentally Disabled, 74–76

relationality. *See under* leadership

religion, 1–2; African diasporic, 105–6, 119–20; and activism, 103–5, 120–21; apostolic, 49; and authority, 20; and Black religious expressions, 33; Black women's participation in, 3–4, 20–21; and changing denominations, 27–29; and collaboration, 153–54, 159; and community, 111; and exile, 26–27, 32–36, 105–6; and gender, 126–27; and homophobia, 83–85; and joy, 6–7; and leadership, 3, 172; and oppression, 17–18; and queer history, 2; and racism, 29, 33; and radical inclusivity, 29, 35–36, 94, 161–62, 178–79, 193n2; and revolution,

religion (continued)
98–99; and salvation, 95–96; and
sexism, 34–35, 54, 83–85; and sexuality, 2–3, 6–7, 21–29, 31–33, 42–44, 49,
52–61, 89–91, 172–73, 192n27, 193n2;
and social justice activism, 2–5, 14,
35–36, 44–46, 51–55, 58–60, 68–71,
77–83, 86–92, 98–102, 137–39, 148–49,
174; "stained glass ceiling," 6, 18, 29;
and trans inclusion, 99–100, 157, 162;
and womanism, 12–13, 178–79; versus
spirituality, 92, 104–9, 195n25. See also
leadership; spirituality
Religious Coalition for Reproductive
Choice, 55–58. See also Jackson, Rev.
Dr. Cari
Religious Institute, Programs for Reproductive
Justice and Sexuality Education, 61, 77
Religious Science philosophy, 106–9, 121–23.
See also New Thought community
resistance, 9–10, 14, 18; Black women's,
69–71; during enslavement, 69–70;
embodied, 185; everyday forms of,
68–69, 72–74; existence as, 38–39, 65;
of naming, 40; narratives of, 67; beyond
protests, 69–70; and religion, 71; sexual-
ity as, 39–40; and storytelling, 37; and
"talking back," 36–37. See also activism;
organizing
respect, respectability, 19, 22–23, 96, 114,
183–84
Rhode, Deborah, 131
Rhue, Dr. Sylvia, 29, 74–77; All God's
Children, 29, 74–76; biography, 74;
Women in Love: Bonding Strategies of
Black Lesbians, 74–76
Rich, Adrienne, 39–40
Roman Catholic Church, 136–37
Rose, Tricia, 1–2, 9
Ross, Rosetta, 77
Rushin, Donna Kate, "The Bridge," 145
Rustin, Bayard, 70–71, 138–39, 147

Sacred Souls Community Church, 148–49,
156
Sallie Bingham Center for Women's History
and Culture (Duke University Libraries), 8–9

salvation, 97–98, 101
sampling, 5–7, 189n5
Sanctified Church, 21
Schomburg Black Gay and Lesbian Archive
Project, 183
Science of the Mind, 107–8
self-determination, 6, 61, 65–66
self, 30–31, 38–39, 42, 56–67, 117; fragmented, 50, 61, 63. See also authenticity;
identity
Seventh Day Adventist, 29, 74
sexuality, 1–2; and aging, 145–47; and
alternative religions, 173; and archives,
189n3; and "coming out," 3, 6–9, 24–25,
38–39, 42–43, 46, 58–60, 63; and Black
Lives Matter movement, 82–83; and
Buddhism, 115–16; and changing
religious denominations, 26–29; and
community, 111; criminalization of,
42–43; and deviance, 40; and gender,
gender expression, 23–25, 174; and
heterosexism, 3–4, 8–9, 17–18, 21–25,
37; historical narrative of, 39–40; and
HIV/AIDS pandemic, 129–30; and
homophobia, 6–7, 23–25, 83–85, 174;
and identity, 5, 39–40, 44; and Judaism,
112–13; and leadership, 5–6, 14, 21–22,
129–31, 168–70, 173, 200n15; and metaphysical communities, 109; and oral
history, 10–11; and passing, 23–25; and
race, 6–7, 40, 46–47, 50, 90–91, 155–56,
172–73, 191n17, 193n1; and religion, 2,
6–7, 21–29, 31–33, 44, 49, 52–61, 89–91,
172–73, 192n27, 193n2; and resistance,
39–40; and respectability, 22–23; and
sex therapy, 74–76; and being silenced,
37; and womanism, 12–13. See also gender; queer, queerness
Sharpton, Rev. Al, 83, 104
Shockley, Ann Allen, 25–26
silence, 9–10, 13, 37, 39, 44, 139, 148, 155,
178–79
SisterReach, 74
Small, Mary, 20
Smith, Albert, 168
Smith, Barbara, 23, 36–37
Smith, Christine, 37
Social Justice Survey Project, 24–25

social media, 69–70, 195n19
solidarity, 18, 119, 138–39
Southerners on New Ground (SONG), 137–38
spirituality, 104, 195n25, 197n28; alternative, 6–7, 103–10, 173; and activism, 92–94, 103–4, 118–24; as communal, 117; during enslavement, 19; as holistic, 116; and identity, 93; indigenous, 116–19; as individualized, 92; as space of monarchy, 19; woman-centered, 25–26; and womanism, 92
"stained-glass ceiling," 6, 18, 29
stereotypes, 6–7, 9–10, 21, 23–25. *See also* myths
storytelling, 37, 182. *See also* history, oral; testimony, testifying
Student Nonviolent Coordinating Committee, 136–37
subjectivity, 18, 38–39, 66–67, 171
subjugation, 6, 9–10, 65–66, 129, 194n27
substance abuse, 149–50
suffrage, 69–70
survival, 9–12, 14, 59–60, 66–67, 89–90, 97–98, 115–16, 124–25, 131–32, 170–71, 177–78, 180–81, 182
sustainability, 36, 78–79, 91, 153–54, 157–58, 163–65

T'ruah (Rabbinical Voice for Social Justice), 120–21
Taylor, Charles, 61, 64–65
technology, 184
Terrell, Mary Church, 69–70
testimony, testifying, 9–10, 36–37
Tharpe, Sister Rosetta, 5–6
therapy, 74–76
Thurman, Howard, 128–29, 152, 167
Tometi, Opa, 83
Townes, Rev. Dr. Emilie, 12–13, 30, 80–82, 117, 124, 135, 164, 179–80, 198n12; biography, 80
trans community, 5, 99–100, 119, 157, 162
Transgender Day of Remembrance, 87–89
Transgender Faith and Action Retreat, 162. *See also* Rawls, Bishop Tonyia
trauma, 6, 73, 87–89
Trinity United Church of Christ, 30–31

kentrust, 140–41. *See also* charisma
truth, truth telling, 11, 18, 36–37, 58–60, 66–67, 72–73, 147
Truth and Reconciliation Commission (South Africa), 11–12
Truth, Sojourner, 69–70, 167, 191n2
Tubman, Harriet, 69–70

United Church of Christ (UCC), 27–30, 52, 54–56, 58, 87–89, 136–37, 166–67
United Methodist Church, 26–30, 55–56, 80–81, 83–85, 90–91, 195n21; *Book of Discipline*, 90–91
United Theological Seminary, Interreligious Chaplaincy program, 119–20
Unity churches, 106. *See also* metaphysical communities
Unity Fellowship Church Movement, 28–29, 31, 33–34, 47, 52–54, 98–99, 150–51, 156, 162–63, 166–67; and experiences of sexism, 34–35
Universal Fellowship of Metropolitan Community Churches. *See* Metropolitan Community Church

violence: domestic, 149–50; police, 83–89, 104, 119, 160–61; sexual, 69–70
visibility, 19–25, 40, 43–44, 51–52, 65–67, 115–16, 150–51, 184
Vodun, 105–6
voice, 6, 9–10, 13, 22–23, 37, 50–51, 62–65, 68–69, 73, 86–87, 121, 148, 185–86
Voice of Witness (human rights organization), 10–11
vulnerability, 12, 81–82, 118, 131, 148, 165–67

Walker, Alice, 12–13, 66, 91, 109–10, 131–32, 178–79, 197n28. *See also* womanism
War Resisters League, 30, 137–39
Washington-Leapheart, Rev. Kentina, 7–9, 30–31, 61–65, 77–79; biography, 61–62
Washington-Leapheart, Rev. Naomi, 7–8, 28, 58–61, 87–89; biography, 58
Weber, Max, 141
Wells-Barnett, Ida B., 69–70, 81–82
wholeness, 14, 38–40, 45–51, 57–60, 78–82, 91, 111, 116–17, 121–23, 131–32, 152, 175–79. *See also* identity; self

Wiggins, Daphne, 21, 190n24
Wilcox, Melissa, 173–74
Williams, Bishop Emeritus Diana, 34–35
Williams, Khalia Jelks, 116
Williams, Matthew, 148, 152–53, 164
Williams, Rev. Cecil, 114–15
witnessing, 50–51
womanism, 8–9, 12–13, 190nn24–25, 197n42;
    and alternative spiritualities, 109–10,
    117; and authenticity, 38–39, 65–67; and
    Buddhism, 117–20; and community,
    178–79; and creative social transforma-
    tion, 97–98, 101; and ethical leadership,
    1–3, 13–14, 127, 131–35, 148, 152, 163–64,
    167, 170–71, 179, 198n12; and histori-
    ography, 12–14; and hopeful futures,
    179–81; and moral wisdom of Black
    women, 124–25; and queer leadership
    models, 177–79, 184–85; and religion,

12–13, 178–79; and resistance narratives,
67; and sexuality, 12–13, 91; and social
justice activism, 85–86, 91; and specificity of experience, 101; and spiritual
activism, 68–69, 91–94, 101–4, 118–19,
195n25, 196n26, 197n28; and "standing
in," 51–52. *See also* Black feminism
Woody, Dr. Imani, 33, 145–46; biography,
    145–46
World AIDS Day, 95–96
World Council of Churches, 31

Yeboah, Angelina Amoako, 180–81
Yetunde, Dr. Pamela "Ayo," 113–16, 118–20,
    124–25, 171–72, 197n42; biography,
    113–14
Yoruba, 105–6

Zen Hospice Project, 115